CW00602473

Computer Graphics and CAD Fundamentals

BBC Micro Version

Computer Graphics and CAD Fundamentals
BBC Micro Version

Noel M Morris

Pitman

Pitman Publishing Limited
128 Long Acre, London WC2E 9AN

A Longman Group Company

© Noel M Morris 1986

First published 1986

British Library Cataloguing in Publication Data

Morris, Noel M.
  Computer graphics and CAD fundamentals :
  BBC Micro version.
  1. Computer graphics   2. BBC Microcomputer
    — Programming
    I. Title
    006.6'86   T385

    ISBN 0 273 02517 1

All rights reserved. No part of this publication may be reproduced,
stored in a retrieval system, or transmitted, in any form or by any
means, electronic, mechanical, photocopying, recording and/or
otherwise, without the prior written permission of the publishers.
This book may not be lent, resold, hired out or otherwise disposed of
by way of trade in any form of binding or cover other than that in
which it is published, without the prior consent of the publishers.

Printed at The Bath Press, Avon

Contents

Preface

Computer graphics are, without doubt, the most exciting application of computers. Not only can they be used to present facts and figures in an informative and interesting way, but they also allow representation of complex facts and equations.

This book is intended to fill the gap between elementary 'how to draw lines and shapes' books and advanced books on computer-aided design. The level of mathematics in the first eight chapters does not go beyond school trigonometry, and each step is explained as it is reached. The final chapter on Computer Graphics Mathematics gently leads to an appreciation of fascinating and exciting areas of mathematics that can be used in program development.

The book is particularly suitable for all levels of study, including GCSE, 'O' and 'A' level computer-based topics (including Computer-Aided Learning or CAL), BTEC courses (ONC, HNC and HND), and also degree courses (including computer science, information technology, electronics, mechanical engineering, etc). It also serves as a sourcebook of ideas for projects, and is well suited to the needs of the computer 'buff' who wishes to extend his/her knowledge and experience in graphics and CAD.

Whilst a knowledge of programming in the BASIC language is assumed, the book begins at a level which anyone can understand. As far as is possible with any microcomputer, the programs have been written so that they are reasonably 'transportable' between microcomputers.

Eighty program listings are contained within the covers of this book, the twenty-four most important and complex programs being available on a disc that can be obtained from Pitman Publishing. It is estimated that the cost of the programs on the disc, if purchased from a software house, would be many times the cost of the book!

Chapter 1 introduces aspects of modular programming and top-down program design. Many features of the microcomputer are introduced in this chapter, including the process of merging programs and writing menu-driven programs. Also included are timing of program operations, 'error' trapping, program 'trace' facility, and speeding up of BASIC programs. One of the limitations of most personal microcomputers (the BBC micro being no exception) is that large programs can run out of memory space. A method of 'overlaying' programs from a disc is described in Chapter 1; using this technique, it is possible to handle very large programs indeed.

Chapter 2 introduces fundamental drawing features, including the drawing of 'wire frame' shapes and specifying user-defined characters. The progrmaming of 'soft' keys or user-defined keys is introduced, and the chapter shows how they can be incorporated into a program. The operation of a graphics 'ruler' is described, explaining how to make measurements on the screen. Finally, text and graphics 'windows' are introduced.

Chapter 3 deals with a very important feature of graphics, namely colour and the filling of shapes with colour. The way in which a microcomputer handles colour is demonstrated by several programs, including the way in which 'logical' operations are carried out on colours. The chapter concludes with an animation program that uses features developed in the chapter.

The use of text on diagrams and drawings is very important in CAD programs. Chapter 4 includes routines that introduce the techniques involved in printing enlarged text at any position on the screen and at any angle, or even around the arc of a circle!

The presentation of data in art, commerce, industry and engineering is vital to the everyday running of organizations (even small clubs find that the graphical presentation of data is invaluable). Chapter 5 introduces concepts associated with drawing graphs, histograms or bar charts, and pie charts. A number of practical effects are covered in the chapter, including different methods of drawing graphs, as well as three-dimensional bar charts, and drawing pie charts with a 'slice' displaced from the chart.

Chapter 6 introduces a line-drawing program which makes it possible to use the keyboard to draw diagrams constructed from straight lines and dots; this is the basis of many computer-aided drawing (CAD) programs. Many important features are dealt with, including methods of 'rubbing out' mistakes on the screen. The use of icons or images is incorporated in the program; in this chapter they are positioned on the screen by a method known as 'picking and placing'.

An area of considerable prominence in graphics and CAD is that of drawing three-dimensional shapes. A number of programs that are developed in Chapter 7 allow the keyboard to be used to manipulate both 'wire-frame' and 'solid' three-dimensional shapes. The basic program, which is extended as the chapter unfolds, incorporates perspective, zooming, translation and rotation. You are shown how to configure your own shapes, a rocket or space vehicle being used as an example. The program is developed to display stereoscope 'wire-frame' three-dimensional shapes which can be made to look as through they 'come out of the screen'! The mathematics of vectors is brought to life in Chapter 7 by extending the program to draw a 'solid' three-dimensional shape including the features of perspective, zooming, translation and rotation. The chapter includes a program which allows a character to be 'embossed' (a letter from the alphabet is used to illustrate the principle) on one face of a 'solid' three-dimensional object, and it concludes with a discussion of the elimination of 'hidden' lines.

An extensive and practical computer-aided drawing program is developed in Chapter 8. The program further extends the use of the user-defined keys — over thirty different effects are achieved by this means. The program also leaves more than ten other 'soft' keys available for the user's own special effects. Features included in the program are: 'rubber-band' drawing of circles, polygons and rectangles; moving rubber-banded shapes around the screen; deleting rubber-banded shapes; drawing lines and arcs; centring the cursor; using a 'ruler' to measure lengths and angles on the screen; using a 'rubber' or 'eraser'; global erasure of the diagram on the screen; adding text to the diagram (at an angle if needed); drawing dots, 'blobs' and arrowheads (the latter at an angle if needed); 'filling' and shading shapes; drawing a graticule on the screen; centring the cursor; 'picking and dragging' icons; 'saving' a diagram either on tape or on disc; 'loading' a diagram on tape or disc onto the screen.

Chapter 9 opens the door not only to the basic mathematics associated with graphics, but also to some of the mathematics used in advanced CAD programs. This chapter deals with trigonometry, compound angles, complex numbers and matrices — mathematical techniques that are vital to the manipulation of lines and shapes in graphics programs and are widely used in art, commerce and industry.

This book could not have been written without the help of many people and organizations, and it is difficult to name everyone who has contributed to it in some way. In particular, I would like to thank the students on whom many of the programs were 'tested', and also Mr F. W. Senior, MSc, and his son Andrew. I am indebted to the Computer Services Unit of the North Staffordshire Polytechnic for advice and assistance, in particular to Mrs C. Faul and her colleagues. I would also like to thank the staff of *Beebug* magazine, and I am grateful to Acorn Computers for permission to reproduce data relating to the BBC microcomputer.

As ever, I gratefully acknowledge my wife's assistance, help and encouragement during the writing of this book.

Developing the programs in the book was not without its moments of difficulty: Mr L. A. Meredith, B.A., reports the following graffiti on the wall of a university computing laboratory. We should reflect on its sentiments!

I'm fed up with this computer,
I wish that they would sell it.
It never does what I want,
Only what I tell it!

North Staffordshire Polytechnic   Noel M. Morris

Introduction

The twin topics of computer-aided drawing and computer-aided design are emerging in a variety of fields of study including science, engineering, computing, architecture and many others. It is perhaps unfortunate that both computer-aided drawing and computer-aided design have been described as CAD! The book begins by introducing the reader to the general concepts of the former and, in later chapters, leads towards the latter, namely the use of graphics in the design process.

The book aims to provide students and teachers with material which explains the principles of CAD programming, and is highly appropriate to any course of study involving design technology with a computing element.

It is possible that the reader may not have a background of mathematics or geometrical drawing. This possibility was borne in mind when the book was written and, to this end, the more complex aspects of mathematics are dealt with in the final chapter. This prevents the mathematics from getting in the way of understanding the graphics techniques.

Since it is recognised that only a few readers will have access to sophisticated support devices such as a 'mouse' or a 'bit-stick', the book has been written around a stand-alone BBC microcomputer with, perhaps, a dot matrix printer as a 'hard copy' output device. It is hoped that, in this way, the book will appeal to any reader with an interest in computer graphics.

As any computer user knows, the documentation provided with the computer is often difficult to read and even more difficult to understand! For this reason, a minimum amount of information about the BBC micro has been included in the text, consistent with the reader being able to understand what he is doing. To enable the reader to make full use of the micro, one or two specialized techniques are also discussed in the text. Among these is the use of the 'overlay' method, which overcomes many of the difficulties associated with the limited amount of memory of a standard personal computer.

It is hoped that between the covers of this book, the reader will find much that is interesting and exciting in the field of mathematics, for it is this subject which permeates every field of study.

Some important statistical methods of treating experimental data are touched on; one such application is a method of producing the 'best' straight line from a set of experimental data. Many items of commercial software make a feature of this technique, and some go to the trouble of extending it into 'curve fitting' software which produces a mathematical equation which best fits the results. It is hoped that the bok will lead readers to develop their own techniques for handling these problems.

Fascinating areas of graphics, including the design and manipulation of three-dimensional shapes, and the production of engineering and architectural drawings, are introduced. The mathematical techniques involved are kept fairly low-key in the early chapters, but those with a mathematical bent can use some of the matrix methods in the final chapter to produce some dramatic effects!

Since BASIC is the most popular programming language, it has been used as a vehicle to develop the programs in this book. However, if trigonometrical ratios are involved in a graphics program, they have the effect of slowing down its operation. For example, a standard (but easily understandable) circle drawing program is used in the early chapters of the book, but it has the drawback that it needs to compute many trigonometrical values. Later in the book a faster (but not so easily understandable) method is introduced; although the speed increase is not dramatic, it serves to illustrate that there is always an alternative method of solving a given problem.

Each computer has its own dialect of the BASIC language, and the BBC micro is no exception. So far as is possible, the progrmas have been written so that they are structured, logical and understandable. It should be possible for a computer-literature programmer to convert the programs into the BASIC dialect of another computer.

At various points in the book, certain problems are left unsolved, and the reader is invited to think about possible solutions. In most cases, the problems are returned to at a later stage, and a solution is offered. In this way, the book offers an educational challenge to those who wish to test their knowledge.

As with most aspects of life, education is a process of increasing perception, and the book leads the reader gradually forward to a deeper understanding of the relationship between art or graphics and the associated mathematics.

The programs on the disc have run successfully on the Model B, the Model B+ and the Master series, with the exception that for the Master series in program P8 it is necessary to change the calling address for the operating system in the screen saving and screen loading routines. The information relating to the addresses is available in the User Guide for the Master series.

Introduction to Programming Techniques

1.1 Modular Programming or 'Top-down' Programming

An advantage of the BBC BASIC language over many other forms of BASIC is that it contains many features which allow highly structured programs to be written. A technique known as **modular programming** using a **top-down** method can be adopted which enables programs not only to be easily understood but also quickly debugged so that errors can be removed.

A program written on these lines employs a relatively short **executive program** whose function it is to "call" a sequence of **procedures** or modules into use. In turn, each of these procedures may call other procedures, and so on; this is known as **nesting** the procedures.

A textbook is a good example of a top-down design. When you first open the book you see the list of contents; this is the executive program of the book which presents you with the list of chapters in the book (these can be thought of as the procedures or modules in the book). It is in the chapters that the real detail and activity takes place. Each chapter may be self-contained or it may call on other chapters for further information, in much the same way that one procedure in a program may call on another.

Modular programming offers a number of advantages over a large single program as follows:

1   Each procedure or module can be individually tested.
2   Errors within a procedure can be easily located.
3   Testing any one procedure can proceed independently of the others.
4   The program can easily be extended by adding new procedures as necessary.

1.2 A Simple 'Top-down' Designed Program

We now consider the process of writing a program in BBC BASIC which calls upon two simple procedures, one using the graphics facility of the computer and the other using the SOUND facility. The graphics procedure simply draws a rectangle, and the SOUND procedure produces a siren-like noise. Initially, we will see how each procedure is written and tested using its own executive program. Finally (in section 1.4) we will merge the two procedures into a single program.

The graphics program is given in *listing 1.1*. The executive program is in lines 10 to 50 inclusive, the purpose of each line being as follows:

10 defines the program name.
20 gets rid of the screen jitter.

30 puts the computer into screen MODE 1 which gives reasonable graphics display combined with a 40-character text width.

40 calls the procedure PROC_rectangle into use, which causes a rectangle to be drawn on the screen.

50 ENDs the executive program.

60 the colon acts as a separator between the end of the executive program and the begining of PROC_rectangle.

Listing 1.1

```
   10  REM****PROGRAM"P1.1"****
   20  *TV0,1
   30  MODE 1
   40  PROC_rectangle
   50  END
   60  :
10000  DEF PROC_rectangle
10010  CLS
10020  MOVE 100,100
10030  DRAW 100,900:DRAW 1100,900
10040  DRAW 1100,100:DRAW 100,100
10050  ENDPROC
10060  :
```

The procedure PROC_rectangle for drawing the rectangle commences in line 10000.There are good reasons for writing procedures which commence with a high line number; this is explained in section 1.3.

The first line in every procedure is a DEFinition of its name, e.g. DEF PROC_rectangle. Since the BASIC programming language has a number of *reserved names* which cannot be used in defining procedure names (these are names involved with program instructions such as MOVE and DRAW,

you are most strongly advised to use lower-case letters for procedure names.

For example you can, if you wish, call a procedure PROC_draw, but you cannot call it PROC_DRAW. The purpose of the lines in PROC_rectangle is as follows:

10010 clears the screen.

10020 MOVEs the graphics cursor to a point close to the bottom left-hand corner of the screen.

10030 and 10040 DRAWs the rectangle.

10050 ENDs the PROCedure (DO NOT USE an END instruction for this purpose, otherwise the computer thinks it has reached the end of the executive program).

Run the program and see the rectangle drawn on the screen. If you have made an error in writing the program, it is a relatively easy matter to put it right at this stage.

The program which produces the SOUND effect is *listing 1.2*. The executive program again commences at line 10, and the only purpose of the executive program is to bring PROC_siren into use. Once again the procedure commences at line 10000; the procedure causes the computer to output data to the sound chip (integrated circuit) which gives rise to a siren-like sound for a period of time. Once again, the procedure can be tested independently and any errors quickly corrected.

Listing 1.2

```
   10  REM****PROGRAM "P1.2"****
   20  PROC_siren
   30  END
   40 :
10000  DEF PROC_siren
10010  FOR C=1 TO 5
10020    FOR P=70 TO 100:SOUND 1,-15,P,1:NEXT P
10030    FOR P=100 TO 70 STEP -1:SOUND 1,-15,P,1:NEXT P
10040    NEXT C
10050  ENDPROC
10060 :
```

1.3   *SPOOLing and *EXECing Programs

In the previous section you encountered and tested two independent modules or procedures which we will now merge into one complete program. When you have written *any* program you can SAVE it on tape or disc (the latter being much quicker). However, when you save a program using the SAVE instruction, it is stored on tape or disc in what is known as a *tokenized* or *compressed* form. That is, certain words are stored in the form of a single character; for example, the basic word PRINT is stored as the token P. However, when you are storing a program or procedure which is to be merged or joined with another program, it is necessary to store each word in exactly the same form as it is typed into the computer. That is, the word PRINT needs to be stored as five characters or five ASCII characters (American Standard Code for Information Interchange).

The operating system command *SPOOL is used to store programs and procedures in ASCII or uncompressed form as follows. Suppose that you wish to *SPOOL the procedure PROC_rectangle so that it can be used as part of a larger program at a later stage (see section 1.4). You now need to retain in the memory of the computer only the part of the program you wish to SPOOL; it is therefore necessary to DELETE lines 10 to 60 of program *P1.1* using the DELETE 10,60 command, leaving only lines 10000 onwards in the memory.

You must give the file to be SPOOLed a name; let us call it "RECTANG". To avoid confusion betwen files that have been SAVED and files that have been SPOOLed, the author has found it useful to precede the filename with "S". Thus, we will call the *SPOOLed version of PROC_rectangle "S.RECTANG". To SPOOL the file you simply type *SPOOL "filename", that is

    *SPOOL "S.RECTANG"

and press the Return key. This has the effect of "opening" a file. Next you must type

    LIST

and, as the program is listed on the screen, it is also written into a file named S.RECTANG. You must then "close" the file and terminate SPOOLing by typing

    *SPOOL

The latter operation is very important, otherwise the file remains open. You can then verify that the file has been saved by typing *CAT and verifying that the program S.RECTANG is stored.

When SPOOLing a procedure, it is advisable to leave the ":" separator which follows each procedure (see line 10060 in *listings 1.1* and *1.2*). The reason for this is that, when several PROCedures are merged using the *EXEC command, each procedure will be separated from the next one by a ":" symbol, allowing the start of each procedure to be easily identified.

Once a file has been SPOOLed onto tape or disc, it can be returned to memory by typing *EXEC "filename" followed by ⟨RETURN⟩. In this case you type

    *EXEC "S.RECTANG"

Whilst the program is being *EXECed, it appears line-by-line on the screen of the monitor as though you were typing it at high speed. However, a SPOOLed program CANNOT be LOADed into the memory of the computer using the LOAD command; if you try to LOAD "S.REC-TANG", the computer will reply with "Bad Program".

When you have *EXECed a program, the computer terminates the display by printing "Syntax Error". This arises because of the > symbol which precedes the *SPOOL instruction; you can ignore the syntax error statement.

If you wish to look at the listing of a SPOOLed file, simply type *LIST "filename", that is

    *LIST "S.RECTANG"

The *LIST command causes the computer to LIST a named ASCII file; in this case the quotation marks around the filename are optional and may be omitted.

1.4 Merging Programs

Suppose that you wish to merge the procedures in programs *P1.1* and *P1.2* into a single program called *P1.3*. Firstly, you must SPOOL PROC_rectangle in the manner described in section 1.3; that is, LOAD program *P1.1* into the memory of the computer and DELETE lines 10 through 50. Next, type the following (pressing ⟨RETURN⟩ after each line):

    ∗SPOOL "S.RECTANG"
    LIST
    ∗SPOOL

You must then LOAD program *P1.2* into the memory and DELETE lines 10 through 40, and type the following:

    ∗SPOOL "S.SIREN"
    LIST
    ∗SPOOL

At this stage the programs S.RECTANG and S.SIREN are SPOOLed onto disc or tape.

You now need a new executive program which calls the two procedures into use. A simple example of this is given below (however, you must make sure that the memory is initialy cleared by typing NEW).

    10 REM∗∗∗∗PROGRAM "P1.3"∗∗∗∗
    20 ∗TV0,1
    30 MODE 1
    40 PROC_rectangle
    50 PROC_siren
    60 END
    70:

Next, you must merge the two SPOOLed procedures onto the end of the new executive program. PROC_rectangle is merged by typing

    ∗EXEC "S.RECTANG"

As the program is EXECed, you will see it appear line-by-line on the screen; remember, ignore the "Syntax Error" message printed by the computer. To complete the merging process type

    RENUMBER

followed by ⟨RETURN⟩. This command renumbers the complete program including the EXECed PROCedure. To verify that this has been done, LIST the program to see what it looks like. The reason for RENUMBERING the program is that is you ∗EXEC a number of PROCedures, each commencing at line 10000, then each EXECed PROCedure is written over the top of the earlier program, and deleted by it.

You must now append PROC_siren by typing

    ∗EXEC "S.SIREN"

followed by RENUMBER. The complete program appears as shown in *listing 1.3.* When you RUN the program, the computer draws a rectangle and makes a siren-like sound.

Listing 1.3

```
10 REM****PROGRAM "P1.3"****
20 *TV0,1
30 MODE 1
40 PROC_rectangle
50 PROC_siren
60 END
70 :
80 DEF PROC_rectangle
90 CLS
100 MOVE 100,100
110 DRAW 100,900:DRAW 1100,900
120 DRAW 1100,100:DRAW 100,100
130 ENDPROC
140 :
150 DEF PROC_siren
160 FOR C=1 TO 5
170    FOR P=70 TO 100:SOUND 1,-15,P,1:NEXT P
180    FOR P=100 TO 70 STEP -1:SOUND 1,-15,P,1:NEXT P
190    NEXT C
200 ENDPROC
210 :
```

1.5 Saving, Loading, Running and Chaining Programs

A program (or part of a program) can be SAVEd on either tape or disc simply by typing SAVE "filename" ⟨RETURN⟩, e.g. SAVE "P1.3". In the case of BBC BASIC, the quotation marks are mandatory; with a tape system, you must obey the prompts appearing on the screen. As mentioned earlier, the program is saved in a tokenized form.

Any program that has been SAVEd can be LOADed into memory simply by typing LOAD "filename", e.g. LOAD "P1.3". The operation of LOADing a new program into memory has the effect of deleting any program already there. You are now free either to amend the program or to RUN it simply by typing RUN ⟨RETURN⟩.

Alternatively, the commands LOAD and RUN can be executed automatically by typing CHAIN "filename" or CH. "filename", e.g.

CH. "P1.3"

1.6 Introduction to Menu-driven Programs

A **menu-driven program** is one which present the user with a "menu" of options or variations from which a choice can be made. Consider a menu-driven program which offers two options, namely "shapes" and "sounds"; a *flow-chart* illustrating the basis of the menu-driven program is shown in Fig. 1.1.

Fig. 1.1 The basis of a
menu-driven program

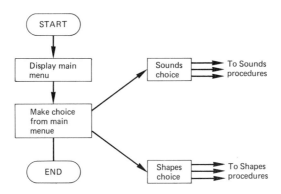

If the shapes option is chosen, the computer removes the main menu and offers a supplementary menu which asks you to make a choice from certain shapes. When you have selected the shape, control is transferred to a PROCedure which draws the shape. In much the same way, the sounds option gives you the choice of a range of sounds. It is rather like going to a high-class restaurant and choosing a meal from a wide menu!

However, in real life you are offered an "escape" clause which allows you to say either that you have made a mistake in your selection or that you wish to leave (quit) the program. In as far as it is possible to cover all the possibilities, the program should offer the quit facility.

Listing 1.4 shows a simple menu-driven program. The executive program (lines 10 through 110) causes the main menu to be displayed on the monitor screen and waits for you to type in your selection (KEY$ in line 70). When you have done this, it calls for PROC_select_from_menu which compares the word (or letter) typed in with one of the word listed in its memory (lines 220 through 280); you are also given the opportunity to type Q to quit the program.

If you type SOUNDS, control is transferred to PROC_sounds, which offers you a secondary menu giving a selection of sounds to choose from. One of these is the SIREN sound with which you are familiar (it is, in fact, a slightly modified procedure), and the other sound is like a gunshot. Depending on your selection, program control is transferred either to PROC_siren2 or PROC_shot.

The penultimate line of each PROCedure causes a "repeat" counter value to be stored (this is the value R in lines 510, 580, 660 and 720). The purpose of this value is to "tell" the computer which procedure was last executed. Just before leaving your selected PROCedure, another PROCedure called PROC_repeat is called (the method by which one procedure can call another is known as **nesting**). This procedure asks you if you want to repeat the last procedure, and if you do it uses the value of R stored in its memory to recall which procedure you last used. Should you decide not to repeat the last procedure, PROC_repeat gives you the option of either returning to the main menu or quitting the program.

Should you choose the shapes option, it allows you to draw either a rectangle or a triangle on the screen.

The function of this program is to introduce you to the exciting possibilities of menu-driven programs. Clearly, many other variants of this program are possible including, for example, altering the position, size and colour of the shapes, or altering the type of sound.

Listing 1.4

```
10  REM**** PROGRAM "P1.4" ****
20  REM**** MENU-DRIVEN PROGRAM ****
30  *TV0,1
40  MODE 1
50  PROC_main_menu
60  REPEAT
70    INPUT KEY$
80    PROC_select_from_menu
90    UNTIL KEY$="Q"
100 CLS
110 END
120 :
130 DEF PROC_main_menu
140 CLS
150 PRINT TAB(0,3)"TYPE M FOR MAIN MENU":PRINT
160 PRINT"TYPE SOUNDS FOR SELECTION OF SOUNDS":PRINT
170 PRINT"TYPE SHAPES FOR SELECTION OF SHAPES":PRINT
180 PRINT"TYPE Q TO QUIT THE PROGRAM":PRINT
190 ENDPROC
200 :
210 DEF PROC_select_from_menu
220 IF KEY$="SOUNDS" THEN PROC_sounds
230 IF KEY$="SHAPES" THEN PROC_shapes
240 IF KEY$="SIREN" THEN PROC_siren2
250 IF KEY$="SHOT" THEN PROC_shot
260 IF KEY$="RECTANGLE" THEN PROC_rectangle2
270 IF KEY$="TRIANGLE" THEN PROC_triangle
280 IF KEY$="M" THEN PROC_main_menu
290 ENDPROC
300 :
310 DEF PROC_sounds
320 CLS
330 PRINT TAB(5,3)"SELECTION OF SOUNDS":PRINT
340 PRINT"TYPE SIREN FOR A SIREN SOUND":PRINT
350 PRINT"TYPE SHOT FOR A SHOT SOUND":PRINT
360 ENDPROC
370 :
380 DEF PROC_shapes
390 CLS
400 PRINT TAB(10,3)"SELECTION OF SHAPES":PRINT
410 PRINT"TYPE RECTANGLE FOR A RECTANGULAR SHAPE":PRINT
420 PRINT"TYPE TRIANGLE FOR A TRIANGULAR SHAPE":PRINT
```

```
430  ENDPROC
440  :
450  DEF PROC_siren2
460  CLS
470  FOR C=1 TO 2
480    FOR P=70 TO 100:SOUND 1,-15,P,1:NEXT P
490    FOR P=100 TO 70 STEP -1:SOUND 1,-15,P,1:NEXT P
500    NEXT C
510  R=1:PROC_repeat
520  ENDPROC
530  :
540  DEF PROC_shot
550  CLS
560  FOR V=-15 TO 0 STEP 2
570    SOUND 0,V,4,2:NEXT V
580  R=2:PROC_repeat
590  ENDPROC
600  :

610  DEF PROC_rectangle2
620  CLS
630  MOVE 100,100
640  DRAW 100,500:DRAW 1100,500
650  DRAW 1100,100:DRAW 100,100
660  R=3:PROC_repeat
670  ENDPROC
680  :
690  DEF PROC_triangle
700  CLS:MOVE 100,100:DRAW 900,100
710  DRAW 500,500:DRAW 100,100
720  R=4:PROC_repeat
730  ENDPROC
740  :
750  DEF PROC_repeat
770  PRINT:PRINT"DO YOU WANT TO REPEAT ?":PRINT
780  INPUT "TYPE Y FOR YES OR N FOR NO";repeat$
790  IF repeat$="N" GOTO 840
800  IF repeat$="Y" AND R=1 THEN PROC_siren2
810  IF repeat$="Y" AND R=2 THEN PROC_shot
820  IF repeat$="Y" AND R=3 THEN PROC_rectangle2
830  IF repeat$="Y" AND R=4 THEN PROC_triangle
840  CLS
850  PRINT TAB(0,3)"TYPE M TO RETURN TO MAIN MENU":PRINT
860  PRINT"OR Q TO QUIT":PRINT
870  ENDPROC
880  :
```

1.7 Timing the Operation of a Program

The BBC micro contains an electronic clock which counts time in 0.01 second intervals; you can use this either as an **interval timer** or as a **real time clock.**

Certain techniques used in graphics programs to produce a particular effect are faster than other methods, and you can easily build a short routine into your program to determine the time taken to, say, draw a triangle. If you modify your program to perform a function in several ways, you can use the routine to determine the time taken by each method.

The number of 0.01 s time intervals counted from the moment that the computer is switched on is stored in the variable TIME in the computer. You can determing the time taken to, say, draw a rectangle using program *1.1* by inserting the following lines in it:

```
35 T=TIME
45 PRINT"TIME = ";(TIME–T)/100;" SECONDS"
```

or, alternatively,

```
35 TIME=0
45 PRINT"TIME = ";TIME/100;" SECONDS"
```

The first method allows TIME to store the total number of 0.01 s intervals from the instant the computer is switched on, whilst the second forces TIME to store zero at the outset of the timing test.

If the program takes a long time to run (say several minutes), it can be timed by intially setting the timer to zero (using TIME=0) and adding a short routine at the end of the main program to calculate the time taken. This is illustrated in *listing 1.5*. Line 30 sets the variable TIME to zero, and

Listing 1.5

```
10  REM**** PROGRAM "P1.5"****
20  CLS
30  TIME = 0
40  PRINT"PROGRAM RUNNING"
50  REM MAIN PROGRAM STARTS HERE
60  FOR N=1 TO 100000:NEXT N
70  REM MAIN PROGRAM FINISHES HERE
80  REM AND RUN TIME IS CALCULATED
90  T=TIME
100 S2 =(T DIV 100)MOD 60 + T/100 -(T DIV 100)
110 S2=(INT(S2*100+0.5))/100
120 MIN=(T DIV 6000)MOD 60
130 PRINT"TIME = ";MIN;" MIN ";S2;" SECONDS"
```

a simulated main program in the form of a time delay program is given in line 60. Line 90 determines the number (T) of 0.01 s time intervals counted by the computer hardware. The data is used in line 100 to calculate the number of seconds (and its fractional part), which is rounded up in line 110 to the nearest 0.01 s. Line 120 calculates the number of minutes, and line 1300 prints the number of minutes and seconds taken to execute the program. (The author's computer took 1 m 7.47 s to complete the program.)

1.8 An Error Trap

When writing (or even copying) a program, it is all too easy to miss something out such as a comma or other punctuation mark. Unless the program contains some form of **error trap**, the computer may stop the program during its run time and suggest that an error exists in a particular line (some errors cause the computer to state a line number which does not even exist!). A common error trap commences by inserting the following line at an early point in the program:

15 ON ERROR GOTO nnnn

where nnnn is a line number either at the end of the program (although it could be earlier than this) or a line which is well beyond the anticipated end of the program, e.g. line 8000. This line should contain a PRINT statement which causes the computer to print an error message indicating the nature of the error. A typical example may be

8000 IF ERR⟨ ⟩17 REPORT:PRINT" AT LINE ";ERL

Error number 17 (see the User Guide for details) corresponds to the BREAK key being pressed, and this information is not normally needed by the user. In general, error traps have been included in programs in this book if thought necessary. The REPORT command prints the error message, and ERL returns the program line number at which the error occurred. To check the operation of the error trap, insert the above instructions in one of your programs together with a known error (for example, change a correct BASIC instruction to an incorrect one) and RUN the program.

1.9 Program TRACE Facility

Most microcomputers, including the BBC micro, have a **program trace** facility which prints on the monitor screen each *line number* as it is executed. This feature is very useful if your program executes complex loops or if you use PROCedures or subroutines. You invoke the trace facility by typing

TRACE ON ⟨RETURN⟩

after which you RUN the program. IF you do this for program *P1.5*, it displays

[30][40]PROGRAM RUNNING
[50][60]

at which point it remains for the duration of the time delay, after which it displays the remaining line numbers as they are executed (lines 70 through 130), together with the elapsed time. If you have an error in the program, the TRACE facility allows you to debug the program. The TRACE facility is turned off either by typing TRACE OFF ⟨RETURN⟩ or by pressing the ⟨ESCAPE⟩ key.

One disadvantage of this method when debugging graphics programs is that the line numbers are printed on the screen over the top of the graphics!

1.10 Speeding Programs Up

The BBC micro is a relatively fast computer but, even so, many graphics programs do not run as quickly as you would like. A few techniques which enable you to speed up the programs on the BBC micro are listed here. Many of them are particular to the BBC micro but, so that the programs and principles in this book are (as far as possible) adaptable to other personal computers, only a limited number of them are used later. In a number of cases it is possible to adopt clever programming techniques to speed up graphics programs. However, this frequently leads to the program being difficult to read and understand; once again these techniques have been discarded in preference to straightforward programming methods.

1 Perhaps the best time saver of all is the use wherever possible of **integer variables** rather than *real variables*. An integer or whole number variable is distinguished from a real variable (which can contain a fractional part) by adding a % sign after the variable. Thus A% is an integer variable whilst A is a real variable. The program of *listing 1.6* uses the TIME instruction described in section 1.7 to compare calculations using two numbers of the same size. Both calculations are fast, but the real variable calculation takes 50 per cent longer than the integer variable calculation! Since the answer (variable C) has a fractional part, it is defined as a real variable.

Listing 1.6

```
 10  REM**** PROGRAM "P1.6" ****
 20  CLS
 30  TIME = 0
 40  A=100000:B=100000:C=(1/A)+(1/B)+A/B:PRINT C:PRINT
 50  T=TIME
 60  PRINT"TIME = ";T/100;" SEC.":PRINT
 70  TIME = 0
 80  A%=100000:B%=100000:C=(1/A%)+(1/B%)+A%/B%:PRINT C:PRINT
 90  T=TIME
100  PRINT"TIME = ";T/100;" SEC.":PRINT
110  END
```

A feature of the BBC micro is that, so long as the micro is switched on, integer variables are almost impossible to erase from the memory of the computer! For example, if you either type NEW or press ⟨BREAK⟩ after running program *P1.6*, you can always determine the values of the integer variables (check this by pressing ⟨BREAK⟩ and typing PRINT A%).

2 When writing graphics programs, PLOT commands (described later in the book) are frequently faster than MOVE and DRAW instructions, but have the disadvantage that they make the program difficult to follow.

3 Also, when using graphics, a PROCedure is often faster in operation than using a subroutine via a GOSUB instruction; in any case, PROCedures are more structured and elegant than subroutines.

4 You can also use special instructions in the BBC micro to alter the time balance between the computer's use of the keyboard and processing. To speed up processing at the expense of making the keyboard response very slow, type

　　?&FE45=1:?&FE46=0

To slow down processing, allowing the keyboard response to be very quick, type

　　?&FE45=255:?&FE46=255

To revert to the normal processing speed after either of the above commands, type

　　?&FE45=11:?&FE46=14

5 Another tip which may prove useful, though not directly related to improving the speed of operation, is a special instruction which can be used to disable the ESCAPE key. Pressing this key can be a nuisance in some programs, and it is disabled by typing

　　∗FX200,1

The key is re-enabled by typing ∗FX200,0.

1.11   BOOTING Programs from a Disc

Practically all computers with a disc drive have some method of enabling the user to BOOT or AUTO BOOT a program from a disc. This enables a specified program to be loaded into the memory and run. The BBC micro disc system is no exception in this respect, and the way in which it is implemented is described below.

　Place a formatted disc into drive 0 and type

　　∗OPT 4,3 〈RETURN〉

This is a disc filing system command (not to be confused with the BASIC OPT command) which enables you to perform the auto-BOOT operation; it has the effect of causing the statement "Option 3 (EXEC)" to appear at the top right-hand side of the VDU screen when you ∗CATalogue the disc [prior to selecting option 3, you will have seen the heading "Options 0 (off) in this position]. Next, you must type

　　∗BUILD !BOOT 〈RETURN〉

This creates or begins to build a file !BOOT into which subsequent entries are written. Line numbers (commencing with 1) are displayed on the screen each time you press Return. Suppose that you wish to BOOT program *P1.1* into use after switch-on. At line 1 of the !BOOT program you simply type

　　CHAIN "P1.1"

The computer replies by displaying line number 2. If program *P1.1* is the only file you wish to BOOT into use, simply close the file by pressing the ESCAPE key. When you ∗CATalogue the disc, you will find a file named

!BOOT in the directory. The program can be BOOTed into action as follows:

1 Hold the SHIFT key down and press the BREAK key.
2 Release the BREAK key and then release the SHIFT key.

The disc drive then runs and BOOTs program *P1.4* onto the screen. To check what any !BOOT file contains, simply type

＊LIST !BOOT

and the contents of the file !BOOT are displayed on the screen.

Should you wish to cause the !BOOT file to CHAIN other programs, you have one of two options.

Option 1 You could simply type the name of the file you wish to call into memory at the next line number of !BOOT, e.g. 2 CHAIN "P1.2", etc.

Option 2 You could include a CHAIN instruction at the end of *P1.4*, i.e. 105 CHAIN "P1.2".

1.12 Overlaying Programs in the BBC Micro

One of the problems with very long programs is that the computer begins to run out of memory space. In a number of cases this problem can be overcome by taking a look at your program to see whether you need to have all of it in the memory all the time. If this is not the case, the program can be split into segments or **overlays**. The computer needs only to store the executive overlay or **zero overlay** all the time, the other segments or overlays being stored on disc, and can be called into the memory as required.

The zero overlay contains instructions which call into use various **primary overlays** which perform specific functions as required by the zero overlay. This concept can be extended further by allowing a primary overlay to call a secondary overlay, and so on. However, we will limit ourselves here to the use of primary overlays.

Before proceeding further, you need to understand the **memory map** of the computer, which is a diagram showing the use to which the memory of the computer is put. This is illustrated for the BBC micro in Fig. 1.2 in which

PAGE = bottom of your program (zero overlay)
TOP = top of your program (zero overlay)
LOMEM = bottom of the area storing the program variables
HIMEM = top of the usable RAM

Using BASIC instructions, you can alter the address of PAGE, LOMEM and HIMEM, but the address of TOP depends on the length of the program. The executive segment or zero overlay occupies the area of memory between PAGE and TOP.

Once you know how much memory space is needed *by the largest primary overlay*, you can raise LOMEM to a value which allows sufficient space for any of your primary overlays.

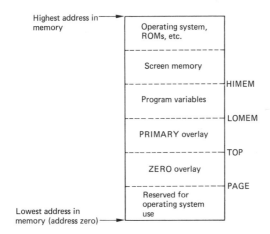

Fig. 1.2 BBC Model B
memory map

Since we have not written a long program yet, we will illustrate the technique using some of the short programs already developed. The zero overlay program is given in *listing 1.7*. The program proper commences in line 50, where LOMEM is set to TOP+&8D, in which &8D is the size of the largest primary overlay (expressed in hexadecimal) to be called by the zero overlay. The way in which this value is determined is explained a little later.

Listing 1.7

```
10   REM****OVERLAY PROGRAM "P1.7"****
20   REM ****OVERLAY 0****
30   *TV0,1
40   MODE 4
50   LOMEM=TOP+&8D
60   REM ****CALL PO1****
70   $&900="LOAD PO1 "+STR$~(TOP-2)
80   X%=0:Y%=9:CALL &FFF7
90   PROC_rectangle
100  REM ****CALL PO2****
110  $&900="LOAD PO2 "+STR$~(TOP-2)
120  X%=0:Y%=9:CALL &FFF7
130  PROC_siren
140  PRINT"END OF PROGRAM"
150  END
160  :
```

The zero overlay calls, in this case, for two primary overlays which respectively contain a copy of PROC_rectangle and PROC_siren (see programs *P1.1* and *P1.2*).

Firstly, you must type in lines 10 to 160 of the zero overlay (*listing 1.7*) and save it on disc as "P1.7". Next, type NEW to clear the memory and type in *listing 1.8* and save it as "PO1". Finally, clear the memory once more and save *listing 1.9* as "PO2", giving three files saved on disc.

Listing 1.8

```
10000  DEF PROC_rectangle
10010  REM ****OVERLAY PO1****
10020  CLS
10030  MOVE 100,100
10040  DRAW 100,900:DRAW 1100,900
10050  DRAW 1100,100:DRAW 100,100
10060  ENDPROC
10070  :
```

Listing 1.9

```
10000  DEF PROC_siren
10010  REM ****OVERLAY PO2****
10020  FOR C=1 TO 5
10030    FOR P=70 TO 100:SOUND 1,-15,P,1:NEXT P
10040    FOR P=100 TO 70:SOUND 1,-15,P,1:NEXT P
10050    NEXT C
10060  ENDPROC
10070  :
```

To run the complete program you either LOAD "P1.7" and then RUN it, or you CHAIN "P1.7". These sequences load and run the zero overlay, which sequentially loads and runs PROC_rectangle and the PROC_siren, both being called into memory from disc by the zero overlay. The way in which this operates is as follows.

Lines 70 and 80 of the zero overlay are equivalent to a *LOAD instruction, which differs from a LOAD instruction in that a sector of the program is loaded into the memory commencing at a specified starting address. The purpose of each of the lines is explained below.

The $ statement at the beginning of line 70 is interpreted by the computer as "write a string (text) to the computer memory starting at the location specified", the address specified in the line being &900 (hexadecimal). The string referred to is specified on the right of the equals sign in line 70.

In line 80, the X-register and the Y-register (specified as X% and Y% respectively) of the central processing unit are loaded with zero (00 hex) and nine (09 hex) respectively, and these are combined in the computer to form the hexadecimal address 0900, i.e. the address given in line 70.

The instruction CALL &FFF7 in line 80 transfers control to the Command Line Interpreter (CLI), which executes the instruction in line 70, namely LOAD PO1 at address (TOP-2). The reason for the rather curious address (TOP-2) is that the final two bytes in the zero overlay, i.e.

at TOP, contain an *end-of-program marker*. By loading overlay PO1 at this address, it strips the end-of-program marker off, making the end of overlay PO1 the end of the program.

The net result is that the zero overlay calls for program PO1 to be loaded from disc, and for it to be overlayed at the end of the zero overlay. The instruction in line 90 then calls for PROC_rectangle in overlay PO1 to be run. Using the same method, lines 110 and 120 call for overlay PO2 to be loaded (thereby deleting PO1 from the memory), and line 130 causes PROC_siren in overlay PO2 to be run.

If you LIST the program when the program has finished, you will find the zero overlay together with PO2 in the memory of the computer.

It only remains to explain how the size of each primary overlay (see line 50 of the zero overlay) is determined. You can use either of two methods described below.

The first is to load each overlay into the "empty" memory by typing the following instructions for *each* overlay:

    NEW
    LOAD "overlay"   i.e. LOAD "PO1"
    PRINT ~TOP-PAGE

The final line causes the hexadecimal value of the overlay memory size to be printed on the VDU.

The second method is quicker and deals with all the overlays simultaneously. With the disc containing all the overlays in drive zero, type

    *INFO *.*

This causes information relating to all the files on the disc to be printed on the screen. The value in the third column from the left is the size of the overlay. The sizes of PO1 and PO2 (neglecting non-significant zeros) are 7F and 8D; the latter value is inserted in line 50 of the zero overlay and is the largest of these, namely 8D. Of course, if you so wish, you can select a value which is greater than 8D. For example, try

    50 LOMEM=TOP+1000

Graphics Operations and User-defined Characters

2.1 Positioning the Display on the Screen

The BBC micro has eight screen MODES (numbered 0–7) offering several formats or arrangments for the display of text and graphics; they are listed in Table 2.1.

Table 2.1 Screen MODES of the BBC micro

Mode	Text on screen	Memory used by micro	Number of colours	Number of pixels	Pixel size
0	80×32	20K	2	640×256	2×4
1	40×32	20K	4	320×256	4×4
2	20×32	20K	16	160×256	8×4
3	80×25	16K	2	———	—
4	40×32	10K	2	320×256	4×4
5	20×32	10K	4	160×256	8×4
6	40×25	8K	2	———	—
7	40×25	1K	TELETEXT	———	—

Depending on the **screen MODE** used, the computer needs a certain amount of memory to store the data relating to the screen display, and you have to make a choice between the MODES when writing your program. You should note that, if you change the MODE in the middle of a program, anything on the screen will disappear! You should therefore select the screen MODE to be used at the outset (the default is MODE 7).

MODES 3, 6 and 7 are generally unsuited to high-quality graphics programs (chunky graphics can be obtained). If you write a program using text, you can choose between a viewing **field** of 80 characters wide (MODE 0 or 3), of 40 characters wide (MODE 1,4,6 or 7), or of 20 characters wide (MODE 2 or 5).

An 80 character width is best suited to a professional word-processing system, for which you will need a medium-resolution or a high-resolution monitor to see the characters (they are merely a blur on a standard TV screen). The "normal" width of display using the BBC micro is 40 characters.

The 20-character width displays are best suited to producing a rather striking text display, but you are limited to the amount you can put on the screen. There are, of course, special programs which enable you to use several screen MODEs simultaneously, but are beyond the scope of this book.

Having chosen the *character width* of the display, you must then choose the **number of colours** needed in the display. You have a choice of 2, 4 or 16 colours. (Strictly speaking, the 16-colour mode is an 8-colour mode, with the provision that eight of the colours flash between a pair of the fixed colours.) You should remember that the standard BBC model B micro has 32K of memory, and an increased amount of memory usage by the computer (see Table 2.1) leaves less for your program.

There are however, at a cost, methods of increasing the **memory size**. One method is to add a shadow RAM board, which deals with the screen display, and leaves you the same amount of memory for your program in any operating MODE. If you have a disc system, an alternative method is to use the overlay method of segmenting the program (see Chapter 1).

The way in which information is sent to the screen of the monitor depends on whether you are dealing with text (using PRINT and TAB instructions, etc.) or with graphics (using MOVE, DRAW and PLOT instructions, etc.).

If you are handling **text instructions**, you view the screen as though it were a piece of writing paper, the origin being at the top left-hand corner (see Fig. 2.1*a*). The rows and columns are numbered from the top left-hand corner, commencing with row and coloum 0. If you wish to print a character (say the letter C) in row 2 (the 3rd row from the left of the screen) column 1 (the 2nd column from the left of the screen), you type

PRINT TAB(2,1);"C"

where TAB tells the computer to tabulate to the text position (2,1) on the screen. The semicolon before the "C" tells the text pointer to remain at the TAB position (2,1) whilst it prints the letter C.

If you are handling **graphics instructions**, you look at the screen as though it were a piece of graph paper, the origin being at the bottom left-hand corner of the screen (see Fig. 2.1*b*). In each of the normal graphics MODES (MODES 0, 1, 2, 4 and 5), the screen is divided into 1280 *addressable columns* (columns 0 through 1279) and 1024 *addressable rows* (rows 0 through 1023). Although you can theoretically address or identify any of the 1280 × 1024 addressable locations on the screen, in fact the computer illuminates a complete **pixel** rather than a single addressable spot when you address a single location.

For example, a MODE 0 pixel contains 2 × 4 addressable locations (see Table 2.1 and Fig. 2.1*b*). If your program addresses any one of the spots within a pixel, it causes the whole pixel to be illuminated. Thus the graphics instruction

MOVE 500,600

causes an invisible graphics cursor to move to a position which is 500 addressable points to the right of the graphics origin and 600 addressable points above it. Should you cause a spot to be illuminated at that point, the complete pixel is illuminated. You will note from Table 2.1 that the pixel height is the same for all graphics MODES, but the width may be 2, 4 or 8 addressable spots.

Fig. 2.1 Addressable
locations for *a)* text, *b)*
graphics

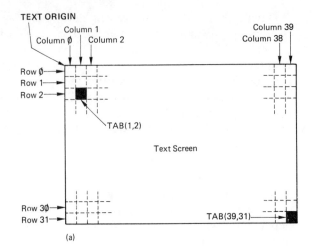

(a)

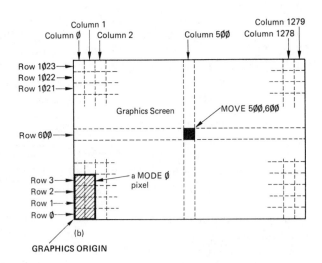

(b)

2.2 Drawing a Line

A line can be drawn by MOVEing the graphics cursor to the starting point
of the line, and then DRAWing a line between it and the finishing point.
This is illustrated in the program in *listing 2.1* (see also Fig. 2.2).

Listing 2.1

```
10   REM****PROGRAM "P2.1"****
20   REM****LINE DRAWING****
30   FOR M=0 TO 7
40     MODE M
50     PRINT TAB(5,2);"MODE ";M
60     MOVE 200,300:REM MOVE TO THE STARTING POINT
70     DRAW 900,800:REM DRAW A LINE
80     FOR C=1 TO 4688:NEXT C
90   NEXT M
100  RUN
```

Fig. 2.2 PLOT instructions

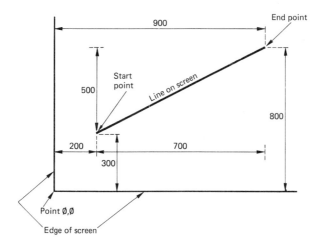

The program sets out to draw a line in each of the graphics MODES from a point which is 200 **graphics units** from the left-hand side and 300 graphics units from the bottom, to a point which is 900 graphics units from the left-hand side and 800 graphics units from the bottom (see lines 60 and 70).

When you RUN the program you should note that the line *is not drawn in MODES 3, 6 and 7) because they are not graphics MODES* (see Table 2.1). Also, the text at the top of the screen takes up a different position from the left of the screen for each of the MODES (but is always on the same text column); this is because the pixel size differs between the MODEs (each letter contains the same number of horizontal pixels). Moreover, both the text and the line drawn on the screen appear to jitter up and down; this is because of the way in which the BBC computer operates, the jitter being due to a feature of the monitor known as *flyback*. For MODES 0 to 6, the flyback can be turned off by inserting the following in program *P2.1*:

```
33 REM TURN FLYBACK OFF
35 *TV0, 1
```

This instruction must be inserted while the computer is in MODE 7 (note: it does not work for MODE 7 itself), after which you must change the MODE to the one you want to operate in (see line 40).

A feature of the program is that it allows you to see what a sloping line looks like in each graphics MODE of the BBC micro. You will see that MODE 0 gives the finest line, and that MODES 2 and 5 give the lowest-quality line (this is confirmed by the pixel size in Table 2.1).

Line 80 of the program gives a time delay of three seconds, enabling you to study the presentation of the line. Line 100 re-runs the program when all the MODES have been tested. Press ⟨ESCAPE⟩ to terminate the program.

2.3 PLOT Instructions

The MOVE and DRAW instructions described above can, alternatively, be replaced by **PLOT instructions**, which are more versatile. There are many PLOT instructions which allow you to draw points, lines and triangles on the monitor screen. Each PLOT statement needs a PLOT number together with a set of X- and Y-coordinates, e.g. PLOT 4,X,Y. The instruction

PLOT 4,200,300

is identical to MOVE 200,300. The instruction PLOT 5,X,Y is identical to a DRAW instruction; the instruction

PLOT 5,900,800

is identical to DRAW 900,800. That is, the MOVE and DRAW instructions in lines 60 and 70 of program *P2.1* can be replaced by PLOT 4,200,300 and PLOT 5,900,800 respectively.

Full details of the PLOT instructions are given in the User Guide, but the following is a summary (note: X and Y are graphics points or addresses on the screen):

PLOT 0,X,Y	move *relative* to the last point.
PLOT 1,X,Y	draw a line *relative* to the last point in the current graphics foreground colour.
PLOT 2,X,Y	draw a line *relative* to the last point in the logical inverse colour.
PLOT 3,X,Y	draw a line *relative* to the last point in the current graphics background colour.
PLOT 4,X,Y	move to the specified *absolute* point on the screen.
PLOT 5,X,Y	draw a line to the specified *absolute* point in the current graphics foreground colour.
PLOT 6,X,Y	draw a line to the specified *absolute* point in the logical inverse colour.
PLOT 7,X,Y	draw a line to the specified *absolute* point in the current background colour.

The first four PLOT instructions refer to an operation which is **relative** to the last point on the screen. If, for example, the current position of the graphics cursor is at the graphics address X = 400, Y = 500, the cursor can be moved to the graphics address X = 600, Y = 800 by means of a

PLOT 0,200,300

This causes the graphics cursor to move by 200 graphics spots (points) to the right of the current position and 300 graphics spots above the current position.

To draw a line in the current graphics foreground colour to the graphics address X = 900, Y = 600, you can use the instruction

PLOT 1,300,−200

This causes the computer to draw a line to the point which is 300 graphics spots to the right of the current graphics position on the screen and 200 graphics spots below it. That is, it draws a line in the graphics foreground colour from the point (X = 600, Y = 800) to the point (X = 600 + 300 = 900, Y = 800 − 200 = 600). If, for example, you insert the following instruction in program *P2.1* and RUN it you will see that the display is unchanged from the earlier version:

    32 MOVE 0,0
    60 PLOT 0,200,300
    70 PLOT 1,700,500

PLOT 2 draws a line relative to the last point in what is known as the *logical inverse colour*. Colours are dealt with in Chapter 3, but we can see its effect here. Insert the following instruction in program *P2.1* and RUN it:

    75 PLOT 2,0,−500

PLOT 3 draws a line relative to the last point in the current background colour. At the moment you are working with a white foreground and a black background, and this command draws a line in black! This is useful for "rubbing out" lines already drawn. This is illustrated by adding the following lines to your already modified program *P2.1* and RUNning it:

    76 FOR C=1 TO 1000:NEXT C
    77 PLOT 3,0,500

Line 76, above, is a time delay to allow you to observe the two lines on the screen, after which line 77 rubs out the vertical line by drawing a line in black over the top of it!

The PLOT 4 to PLOT 7 instructions repeat the functions of PLOT 0 to PLOT 3 respectively, but refer to an **absolute address** in graphics units on the screen.

There is a very wide range of other plot instructions which we cannot go into in detail, but are summarized below.

PLOT 8–15   as PLOT 0–7 but with the last point in the line omitted.
PLOT 16–23   as PLOT 0–7 but with a dotted line.
PLOT 24–31   as PLOT 0–7 with a dotted line, the last point being omitted.
PLOT 64–71   as PLOT 0–7 but only a single point is plotted.
PLOT 80–87   as PLOT 0–7 but plots and fills a triangle. The triangle is drawn between the coordinate specified and the last two points visited.

The PLOT 80–87 instructions may seem unusual, but are very useful not only in filling a wide variety of shapes with colour, but also in drawing wide lines on the screen (see section 2.4).

2.4 Altering the Width of the Line Drawn on the Screen

One method of drawing or "painting" lines of various widths on a screen (which you need in certain types of drawing) is to use the PLOT 85 instruction. This instruction draws and fills a triangle with colour (which is white unless you have specified some other colour). The steps involved are:

1 MOVE the graphics cursor to one of the corners of the triangle (say point 1 in Fig. 2.3).
2 MOVE the graphics cursor to another corner (say point 2).
3 PLOT 85 to the third corner (point 3), this instruction including the graphics coordinates of point 3.

The final instruction fills in the triangle 1,2,3 in Fig. 2.3 with colour. Write and run the following single-line program and you will see a filled triangle quickly appear on the screen:

10 MOVE 100,100:MOVE 800,500:PLOT 85,10,900

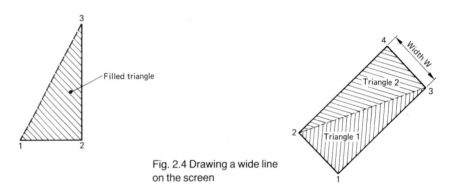

Fig. 2.3 The use of PLOT 85,X,Y

Filled triangle

Fig. 2.4 Drawing a wide line on the screen

This technique can be used to draw a wide line on the screen as shown in Fig. 2.4. Suppose that a line of width W graphics units is to be drawn from end 1,2 to end 3,4; a sequence of events which causes this to happen is described below:

1 MOVE to point 1: MOVE to point 2: PLOT 85 to point 3.
2 PLOT 85 to point 4.

Step 1 draws and fills in the triangle 1,2,3. Step 2 fills in the triangle between point 4 and the last two points visited, namely ponts 2 and 3. The net result is a line between end 1,2 and end 3,4 of width W. Program *P2.1* can be modified to show this by inserting the following lines:

25 INPUT "LINE WIDTH = ";W
65 MOVE(200+.581*W),(300−.814*W):PLOT 85,900,800
70 PLOT 85,(900+.581*W),(800−.814*W)

Line 25 asks you to give the line width W in graphics units, and lines 65 and 70 result in the wide line being drawn in each of the graphics MODEs. The values 0.581 and 0.814 are trigonometric values to make the end of the line square for any width of line.

2.5   Drawing a Wire-frame Shape

A simple **wire-frame shape** can be drawn using a sequence of MOVE and DRAW (or PLOT) instructions. Procedures for drawing a box and a triangle were introduced in Chapter 1; these diagrams were, of course, plane or flat.

Simple three-dimensional shapes can be produced using similar techniques. For instance, the program in *listing 2.2* draws an aerial view of a pyramid (see Fig. 2.5). Other shapes can be drawn using this technique.

Listing 2.2

```
10  REM****PROGRAM "P2.2"****
20  REM****SIMPLE SHAPE****
30  *TV0,1
35  *TV0,1
40  MODE 1
50  MOVE 800,200:DRAW 200,200:DRAW 500,800
60  DRAW 800,200:DRAW 1000,500:DRAW 500,800
70  END
```

Table 2.2   Graphics coordinates of the points in Fig. 2.5

Point number	Coordinates	
	X	*Y*
1	800	200
2	200	200
3	500	800
4	1000	500

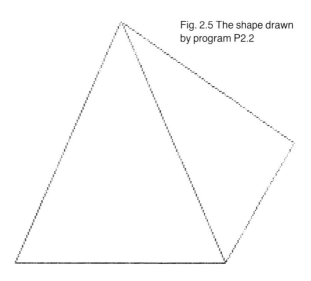

Fig. 2.5 The shape drawn by program P2.2

The disadvantage of this method is that each program must be individually tailored to the shape you need to draw. *Listing 2.3* is a drawing program containing a number of procedures which allow you to draw almost any shape you like on the screen and in any position. This program uses **arrays** to store data.

Lines 60, 80 and 100 and 120 of the executive program contain the DATA relating not only to the number of points and their screen location, but also to the number of lines to be drawn, and which points are to be

Listing 2.3

```
10   REM****PROGRAM "P2.3"****
20   REM****PRACTICAL DRAWING PROGRAM****
30   *TV0,1
40   MODE 1
50   REM****NUMBER OF POINTS ON DRAWING****
60   DATA 4
70   REM****X AND Y COORDINATES OF POINTS****
80   DATA 800,200, 200,200, 500,800, 1000,500
90   REM****NUMBER OF LINES ON DRAWING****
100  DATA 5
110  REM****PAIRS OF POINTS TO BE JOINED BY LINES****
120  DATA 1,2, 2,3, 3,1, 1,4, 4,3
130  PROC_points
140  PROC_lines
150  PROC_draw
160  END
170  :
180  DEF PROC_points
190  REM**READ NUMBER OF POINTS ON DRAWING
200  READ NP
210  REM**READ X AND Y COORDINATES OF EACH POINT
220  DIM X(NP),Y(NP)
230  FOR C=1 TO NP
240     REM**READ COORDINATES OF EACH POINT
250     READ X(C),Y(C)
260     NEXT C
270  ENDPROC
280  :
290  DEF PROC_lines
300  REM**READ NUMBER OF LINES ON DIAGRAM
310  READ NL
320  REM**READ STARTING (S) AND FINISHING (F) POINTS OF LINES
330  DIM S(NL),F(NL)
340  FOR C=1 TO NL
350     REM**READ STARTING AND FINISHING POINT OF EACH LINE
360     READ S(C),F(C)
370     NEXT C
380  ENDPROC
390  :
400  DEF PROC_draw
410  CLS
420  FOR C=1 TO NL
430     REM**MOVE TO START OF LINE
440     MOVE X(S(C)),Y(S(C))
450     REM**DRAW LINE
460     DRAW X(F(C)),Y(F(C))
470     NEXT C
480  ENDPROC
```

joined by lines. Program *P2.3* is written to repeat the pyramid shape in Fig. 2.5. The X- and Y-coordinates of each of the four points in Fig. 2.5 are listed in Table 2.2 Now, the computer not only has to know where the points on the screen are, but also which points are to be joined together. The four points are joined together by five lines as follows:

1 to 2, 2 to 3, 3 to 1, 1 to 4, 4 to 3

The executive program calls on PROC_points to read not only the number of points (NP) but also the X- and Y-coordinates of each point in sequence. Thus, the DATA in line 60 corresponds to the number of points (NP = 4) on the drawing. Next, the procedure reads pairs of data values (from line 80) of the X- and Y-coordinates of the points 1, 2, 3 and 4 in the diagram (in that sequence), and stores the X-values in an array called X, and the Y-values in an array called Y.

Next, line 140 transfers control to PROC_lines which reads the number of lines (NL) on the diagram (see line 100) and the pairs of points between which the lines are to be drawn (see line 120). Line 120 contains ten items of data (five pairs of values), the first of each pair of data values being the *starting point* S of the line and the second of each pair being the *finishing point* F. That is, lines are to be drawn from point 1 to point 2, then from point 2 to point 3, etc. On completion of PROC_points and PROC_lines, the computer stores the following data:

$$NP = 4, NL = 5$$

X(1) = 800, Y(1) = 200	S(1) = 1, F(1) = 2
X(2) = 200, Y(2) = 200	S(2) = 2, F(2) = 3
X(3) = 500, Y(3) = 800	S(3) = 3, F(3) = 1
X(4) = 1000, Y(4) = 500	S(4) = 1, F(4) = 4
	S(5) = 4, F(5) = 3

Program control is then transferred to PROC_draw which is described below. The MOVE X(S(C)),Y(S(C)) instruciton in line 440 "lifts" the computer "pen" and MOVEs it to the starting point S of a line. It determines the screen position of this point from arrays X and Y. The DRAW X(F(C)),Y(F(C)) instruction in line 460 draws the line between the starting point of the line and the finishing point F. The MOVE and DRAW sequence is repeated as many times as there are lines on the diagram (5 in this case).

You can modify the shape, size and position of the object merely by altering the data in lines 60, 80, 100 and 120. (For a complex object such as a car, you need to increase not only the amount of data but also the number of lines to draw it.) For example, altering the data lines to

```
 60 DATA 7
 80 DATA 200,200, 200,400, 400,400, 400,200, 341,541, 541,541,
    541,341
100 DATA 9
120 DATA 1,2, 2,3, 3,4, 4,1, 2,5, 5,6, 6,7, 7,4, 6,3
```

causes a box-shaped object to appear on the screen.

2.6 Drawing Geometrical Shapes

Many diagrams use a range of geometrical shapes such as rectangles, triangles, circles, ellipses, etc. In this section we will develop a number of procedures which you can add to any program needing them.

We will start with perhaps the simplest shape, the **rectangle**. *Listing 2.4* contains a procedure which allows you to draw a rectangle of any size and which starts at any point you choose on the screen. The data stored in lines

Listing 2.4

```
 10  REM****PROGRAM "P2.4"****
 20  REM****DRAW RECTANGLES****
 30  *TV0,1
 40  MODE 1
 50  REPEAT
 60    READ xstart,ystart,width,height
 70    PROC_rectangle(xstart,ystart,width,height)
 80    UNTIL xstart = -1
 90  END
100  :
110  DATA 200,200,400,200,  700,300,300,300
120  DATA 500,800,200,200,  -1,0,0,0
130  :
140  DEF PROC_rectangle(X,Y,W,H)
150  MOVE X,Y:DRAW X+W,Y:DRAW X+W,Y+H
160  DRAW X,Y+H:DRAW X,Y
170  ENDPROC
```

110 and 120 are used to fix the position and size of the rectangle, as shown in Fig. 2.6a; the X- and Y-coordinates of the bottom left-hand corner of the rectangle are xstart and ystart, the width of the rectangle is W, and the height is H. These have been converted to X, Y, W and H in PROC_rectangle (see line 140). The program reads the first four items of data from line 110 and, using PROC_rectangle, draws the corresponding rectangle. This is repeated twice more before the program is terminated (which happens when the computer reads a block of data containing xstart = 1).

Fig. 2.6 Coordinates for a) a rectangle, b) a triangle and c) a circle

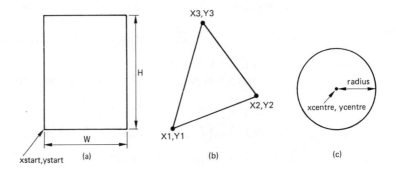

Listing 2.5 enables you to draw a **triangle** whose apexes are given by the points (X1,Y1), (X2,Y2) and (X3,Y3) — see Fig. 2.6*b*. Each time the program reads six items of data corresponding to the X- and Y-coordinates of the three apexes of the triangle, it calls on PROC_triangle to draw the corresponding triangle. The program is terminated when the computer reads a block of data containing X1 = −1.

Listing 2.5

```
10  REM****PROG "P2.5"****
20  REM****DRAW TRIANGLES****
30  *TV0,1
40  MODE 1
50  REPEAT
60    READ X1,Y1,X2,Y2,X3,Y3
70    PROC_triangle(X1,Y1,X2,Y2,X3,Y3)
80    UNTIL X1=-1
90  END
100 :
110 DATA 200,200,400,200,600,300
120 DATA 700,300,1000,400,700,800
130 DATA -1,0,0,0,0,0
140 :
150 DEF PROC_triangle(X1,Y1,X2,Y2,X3,Y3)
160 MOVE X1,Y1:DRAW X2,Y2:DRAW X3,Y3:DRAW X1,Y1
170 ENDPROC
```

Listing 2.6 enables you to draw a **circle** on the screen, the position of the centre of the circle and the radius being respetively defined by the variables xcentre, ycentre and radius (see Fig. 2.6*c*). In line 50, the executive program passes these parameters to PROC_circle. You will find that this program is slower in operation than programs *P2.4* and *P2.5* because it uses trigonometric functions (SIN and COS). These functions are relatively complex to process and take some time to evaluate. If at all possible, trigonometric functions should be avoided (you cannot always do this) because of the time penalty involved when using them.

Listing 2.6

```
10  REM****PROG "P2.6"****
20  REM****DRAW A CIRCLE****
30  *TV0,1
40  MODE 1
50  PROC_circle(500,600,200)
60  END
70  :
80  DEF PROC_circle(xcentre,ycentre,radius)
90  MOVE xcentre+radius,ycentre
100 FOR theta=0 TO 2*PI STEP PI/30
110   X=radius*COS(theta):Y=radius*SIN(theta)
120   DRAW X+xcentre,Y+ycentre
130   NEXT theta
140 ENDPROC
```

Fig. 2.7 illustrates the way in which the circle is drawn. Firstly, the graphics cursor is moved to point M, which has the screen coordinates (xcentre+radius, ycentre). Next, the values of X and Y in Fig. 2.7 are calculated for the angular step of PI/30 radians or 6°. Following this, a line is drawn from M to N. The circle therefore consists of 60 straight lines, each corresponding to a 6° arc.

For some angular steps, you may find that the computer does not quite complete the circle; this is because the computer works in binary and not in decimal or denary, and cannot exactly identify the decimal value corresponding to 2∗PI. In this case, it leaves a small gap at the end of the circle. One method of overcoming this problem is to modify line 100 as follows:

100 FOR theta=0 TO 2∗PI+0.01 STEP PI/30

Fig. 2.7 Steps in drawing a circle (not to scale)

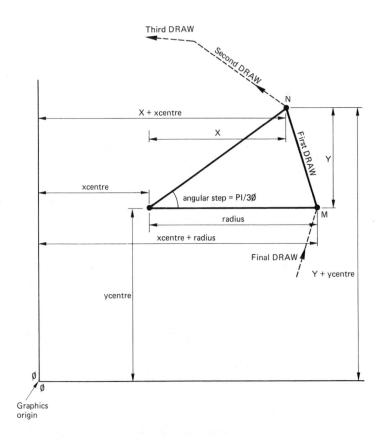

A regular polygon The circle program can be modified to cause it to draw an N-sided shape or regular polygon, e.g. an octagon or hexagon by changing line 100 to

100 FOR theta=0 TO2∗PI STEP 2∗PI/N

where N is the number of sides in the polygon. You must also insert a line in the program which gives the value of N, for example

45 N = 5

2.7   User-defined Characters

Although the readily available characters in the BBC micro are restricted to the keyboard characters, the computer offers the exciting prospect of allowing you to program your own characters. Moreover, large composite characters can be formed by combining programmable characters together!

Each keyboard character displayed on the screen is stored in the computer in the form of an **ASCII code** (American Standard Code for Information Interchange), and when the **VDU driver** of the BBC micro receives an ASCII code, it sends instructions to the screen or to the printer to print the character.

For example, the letter Y has the ASCII code 89 and the letter y has the ASCII code 121. These codes are sent to the display device whenever the appropriate key is pressed.

The BBC micro itself uses the ASCII codes up to and including 223.

> *You are free to use ASCII codes 224 to 255 for your own programmable characters.*

You can define your own programmable characters using the VDU 23 command in any MODE (except MODE 7) as follows:

VDU 23,224,R1,R2,R3,R4,R5,R6,R7,R8

The meaning of each part of this instruction is as follows:

VDU 23   instruction to redefine an ASCII character.
224   the ASCII character number to be redefined.
R1 to R8 the decimal value of each row in the new character (see below).

The shape of the character you produce in any given screen MODE can be slightly larger than one text character in that MODE because text characters have small spaces to separate one from another.

Each character is represented on an 8×8 grid as shown in Fig. 2.8.

Fig. 2.8 An arrowhead which is drawn using the VDU 23 command

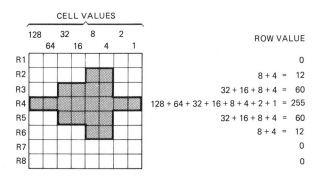

The top (first) row is called R1, the second R2, etc., and the bottom (final) row is R8. Each cell in each row is given a decimal value which doubles as you move to the left. The value of the row is simply the sum of the numbers associated with the filled-in cells in the row (you can, alternatively, use binary numbers rather than decimal values).

Suppose that you need to draw the arrow shown in Fig. 2.8. You must determine the decimal value associated with each of the rows in the character. Since rows R1, R7 and R8 do not have any filled-in cells, the decimal values, or weight, of each of these rows is zero; *this information must be entered into the VDU 23 definition of the character.*

Row R2 has cell values 4 and 8 filled in, so that R2 = 4+8 = 12. The value of row R3 is 32 + 16 + 8 + 4 = 60, etc. The VDU 23 instruction that defines the arrow in Fig. 2.8 is therefore

VDU 23,224,0,12,60,255,60,12,0,0

There are two methods of displaying the stored character on the screen, and these are

PRINT CHR$(ASCII number) i.e. PRINT CHR$(224)

and

VDU ASCII number i.e. VDU 224

However, there is an important difference between the two methods of display, namely *the PRINT instruction causes a line feed and carriage return to occur.* This means that, on completion of the instruction, the cursor always appears at the left-hand side of the screen and below the symbol.

The VDU 24 instruction leaves the cursor on the same line as the character on the screen.

Run the program of *listing 2.7* and you will find that lines 80 and 90 print two separate arrows, followed by two touching arrows (leaving the cursor on the same line as the arrows). You can get the cursor to return to the next line by altering line 80 to VDU 224:PRINT.

Listing 2.7

```
10  REM****PROGRAM "P2.7"****
20  REM****USER-DEFINED ARROW****
30  *TV0,1
40  MODE 1
50  VDU 23,224,0,12,60,255,60,12,0,0
60  PRINT CHR$(224)
70  PRINT CHR$(224)
80  VDU 224
90  VDU 224
100 END
```

It must be pointed out here that the size of the character defined here is constrained within the size of one *text character*, that is the character is *treated as text* rather than as a graphics character. Hence, to position the character on the screen, a text instruction such as PRINT TAB(X,Y) is used.

2.8 A Character-defining Program

The process of calculating the decimal value associated with each line of a user-defined character is rather a chore, and *listing 2.8* is both an interesting and educational program which does this for you.

Listing 2.8

```
10  REM****PROGRAM "P2.8"****
20  REM****CHARACTER DEFINER****
30  *TV0,1
40  MODE 1:VDU 19,0,4;0;:REM BLUE SCREEN
50  DIM CHAR(8,8):REM CLEAR CHARACTER MATRIX
60  PRINT"Cursor keys control cursor."
70  PRINT"Press 1 to fill the square."
80  PRINT"Press 0 to empty the square."
90  PRINT"Press P to print the definition."
100 PRINT"Press COPY to exit from program."
110 PRINT"Press N for new character."
120 INPUT"REQUIRED CHARACTER NUMBER = ";character
130 leftx=340:topy=790:size=72:border=8
140 x=376:y=754:Z=0
150 PROC_matrix:N=0
160 PROC_design
170 END
180 :
190 DEF PROC_design
200 REM COPY AND CURSOR KEYS RETURN NUMBERS
210 *FX 4,1
220 REPEAT
230   K=INKEY(0):REM READ KEYBOARD
240   IF K=136 AND x>380 THEN PROC_rubout_cursor:PROC_block:x=x-size:N=N
-1
250   IF K=137 AND x<875 THEN PROC_rubout_cursor:PROC_block:x=x+size:N=N
+1
260   IF K=138 AND y>255 THEN PROC_rubout_cursor:PROC_block:y=y-size:N=N
+8
270   IF K=139 AND y<750 THEN PROC_rubout_cursor:PROC_block:y=y+size:N=N
-8
280   PROC_cursor
290   PROC_calc
300   IF K=49 THEN CHAR(X,Y)=1:K=0:PROC_fill
310   IF K=48 THEN CHAR(X,Y)=0:K=0:PROC_empty
320   PROC_define_character
330   PROC_character
340   IF K=80 THEN PROC_print
350   IF K=78 THEN RUN
360   UNTIL K=135:REM COPY KEY
370 REM RESTORE KEYS TO NORMAL FUNCTION
380 *FX 4,0
```

```
390  VDU 20:CLS
400  ENDPROC
410 :
420  DEF PROC_define_character
430  CHAR(8,Y)=0
440  FOR I=0 TO 7
450    IF CHAR(I,Y)=1 THEN CHAR(8,Y)=CHAR(8,Y)+2^(7-I)
460    NEXT I
470  PRINT TAB(0,26);"Character definition = "
480  PRINT"VDU 23,";character;
490  FOR I=0 TO 7:PRINT",";CHAR(8,I);:NEXT
500  VDU 23,character
510  FOR J=0 TO 7:PRINT CHR$(CHAR(8,J));:NEXT J:PRINT"  "
520  ENDPROC
530 :


540  DEF PROC_character
550  PRINT TAB(0,30);"Character shape = ";CHR$(character)
560  IF CHAR(X,Y)=1 THEN PROC_fill ELSE PROC_empty
570  ENDPROC
580 :
590 :
600  DEF PROC_matrix
610  FOR N=63 TO 0 STEP -1
620    X=N MOD 8:Y=N DIV 8
630    PROC_fill:PROC_empty
640    NEXT N
650  ENDPROC
660 :
670  DEF PROC_fill
680  GCOL 0,131
690  VDU 24,leftx+X*size;topy-size*(Y+1);leftx+size*(1+X);topy-Y*size;
700  CLG
710  VDU 26:REM RESTORE WINDOWS
720  ENDPROC
730 :
740  DEF PROC_empty
750  GCOL 0,128
760  VDU 24,leftx+border+X*size;topy+border-size*(1+Y);leftx-border+size*
(1+X);topy-(border+size*Y);
770  CLG
780  VDU 26:REM RESTORE WINDOWS
790  ENDPROC
800 :
810  DEF PROC_calc
820  X=N MOD 8:Y=N DIV 8
830  ENDPROC
840 :
```

```
850   DEF PROC_cursor
860   GCOL 4,1
870   MOVE x,y+28:DRAW x,y-30:MOVE x-28,y:DRAW x+30,y
880   ENDPROC
890   :
900   DEF PROC_rubout_cursor
910   MOVE x,y+28:PLOT 7,x,y-30:MOVE x-28,y:PLOT 7,x+30,y
920   ENDPROC
930   :
940   DEF PROC_block
950   IF CHAR(X,Y)=1 THEN PROC_fill ELSE PROC_empty
960   ENDPROC
970   :
980   DEF PROC_print
990   VDU 2:REM ENABLE PRINTER
1000  PROC_define_character
1010  VDU 3:REM DISABLE PRINTER
1020  ENDPROC
```

A typical display produced by the program is shown in Fig. 2.9; the program also offers the option of printing the character definition (in the form of a VDU 23 instruction) on a printer connected to the micro by a parallel (Centronics) interface.

Fig. 2.9 A screen display provided by the character-defining program

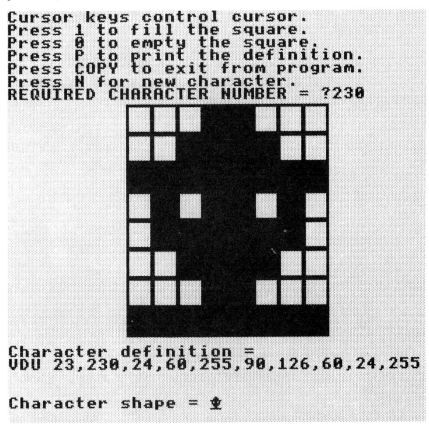

The screen display allows you to fill any cell on a large 8×8 matrix (or to empty the cell) and, simultaneously, at the foot of the screen to build up the character as it is seen on the screen (although the size will depend on which MODE you use in line 40). A summary of the function of each part of the program is given below:

Executive program   Lines 60 to 110 display information about the program, and line 120 asks you for your selected character number (ASCII number). Line 150 calls for PROC_matrix, which draws up an 8×8 matrix on the screen. Line 160 allows you to design your character.

PROC_design   Line 210 causes the cursor and COPY keys to input numerical values to the computer (this allows you to control the position of the cursor on the screen). Lines 240 to 270, inclusive, prevent the cursor moving outside the matrix. Line 280 (PROC_cursor) draws the cursor inside the current cell and line 290 (PROC_calc) calculates which cell the cursor is in. Lines 300 and 310 either fill or empty the cell (depending on whether you press a 1 key or a 0 key). Line 320 (PROC_define_character) calculates the numerical value of the row in the VDU 23 instruction, and line 330 (PROC_character) draws the character in its true size at the foot of the screen. IF you press the P (Print) key at any stage, line 340 provides you with a hardcopy on your printer. If you press the N (New) key, the program repeats itself and enables you to define another character. Finally, you can escape from the program by pressing the COPY Key.

2.9   Joining User-defined Characters Together

Some useful effects can be obtained using relatively simple techniques. For example, several user-defined characters can be joined together in a single VDU statement simply by separating each VDU number by a comma. *Listing 2.9* illustrates this technique. Code 225 in line 50 draws a short line and code 226 in line 60 draws an elongated dot. The two codes are combined in the FOR-NEXT loop in lines 70 to 90, inclusive, to draw a chain-dotted line which can be used, for example, as a centre-line in an engineering drawing.

Listing 2.9

```
10   REM****PROGRAM "P2.9"****
20   REM****CHAIN-DOTTED LINE****
30   *TV0,1
40   MODE 1
50   VDU 23,225,0,0,0,255,0,0,0,0
60   VDU 23,226,0,0,0,24,0,0,0,0
70   FOR C=1 TO 4
80     VDU 225,225,225,226
90     NEXT C
100  VDU 225,225,225:PRINT
110  END
```

VDU codes can also be used to control the position of the cursor on the screen as follows:

VDU code	Effect
8	move the cursor one step to the left
9	move the cursor one step to the right
10	move the cursor down one line
11	move the cursor up one line

The effect of one of these, VDU 10 for example, can be illustrated in program *P2.9* by adding it to the end of line 80 as follows:

80 VDU 225,225,225,226,10

You will see that this has the effect of moving successive dash-and-dot down the screen a distance *equal to one text line*.

Let us use the knowledge acquired so far to draw a larger object. In this case we will use the program in *listing 2.10* to display the bus in Fig. 2.10.

Listing 2.10

```
10  REM****PROGRAM "P2.10"****
20  REM****LARGE USER-DEFINED CHARACTER****
30  *TV0,1
40  MODE 1
50  PROC_define_codes
60  PROC_print_codes
70  END
80  :
90  DEF PROC_define_codes
100  VDU 23,227,0,0,127,66,66,66,66,127
110  VDU 23,228,0,0,255,16,16,16,16,255
120  VDU 23,229,0,0,255,132,132,132,132,255
130  VDU 23,230,0,0,224,32,32,32,32,224
140  VDU 23,231,127,127,127,124,121,123,3,1
150  VDU 23,232,255,255,255,63,159,223,192,128
160  VDU 23,233,255,255,255,252,249,251,3,1
170  VDU 23,234,254,254,254,62,158,222,192,128
180  ENDPROC
190  :
200  DEF PROC_print_codes
210  CLS
220  VDU 10,9,9,9
230  VDU 227,228,229,230
240  VDU 10,8,8,8,8
250  VDU 231,232,233,234
260  ENDPROC
```

The characters defined by the ASCII codes 227 to 234 in lines 100 to 170, respectively of PROC_define_codes are combined in PROC_print_codes to form the shape of the bus.

Fig. 2.10 Joining user-defined characters

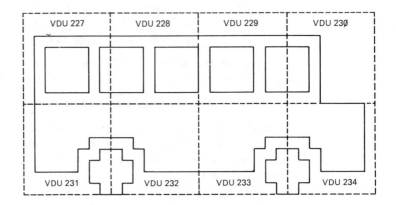

Line 220 positions the top of the bus as follows. The VDU 10 instruction shifts the cursor down one line from the top of the screen, and the three VDU 9 codes cause the cursor to move three text positions to the right. When line 230 is executed, the four user-defined codes cause the top half of the bus to be printed on the monitor screen. Line 240 results in the cursor being moved down one line and four places to the left, and line 250 prints the bottom half of the bus.

Alternatively, you can combine the characters and control codes into a single string and include them in program *P.10* as shown below. This modification prints out six buses which are in line with one another.

```
220  bus$=CHR$(227)+CHR$(228)+CHR$(229)+CHR$(230)
     +CHR$(10)+CHR$(8)+CHR$(8)+CHR$(231)+CHR$(232)
     +CHR$(233)+CHR$(234)
230  FOR X=2 TO 32 STEP 5
240  PRINT TAB(X,3);bus$
250  NEXT X
```

2.10   Controlling the Text Cursor Position

In normal use, the text cursor is a flashing line on the screen which shows where text will appear when it is typed. Its position can be controlled in several ways, including the usual cursor control keys (the four keys in the top right-hand corner of the keyboard), and by using either VDU codes or PRINT CHR$ as explained in section 2.9. Additionally, cursor control can be exercised by other VDU codes including the following:

VDU 12   to clear the text area and return the text cursor to the home position (top left-hand corner of the screen).

VDU 30   to return the cursor to the home position without clearing the screen.

In a number of graphics programs, the flashing cursor can be a nuisance, and it may be turned OFF either by the instruction

>VDU 23;8202;0;0;0;

or

>VDU 23,1,0;0;0;0;

and may be turned ON again either by

>MODE n

where n is the MODE number you select, i.e. 0 to 7, or by

>VDU 23,1,1;0;0;0;

2.11 User-defined Function Keys or Soft Keys

The red user-defined keys or software-controlled keys at the top of the keyboard can be used in the following ways:

1 To store a string of text.
2 To return an ASCII value (number) to the computer.

Method 1 is described here, method 2 being described later in this section (see also Chapter 8).

1 To cause one of the function keys, say f0, **to store a letter or a string of text**, for example the word LIST, you simply type

>*KEY0 LIST ⟨RETURN⟩

Every instruction which is preceded by an asterisk (*) is passed to the operating system (OS) which controls the computer.
You cannot write another BASIC instruction after an OS command
so that either it must be written on a line on its own, or it must be the final instruction in a line.

Thereafter, every time you press the red f0 key, the word LIST appears on the screen as though you had typed it. If you press the RETURN key, a listing of the program currently in the memory of the computer will be displayed on the screen. You can also use this key to LIST a section of the program simply by typing the required starting and finishing lines.

By incorporating appropriate control codes into the *KEYn instruction, you can make the function keys do several things. For example, the vertical line (¦ in MODE 0 to MODE 6 or ‖ in MODE 7) is equivalent to pressing the CTRL key, so that ¦ M (see the VDU summary sheet in the user handbook of the BBC micro) is equivalent to pressing the RETURN button. Thus, if the red f1 key is defined as

>*KEY1 LIST ¦ M

then, every time key f1 is pressed, the program currently in memory is listed on the screen.

Any frequently used string of text can be held in a user-defined key. For instance, when modifying line 220 of program *P2.10* (see section 2.9), it is convenient to define key f2 as

   *KEY2)+CHR$(

When altering *P2.10* it merely remains to type each ASCII code before pressing the f2 key.

   You can usefully write a short program to use the function keys to store your ten most useful BASIC instructions such as SAVE, LOAD, RUN, *CAT, etc. If you RUN this program (or, more usefully, write it as a !BOOT file — see Chapter 1), the user-defined keys provide useful time-saving features.

   Listing 2.11 is a simple example of this kind. The function performed by

Listing 2.11

```
 10  REM****PROGRAM "P2.11"****
 20  REM****SOFTKEY PROGRAMMING****
 30  *KEY0 LIST
 40  *KEY1 OLD¦M LISTO 0¦M LIST¦M
 50  *KEY2 LISTO 7¦M LIST¦M
 60  *KEY3 ¦N¦M
 70  *KEY4 ¦O¦M
 80  *KEY5 REN.¦M
 90  *KEY6 RUN¦M
100  *KEY7 SAVE"
110  *KEY8 LOAD"
120  *KEY9 ¦B¦M LIST¦M ¦C¦M
```

each of the keys after the program has been loaded and run is as follows:

KEY0   This simply prints LIST and waits for you to enter a line number (or numbers) which you require listing on the screen.

KEY1   The words OLD and LISTO0 are printed on the screen, and the current program is listed. The command OLD simply recovers the program if the BREAK key has been pressed, and LISTO0 (LIST Option 0) suppresses the indenting of FOR-NEXT and REPEAT-UNTIL loops in the listing.

KEY2   This LISTs the current program but indents FOR-NEXT and REPEAT-UNTIL loops in the program.

KEY3   Prints nothing on the screen (the cursor merely moves down one line), but switches the monitor into the *page mode*. This is equivalent to pressing the N key with the CTRL key held down; this is very useful when listing long programs, since the screen is scrolled one page at a time.

KEY4   This turns the page mode off and restores *continuous scrolling*. It is equivalent to pressing the O key with the CTRL key held down.

KEY5   RENUMBERs the current program using a 10-line interval.

KEY6   RUNs the program currently in the memory of the computer.

KEY7   Prints SAVE". This saves typing time when saving a program.

KEY8   Prints LOAD". This saves typing time when loading a program.

KEY9   Performs ¦ B ¦ M which enables the printer, after which a listing of the current program is printed on a printer with a parallel interface connected to the printer port. The printer is then disabled by the ¦ C ¦ M command.

However, the BBC micro has only 256 bytes of memory (corresponding to 256 keyboard characters, which includes spaces), reserved for user key definitions. There appears to be no restriction on the way in which this amount of memory is divided between the keys.

2 Returning an ASCII code from user-defined keys This technique is particularly useful in designing computer-aided drawing programs since it allows you to control not only the red function keys but also the four cursor control keys and the COPY key. At this stage we will outline a simple method of redefining the cursor as a cross (+) for use in, for example, a graphics program. The four cursor control keys will be used to move the new cursor around the screen in steps of ten graphics units. In this program the COPY key is redefined to allow you to restore the computer to its normal condition when you want to quit the program. The program is given in *listing 2.12* and is described below.

The executive program calls for PROC_initialize, which sets up the operating conditions of the computer as follows. Line 210 turns the text cursor off, and line 230 makes the cursor control and COPY key return ASCII values which, in this case, are

Key	ASCII value
COPY	135
←	136
→	137
↓	138
↑	139

Finally, line 240 establishes the X- and Y-position of the cursor at the centre of the screen in graphics units.

Next, the executive program transfers control in line 60 to PROC_cursor which draws the new cursor (a cross) on the screen at the position X = 600 graphics units, Y = 500 graphics units. You will note at this time that both the prompt (⟩) and the flashing text cursor are extinguished.

Following this, a REPEAT-UNTIL loop (lines 70 to 140 inclusive) is executed until either one of the cursor control keys or the COPY key is pressed. When a cursor control key is pressed, the current cursor is rubbed out by PROC_rubout_cursor (which uses PLOT 7 instructions), and another cursor is drawn at the new position.

The REPEAT-UNTIL loop is terminated when the COPY key (ASCII code 135) is pressed. After this, the executive program restores the editing and COPY keys to their normal functions (line 160) and the flashing text cursor is turned on (line 170).

You can have the cursor any shape you choose. For example, altering line 280 to

> 280 MOVE X,Y+15:DRAW X−15,Y:DRAW X,Y−15:DRAW
> X+15,Y:DRAW X,Y+15

results in a diamond-shaped cursor being drawn which is centred on the point X,Y (you must remember to alter PROC_rubout_cursor to delete the same shape). You can also make the stepping movement of the cursor either coarser or finer by respectively increasing or decreasing the step change in lines 90 to 120 inclusive. There is no point in reducing the step size to a value which is less than one pixel in the chosen MODE.

Listing 2.12

```
10  REM****PROGRAM "P2.12"****
20  REM****CURSOR DEFINITION AND CONTROL****
30  *TV0,1
40  MODE 1
50  PROC_initialize
60  PROC_cursor
70  REPEAT
80    K=INKEY(0):REM READ KEYBOARD
90    IF K=136 THEN PROC_rubout_cursor:X=X-10
100   IF K=137 THEN PROC_rubout_cursor:X=X+10
110   IF K=138 THEN PROC_rubout_cursor:Y=Y-10
120   IF K=139 THEN PROC_rubout_cursor:Y=Y+10
130   PROC_cursor
140   UNTIL K=135:REM COPY KEY
150 REM RESTORE EDITING KEYS TO NORMAL
160 *FX 4,0
170 MODE 1:REM TURN CURSOR OFF
180 CLS:END
190 :
200 DEF PROC_initialize
210 VDU 23;8202;0;0;0;:REM TURN TEXT CURSOR OFF
220 REM MAKE CURSOR KEYS RETURN ASCII NUMBERS
230 *FX 4,1
240 X=600:Y=500
250 ENDPROC
260 :
270 DEF PROC_cursor
280 MOVE X,Y+15:DRAW X,Y-15:MOVE X-15,Y:DRAW X+15,Y
290 ENDPROC
300 :
310 DEF PROC_rubout_cursor
320 MOVE X,Y+15:PLOT7,X,Y-15:MOVE X-15,Y:PLOT7,X+15,Y
330 ENDPROC
```

2.12   A Graphics Ruler

An important feature of many graphics programs is the ability to use the cursor to measure distances on the screen. To illustrate this, we will modify program *P2.12* to include a **ruler** which prints the movement of the cursor from its origin in graphics units. To do this, simply add the following lines to the program:

```
62 PRINT TAB(0,1)"Cursor X position = "
64 PRINT TAB(0,2)"Cursor Y position = "
65 PRINT TAB(0,3)"Movement of cursor = "
122 PRINT TAB(20,1)"       ";TAB(20,1);X
124 PRINT TAB(20,2)"       ";TAB(20,2);Y
126PROC_calc
340:
350 DEF PROC_calc
360 dx=600−X:dy=500−Y:len=INT(SQR(dx^2+dy^2)*100)/100
370 PRINT TAB(21,3)"       ";TAB(21,3);len
380 ENDPROC
```

Remember to leave seven spaces between the quotation marks in lines 122, 124 and 370. These cause the computer to rub out the old values of X, Y and len, respectively, before it prints the new values.

The points to note about the modified program are as follows. Firstly, the values of the X- and Y-position of the cursor are in screen graphics units and the display flickers. The latter is because the computer is continually measuring the calculating values on each pass of the REPEAT-UNTIL loop. Secondly, you can move the cursor off the screen; at the same time, the position of the cursor (both on screen and off it!) is continually monitored. Thirdly, the movement of the cursor position is calculated to two decimal places in line 360.

Fourthly, if you hold down one of the cursor control keys for any length of time, the cursor continues moving for a short time after you release the key. This is because the computer forms a queue of requests to move the cursor; it continues until the queue has been dealt with. One way of overcoming this is dealt with in a later program.

2.13   Text and Graphics Windows

Up to this point in the book, the whole screen has been used to display both text and graphics. However, there are many occasions in graphics programs where we need to keep the graphics area separate from the text area. To do this, you can create **windows** on the VDU screen which are intended either for text or for graphics. (It is, of course, necessary in some cases to have text on drawings, and special instructions enable you to write text in the graphics window.) The following explains how you create the windows.

In section 2.1 (see also Fig. 2.1) it was shown that the origin of the *text screen* is in the top left-hand corner of the screen, and the origin of the *graphics screen* is in the bottom left-hand corner. These are used as reference points or starting points from which we can define the windows.

Defining a text window A text window (see Fig. 2.11) is defined in terms of two points on the window: namely, the bottom left-hand corner and the top right-hand corner of the window. The locations of these points are used in association with a VDU 28 statement as follows:

VDU 28,a,b,c,d

bottom left X,Y ⎤ ⎣ top right X,Y

Example   VDU 28,5,20,20,5

Notice that the values in the expression are separated by a comma, and that the final value does not have a comma after it. The numbers in the VDU 28 expression are in **text units** or characters. In the example given, the text window has its bottom left-hand corner at a point which is five text character spaces from the left-hand side of the screen and twenty text character spaces from the top.

Fig. 2.11 Defining a text window (in this case, screen MODEs 1 and 4 are implied)

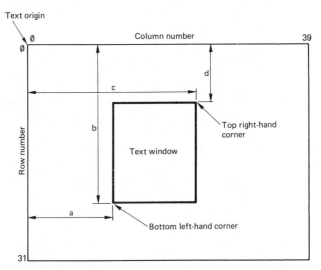

You must never define a text window before you change the screen MODE because changing the MODE causes both text and graphics windows to fill all the screen.

The program in *listing 2.13* shows the use of a text window in each of the eight screen MODEs. Line 30 contains a CLS **text instruction** which *clears the text window*. If both text and graphics windows are equal to the whole screen area (as they are when the micro is switched on), it has the effect of clearing everything from the screen.

The FOR-NEXT loop in lines 40 to 90 inclusive has the following effect:

1 It changes the screen MODE (line 50).
2 It defines the text window (line 60).
3 It prints the MODE number (0–7) eighty times (line 70), thereby filling the text window and causing the text to scroll upwards.
4 It causes the display to dwell for a short period (line 80).

The default windows are restored in line 100.

Listing 2.13

```
10   REM****PROGRAM "P2.13"****
20   REM****TEXT WINDOW****
30   CLS
40   FOR M=0 TO 7
50     MODE M
60     VDU 28,5,15,15,5
70     FOR C=1 TO 80:PRINT"MODE";M;:NEXT C
80     FOR K=1 TO 5000:NEXT K
90     NEXT M
100  VDU 26:END
```

Defining a graphics window   The graphics origin is at the bottom left-hand corner of the screen (see Fig. 2.1). A graphics window is defined in terms of the X- and Y-coordinates of the lower left-hand corner and the upper right-hand corner of the window, and uses a VDU 24 instruction as follows:

VDU 24,a;b;c;d;

bottom left X,Y⌐   ⌐top right X,Y

Example   VDU 24,600;200;1000;800;

You should note here that the X- and Y-measurements are in **graphics units** and are taken from the *bottom left-hand corner of the screen* (see Fig. 2.12).

Fig. 2.12 Defining a
graphics window

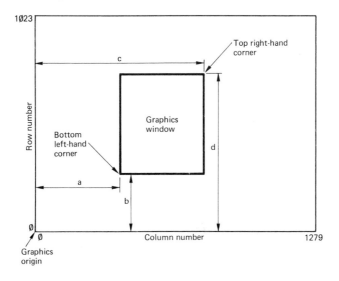

When defining the graphics window,
    *there is a comma after the 24 in VDU 24, and a semicolon after each
    value specifying the X- or Y-coordinates.*

The program in *listing 2.14* gives a simple illustration of the use of both graphics and text windows. Line 60 defines the graphics window, and line 70 fills it with colour (which is either white or red, depending on the screen MODE); details of instructions referring to colour are given in Chapter 3. Line 90 defines the text window and line 110 prints the screen MODE number. Line 120 provides a time delay which allows time to look at the effect.

Listing 2.14

```
10  REM****PROGRAM "P2.14"****
20  REM****GRAPHICS WINDOW****
30  CLG
40  FOR M=0 TO 7
50    MODE M
60    VDU 24,600;200;1000;800;
70    GCOL 0,129
80    CLG
90    VDU 28,5,15,15,10
100   CLS
110   PRINT"MODE ";M
120   FOR K=1 TO 5000:NEXT K
130   NEXT M
140 VDU 26:END
```

You will observe that,
> *even though the text window alters in size with the screen MODE, the graphics window does not.*

This is because the text characters alter in size with the screen MODE, but in graphics operations the screen is always the same size, namely 1280×1024 addressable points.

The program provides some useful information in that it illustrates both types of windows simultaneously. In screen MODEs 0, 1 and 4, the text window does not interfere with the graphics window. In MODEs 2 and 5, the text window overlays the graphics window and blacks out part of it (the reason being that the text window is defined after the graphics window). MODEs 3, 6 and 7 are not graphics MODEs, and the graphics window is ignored.

The effect of overlaying a graphics window on top of a text window can be seen by renumbering line 90 as line 52, line 100 as line 54, and line 110 as line 56; lines 90, 100 and 110 must be deleted from the program. In this case, it is the graphics window which covers up part of the text in MODEs 2 and 5.

2.14 Writing Text in a Graphics Window

There are many applications which need both text and graphics windows, but still have a need for text to be written within the graphics window. This occurs, for example, where some sort of commentary must appear in the text window, whilst (say) a graph together with its axes, scales and labels must be drawn in the graphics window. The writing of text is achieved by means of the VDU 5 command (write text at the graphics cursor).

This is illustrated as follows. Load program *P2.14* (graphics window program) into the computer and alter lines 90 and 100 to the following:

90   VDU 5:REM WRITE TEXT AT GRAPHICS CURSOR
100 MOVE 600,232:REM MOVE THE INVISIBLE GRAPHICS
       CURSOR

These lines allow the computer to print the MODE number at the foot of the graphics window (see also Fig. 2.13). *The text is printed just below and slightly to the right of the position of the graphics cursor.*

After each text character has been printed, the graphics cursor moves the correct distance to the right and prints the next character. Since the text is written in white, and the graphics colour in MODEs 0 and 4 is also white, the text is invisible in these MODEs in the modified program.

Fig. 2.13 Writing text at the graphics cursor (VDU 5)

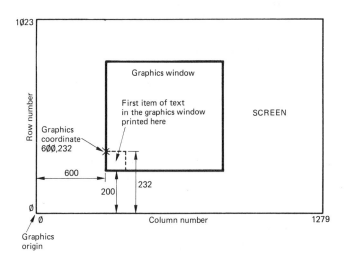

Colour, Colour Filling and Animation

3.1 Colours on the BBC Micro

The number of colours directly available when using the BBC micro depends on the screen MODE you have selected. Some of the MODEs are two-colour modes, some are four-colour modes and one is a sixteen-colour mode. We discuss below the *default colours* of the computer, but you must remember that the BBC micro is a versatile computer and you can use software instructions to change the range of colours (even in a two-colour mode).

Text and graphics use different commands to set up the colour display, and are discussed below.

3.2 Text Colour

The colour not only of text but also its background is established by the COLOUR command. Each COLOUR command has a number associated with it, its value depending on such factors as the colour of the text and of its background.

In a **two-colour mode** (MODE's 0, 3, 4 and 6) the following numbers apply:

Colour	Foreground	Background
Black	0	128
White	1	129

In **four-colour modes** (MODEs 1 and 5) the following apply:

Colour	Foreground	Background
Black	0	128
Red	1	129
Yellow	2	130
White	3	131

In **sixteen-colour mode** (MODE 2) the following apply:

Colour	Foreground	Background
Black	0	128
Red	1	129
Green	2	130
Yellow	3	131
Blue	4	132
Magenta (blue-red)	5	133
Cyan (blue-green)	6	134
White	7	135

Flashing black-white	8	136
Flashing red-cyan	9	137
Flashing green-magenta	10	138
Flashing yellow-blue	11	139
Flashing blue-yellow	12	140
Flashing magenta-green	13	141
Flashing cyan-red	14	142
Flashing white-black	15	143

From the above you can see that

Background colour number = 128 + foreground colour number

At the instant of switch-on, the **default colour number** in any MODE gives white text on a black background. Program *P3.1*(*listing 3.1*) displays the text and background colours in MODE 1 (a 4-colour mode). The program prints lines of text using all four background colours and all four foreground (text) colours. The text cannot, of course, be seen where it has the same colour as the background. Line 110 of the program restores the default colours.

Listing 3.1

```
10  REM****PROGRAM "P3.1"****
20  REM****COLOURED TEXT****
30  *TV0,1
40  MODE 1
50  FOR CF=0 TO 3
60    COLOUR CF:REM FOREGROUND COLOUR
70    FOR CB=128 TO 131
80      COLOUR CB:REM BACKGROUND COLOUR
90      PRINT"FOREGR. COLOUR ";CF;",BACKGR. COLOUR ";CB
100     NEXT CB:NEXT CF
110 VDU 20:REM RESTORE DEFAULT COLOURS
120 END
```

You will find it an interesting exercise to modify program *P3.1* to deal with some of the colours in MODE 2. The colour number associated with the COLOUR instruction is known as the *logical colour number*.

An example of the use of the COLOUR command If you type the following lines when, say, in MODE 1, all subsequent keyboard characters are printed in red on a yellow background when you RUN the program:

10 COLOUR 1:COLOUR 130:END

You will see that only the text and its immediate background appear in this colour, the rest of the screen remaining black.

However, if you want to have the complete text window filled with the same background colour then, after defining the background colour, you must clear the text window with a CLS instruction as follows:

10 COLOUR 1:COLOUR 130:CLS:END

When you RUN the program, the screen background colour is yellow, and any text is printed in red.

If you use both text and graphics windows on the screen, the CLS instruction clears anything (including graphics) *which is in the text window*. This instruction also moves the text cursor to the home position at the top left-hand corner of the text window, the text area remaining in the current background colour.

3.3   Redefining the Text Colour

In some of your programs you may wish to use a particular screen MODE, say MODE 0 for high-definition graphics, but you may want to display text which is not available as a default colour. You can change the colours or *redefine* them in any of the screen MODEs in terms of any of the sixteen colours available in MODE 2 (see section 3.2 for details) using the VDU 19 command. The VDU 19 command is written in one of the following formats:

VDU 19,logical colour number,actual colour number,0,0,0

or

VDU 19,logical colour number,actual colour number;0;

These instructions have the effect of causing the original **logical colour** (wherever it appears) to be changed to the specified **actual colour.**

The *logical colour number* is, in MODE 1 for example, a value in the range 0–3 for foreground colours and 128–131 for background colours. The *actual colour number* is the colour number listed for the 16-colour mode (MODE 2).

The colours for colour numbers in, say, MODE 1, other than colour numbers 0–3 and 128–131 inclusive, are not defined in the User Manual of the computer but, in fact, they produce well-defined colours. For example, in four-colour modes, if you add an integral multiple of 4 to any colour number in the range 0–3 inclusive, you will get the same colour. That is colour numbers 1, 5, 9, 13,... 121, 125 all give red text; colour numbers 3, 7, 11, ... 123, 127 give white text. Similarly, colour numbers 128, 132, 136, etc. give a black background, whilst colour numbers 129, 133, 137, etc. give a red background. In MODE 2 (the sixteen-colour mode), the colour numbers change in blocks of sixteen, so that colour 1 is the same as colour 17, etc.

Program P3.2 (*listing 3.2*) has the effect, in MODE 1, of changing the logical foreground colour 3 (white) into the actual colour 4 (blue) — see line 40 — and of changing the logical background colour 128 (black) into actual colour 136 (flashing black and white). The program can be simplified by combining the two VDU 19 instructions in a single line as follows:

40 VDU 19,3,4;0;19,128,136;0;

second VDU 19 instruction starts here

Line 50 would, of course, have to be deleted.

Listing 3.2

```
10  REM****PROGRAM "P3.2"****
20  REM****CHANGING THE TEXT COLOUR****
30  MODE 1
40  VDU 19,3,4,0,0,0:REM CHANGE TEXT COLOUR
50  VDU 19,128,136;0;:REM CHANGE BACKGROUND COLOUR
60  PRINT"PRESS ANY KEY TO QUIT PROGRAM"
70  K=GET
80  VDU 20:REM RESTORE DEFAULT COLOURS
90  END
```

You can also define one of the red user-defined keys to change the colours as follows:

   *KEY0 VDU 19,3,1;0;19,128,131;0; ¦ M

When you press the red f0 key (when in any of the 4-colour modes), all text will be red on a yellow background. The default colours can be restored either by typing VDU 20 or by defining another user-defined key to return VDU 20 to the computer.

It is interesting to note that if you redefine, say, the MODE 2 colour red to appear as green on the screen, you then have two green colours. One is the logical green and the other is the redefined green (corresponding to logical red). Both result in a green display on the screen.

3.4   Graphics Colours

Graphics colours are specified using a **GCOL command**. Each GCOL command specifies not only the graphics colour but also the way in which it is logically presented on the screen. The form of a GCOL command is as follows:

   GCOL logic number,logical colour

e.g. GCOL 0,2. The logic number is in the range 0–4 inclusive, and specifies a logical action as follows.

Logic number	Action
0	Plot the specified colour.
1	Logically OR the specified colour with the colour already on the screen.
2	Logically AND the specified colour with the colour already on the screen.
3	EXCLUSIVE-OR the specified colour with the colour already on the screen.
4	Logically invert (the logical NOT operation) the colour already on the screen.

The use of the logic numbers is explained in detail in sections 3.5 and 3.6. The logical colour number is the default colour number for the mode you are operating in; that is, in a 4-colour mode (MODE 1 or 5), colour 0 is black, colour 1 is red, colour 2 is yellow, and colour 3 is white (as outlined in section 3.2). You will find that the GCOL command is at the heart of most BBC micro programs using animation.

3.5 Binary numbers

A **binary variable** is a quantity which can have only one of two possible states or conditions. It is rather like the operating state of an electric lamp, that is it can either be ON or it can be OFF. A binary variable is given the logical value 1 when it is ON or it is *true,* and the value 0 when it is OFF or is *untrue.*

Since a binary variable can only have one of the values zero or unity, humans have invented a binary numbering system to deal with numbers other than unity. The general principle is similar to the decimal system; that is, the lowest digit (the *least significant* digit) of a decimal number represents a number in the range zero to nine. The next higher-order digit represents a value in the range $(0 \times \text{ten})$ to $(9 \times \text{ten})$. Hence

$$\text{decimal } 92 = (9 \times 10^1) + (2 \times 10^0) \text{ or } (9 \times 10) + (2 \times 1)$$

When looking at numbers in a conventional book, you accept that the number 11 is the decimal number eleven. However, when dealing with numbering systems in general, you cannot be sure that the number 11 represents decimal 11 or binary 11, or even 11 in some other code. To indicate the **base** or the **radix** of the numbering system involved, we write it as a subscript to the number. For example, decimal 92 is written in the form

$$\text{decimal } 92 = 92_{10}$$

The decimal number 3 can be written in the form

$$\begin{aligned} 3_{10} = 2_{10} + 1_{10} &= (1 \times 2) + (1 \times 1) \\ &= (1 \times 2^1) + (1 \times 2^0) \\ &= \text{binary } 11 = 11_2 \end{aligned}$$

The *least significant binary digit* (binary digit is abbreviated to **bit**) or l.s.b. of the number 11_2 has unity value, and the *most significant bit* or m.s.b. has the decimal value 2. Some binary codes are listed in Table 3.1. Note that the name "eleven" is reserved for use in the *decimal* or *denary* system; 11 in binary is described as "binary one, one". The "length" or number of code combinations in a binary code is given by the equation

$$\text{Number of combinations} = 2^n$$

where *n* is the number of bits in the code. That is, a binary code using four bits has $2^4 = 16$ code combinations ranging from

$$0_{10} \text{ to } 15_{10} \qquad (\text{or } 0_2 \text{ to } 1111_2)$$

The three binary codes in Table 3.1 are used to specify the colour number in the GCOL instruction in the BBC micro. For example, the colour numbering of the first three colours in the 16-colour mode are

Colour number	Binary colour code
0 (black)	0000
1 (red)	0001
2 (green)	0010

Table 3.1
1-bit code

Decimal value (colour number)	Binary value
0	0
1	1

2-bit code

Decimal value (colour number)	Binary value
0	00
1	01
2	10
3	11

4-bit code

Decimal value (colour number)	Binary value
0	0000
1	0001
2	0010
3	0011
4	0100
5	0101
6	0110
7	0111
8	1000
9	1001
10	1010
11	1011
12	1100
13	1101
14	1110
15	1111

Table 3.2   Truth table for the OR function (GCOL 1)

Variables A B	Result f
0 0	0
0 1	1
1 0	1
1 1	1

The m.s.b. of the 4-bit code above can be thought of as the bit which controls the colour flashing effect. When this bit has the value 0 (as it does in colours 0–7 inclusive), the colours are displayed on the screen in their normal form. When the m.s.b. of the binary colour code has the value 1 (as it does in colours 8–15 inclusive), the colour on the screen flashes from one colour to its logical complementary colour.

3.6   Logical Operations on Colour

Logical operations on colours in the BBC micro are as follows:

1   The logical OR operation.
2   The logical AND operation.
3   The logical EXCLUSIVE-OR operation.
4   The logical INVERT or NOT operation.

The numbers 1–4 above correspond to the logic numbers in the GCOL command (outlined in section 3.4). In addition to the functions listed above there is one more logic number, namely 0, which merely causes the specified colour to be displayed on the screen. That is, in a 4-colour mode, the command GCOL 0,2 results in yellow graphics.

Listing 3.3

```
10   REM****PROGRAM "P3.3"****
20   REM ****ILLUSTRATING THE GCOL COMMAND****
30   *TV0,1
40   MODE 1
50   PRINT TAB(0,1);"MODE NUMBER";:INPUT mode:PRINT
60   MODE mode
70   INPUT "LOGIC NUMBER"; logic:PRINT
80   DIM colour(3)
90   PRINT "INPUT THREE COLOUR NUMBERS":PRINT
100  INPUT"FIRST COLOUR NUMBER = ";colour(1)
110  INPUT"SECOND COLOUR NUMBER = ";colour(2)
120  INPUT"THIRD COLOUR NUMBER = ";colour(3)
130  CLS
140  PRINT "GCOL";logic;" FOR COLOURS ";colour(1);", ";colour(2);", ";col
our(3)
150  PRINT:PRINT"MODE ";mode
160  X1=0:Y1=50:X2=1279
170  FOR C=1 TO 3
180    GCOL 0,C
190    MOVE X1,Y1:MOVE X1,(Y1+50):PLOT 85,X2,Y1:PLOT 85,X2,(Y1+50)
200    Y1=Y1+100
210    NEXT C
220  X1=250:Y1=0:Y2=350
230  FOR C=1 TO 3
240    GCOL logic,colour(C)
250    MOVE X1,Y1:MOVE (X1+50),0:PLOT 85,X1,Y2:PLOT 85,(X1+50),Y2
260    X1=X1+300
270    NEXT C
280  END
```

The program in *listing 3.3* enables you to inspect the effect of each of the logic numbers on the colours as they appear on the screen (the effect of each logic number is described later). The computer is initialized in the program in MODE 1 (this is simply a matter of convenience, and any other screen MODE could have been chosen).

Line 50 of the program enables you to select a screen MODE of your choice, and line 60 switches you into that MODE (the MODE change also clears the screen of the monitor. Line 70 of the program allows you to select the logic number (0–4 inclusive) for use with the GCOL instruction, and lines 100 to 120 enable you to nominate three colour numbers which are used in association with your selected GCOL command.

The FOR-NEXT loop in lines 170 to 210 inclusive draw three horizontal bands close to the bottom of the screen. The colour of these bands corresponds to colour numbers 1, 2 and 3 in the screen MODE of your choice. For example, if you choose MODE 1, the horizontal bands are respectively red (at the bottom of the screen), yellow and white. If you choose a 2-colour mode, you will only get black-and-white bands.

The FOR-NEXT loop in lines 230–270 draws three vertical bands in the logic number and colour of your choice, which cross the horizontal bands. A typical display is shown in Fig. 3.1 for the GCOL 0 instruction in MODE 1 for colours 1, 2 and 3 (red, yellow and white respectively). You will see

Fig. 3.1 The GCOL 0 command

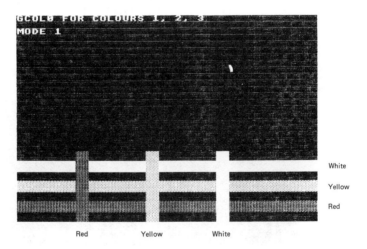

White

Yellow

Red

Red   Yellow   White

that, with the GCOL 0 instruction, where a vertical band crosses a horizontal band, it has the effect of painting over it. That is, the horizontal colour is obliterated. this effect is used in certain types of simple three-dimensional drawings later in the book.

3.7   GCOL 1 — the Logic OR Operation on Colours

The OR function with colours has exactly the same effect as the OR function on binary values. That is, if you have two binary values *A* and *B* then, if either or both of them has the logic value 1, then the result is also binary 1. If the result is represented by the function f, the OR operation is written down as

$$f = A \text{ OR } B = A + B$$

where the $+$ sign represents the OR function. The OR function is described by what is known as its truth table in Table 3.2. A truth table is a list of all the possible combinations of the input variables, together with the OR result (f) for each combination. In this case there are two variables (A and B) so, that there are $2^2 = 4$ combinations of the variables, giving four rows in the truth table. You will see from the truth table that, if either (or both) of the variables has the value 1, then the result f has the value 1.

Your attention is now directed to the effect that the OR function has on the screen colours. At this point you should run program $P3.3$ and select GCOL 1 and a 4-colour mode (say MODE 1). In this mode the colour numbers are

$$
\begin{aligned}
\text{Black} &= \text{colour 0 or } 00_2 \\
\text{Red} &= \text{colour 1 or } 01_2 \\
\text{Yellow} &= \text{colour 2 or } 10_2 \\
\text{White} &= \text{colour 3 or } 11_2
\end{aligned}
$$

The resulting screen display is illustrated in Fig. 3.2. Where the vertical red line passes over the black background of the screen, the two colours are ORed together as follows:

$$
\begin{array}{lcl}
& \text{m.s.b.} \longrightarrow \ \ulcorner \text{l.s.b.} \\
& & \downarrow\downarrow \\
\text{Black} & = & 00 \\
\text{Red} & = & \underline{01} \\
\text{Result (OR)} & = & 01 \ (\text{red})
\end{array}
$$

Fig. 3.2 The GCOL 1 command

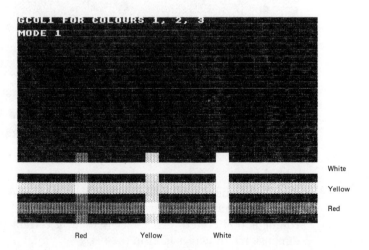

The computer carries out the OR operation on a bit-by-bit basis as follows. Looking at the least significant bit of each of the numbers in the above calculation, the red colour has the value 1, so that the l.s.b. in the result is also 1. In the m.s.b. position, both the red and the black have the value 0, so that the m.s.b. of the result is also 0. Hence the effect of ORing red and black is 01_2, or red, so that, when a red line passes over a black area when the GCOL 1 command is being executed, the resulting colour is red.

In fact, you can quickly show that

> *whenever any colour is logically ORed with black using GCOL 1, the net result is the original colour.*

If you extend the argument to the area where the red vertical line is ORed with the red horizontal line, the result is also red.

Moving further up the red vertical line in Fig. 3.2, you will see that, where the red vertical line passes over (in fact is ORed with) the yellow horizontal line, the result is a white area. The logical calculation is as follows:

$$\text{m.s.b.} \quad \text{l.s.b.}$$

Yellow	=	10
Red	=	01
Result (OR)	=	11 (white)

Where a vertical white band passes over (is ORed with) any other colour, the result is white as shown in the following example:

Yellow	=	10
White	=	11
Result (OR)	=	11 (white)

That is,

> *white will obliterate any other colour using the GCOL 1 command, and any colour obliterates black.*

3.8 GCOL 2 — the Logical AND Operation on Colours

The truth table for the AND function of two variables is given in Table 3.3.

Table 3.3 Truth table for the AND function (GCOL 2)

Variables A	B	Result f
0	0	0
0	1	0
1	0	0
1	1	1

You will see that the result f has the value 1 only when both A AND B are *simultaneously* 1. If either A or B is 0, the result is 0. The AND function is expressed in the form.

$$f = A \text{ AND } B = A.B$$

where the "dot" represents the AND function.

If you run program *P3.3* in MODE 1 for GCOL 2 and colours 1, 2 and 3, you will get the results shown in Fig. 3.3. Where any one of the vertical

Fig. 3.3 The GCOL 2
command

colours passes over (is ANDed with) black, the result is black, as follows:

Yellow	=	1Ø
Black	=	ØØ
Result (AND) =		ØØ (black)

Once again, the logical operation takes place on a bit-by-bit basis, and a logic Ø (in either of the colours) effectively eliminates a logic 1 in the equivalent bit position of the other colour. Consequently,

you will not "see" the vertical coloured bands where they pass over the black background.

Where two similar colours cross one another, e.g. red crossing red, the result is the same colour (red in this case):

Red	=	Ø1
Red	=	Ø1
Result (AND) =		Ø1

Where white crosses another colour (say yellow) the resulting colour is the second colour (yellow in this case):

White	=	11
Yellow	=	1Ø
Result (AND) =		1Ø

Where red crosses yellow, the result is black:

Red	=	Ø1
Yellow	=	1Ø
Result (AND) =		ØØ (black)

3.9   GCOL 3 — the EXCLUSIVE-OR (EOR) Logical Operation

The truth table for the EXCLUSIVE-OR function is given in Table 3.4. It is generally similar to the OR function with the exception that it EX-CLUDES from the truth table the possibility of a result of logic 1 in the final row. (In the OR function truth table, the result is 1 in the final row.) The EOR function is widely used in digital electronics and microcomputers for a number of applications. It is also known as the NOT-EQUIVALENT

Table 3.4 Truth table for the EXCLUSIVE-OR function (GCOL 3)

Variables		Result
A	B	f
0	0	0
0	1	1
1	0	1
1	1	0

function because the result if 1 whenever the values of A and B are NOT EQUIVALENT to one another. (When they are equivalent, the result is 0.)

When you run program *P3.3* using logic number 3 (GCOL 3) in MODE 1 for colours 1, 2 and 3 you will get a very interesting display. Each of your nominated vertical colours has a diagonal line across them (see Fig. 3.4). For the moment we will ignore this effect, but will return to it later.

Fig. 3.4 The GCOL 3 command

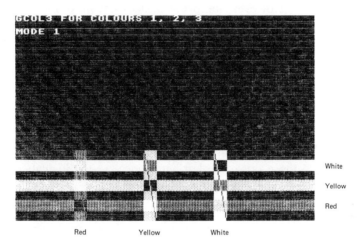

GCOL3 FOR COLOURS 1, 2, 3

MODE 1

White

Yellow

Red

Red   Yellow   White

Where two similar colours cross one anothr (say yellow crossing yellow), the result is (see also Table 3.4)

Yellow	=	10
Yellow	=	10
Result (EOR)	=	00 (black)

Like all logical operations, the EXCLUSIVE-OR function is carried out on a bit-by-bit basis. Where the two bits are the same, the result is logic 0 (see the above result); where they are not the same, the result is logic 1. Consequently,

the resulting colour is black whenever two identical colours cross.

Where any colour crosses black, the colour is unchanged.

Suppose we take red as the colour:

Black =	=	00
Red	=	01
Result (EOR)	=	01 (red)

Where, say, red crosses yellow the result is

Red	=	01
Yellow	=	10
Result (EOR)	=	11 (white)

It is left as an exercise for you to verify the other colours on the screen.

We now return to the diagonal black lines running across the vertical stripes. The reason for this is the way in which the vertical stripes are drawn by the computer. You will recall that, in program *P3.3*, these stripes are drawn using two PLOT 85 commands, each of which fills a triangle with colour. To make sure that the triangle is properly filled, there is a small overlap between them. Thus on, say, a yellow vertical stripe, the second yellow triangle overlaps the first yellow triangle.

You saw at the beginning of this section that, when two identical colours overlap one another using the GCOL 3 instruction, the resulting colour is black. Consequently, there is a black line across each of the vertical stripes drawn using GCOL 3.

However, the problem does not finish there in program *P3.3*, because the colour of the sloping line on the vertical line changes whenever it crosses a horizontal stripe. It has already been shown that, when a black colour crosses any other colour, the colour is unchanged. That is,

where the sloping black line on the vertical stripe crosses a horizontal line, you see the colour of the horizontal line!

A knowledge of the EOR function is particularly valuable when writing animation programs and, for the convenience of the reader, a table for the results of EORing any one of the fifteen available colours with any other colour is given in Table 3.5. The numbers along the top of the table, and those down the left-hand side, are the logical colour numbers which are

Table 3.5 EXCLUSIVE-OR (EOR) Operation

	0	1	2	3	4	5	6	7	8	9	10	11	12	13	14	15
0	0	1	2	3	4	5	6	7	8	9	10	11	12	13	14	15
1	1	0	3	2	5	4	7	6	9	8	11	10	13	12	15	14
2	2	3	0	1	6	7	4	5	10	11	8	9	14	15	12	13
3	3	2	1	0	7	6	5	4	11	10	9	8	15	14	13	12
4	4	5	6	7	0	1	2	3	12	13	14	15	8	9	10	11
5	5	4	7	6	1	0	3	2	13	12	15	14	9	8	11	10
6	6	7	4	5	2	3	0	1	14	15	12	13	10	11	8	9
7	7	6	5	4	3	2	1	0	15	14	13	12	11	10	9	8
8	8	9	10	11	12	13	14	15	0	1	2	3	4	5	6	7
9	9	8	11	10	13	12	15	14	1	0	3	2	5	4	7	6
10	10	11	8	9	14	15	12	13	2	3	0	1	6	7	4	5
11	11	10	9	8	15	14	13	12	3	2	1	0	7	6	5	4
12	12	13	14	15	8	9	10	11	4	5	6	7	0	1	2	3
13	13	12	15	14	9	8	11	10	5	4	7	6	1	0	3	2
14	14	15	12	13	10	11	8	9	6	7	4	5	2	3	0	1
15	15	14	13	12	11	10	9	8	7	6	5	4	3	2	1	0

EORed together. The intersecting point in the table gives the colour number seen on the screen. For example, EORing colour 7 with colour 3 gives colour 4; EORing colour 10 with colour 14 also gives colour 4.

3.10   GCOL 4 — Logical Inversion or the NOT Operation

The truth table for the logical inversion or the NOT function is shown in Table 3.6. In this case there is only one variable, and the result is the

Table 3.6   Logical inversion (GCOL 4)

Variable A	Result f
0	1
1	0

logical inversion or the logical opposite value. That is, the result is NOT equal to the variable value, or

$$1 = NOT\ 0 \quad and \quad 0 = NOT\ 1$$

This is the only GCOL instruction where the colour number has no meaning.

For example, GCOL 4,0 has the same effect as GCOL 4,1, or as the same as GCOL 4,2, etc.

This instruction logically inverts any colour it touches or passes through. Hence, each logic 1 in the colour is changed to a 0, and each 0 is changed to a 1. In MODE 1, for example, the following would occur:

The inverse of 00 (black) is 11 (white).
The inverse of 01 (red) is 10 (yellow).
The inverse of 10 (yellow) is 01 (red).
The inverse of 11 (white) is 00 (black).

When you run program *P3.3* for GCOL 3 in MODE 1 for colours 1, 2 and 3, you will find that the vertical stripes consist of the inverse colours (see above) either of the background (black) or of the horizontal colour (where they cross).

Once again, there is a diagonal line across each of the vertical stripes, whose colour changes at various points. The reason for this can be explained in terms of the discussion in section 3.9.

3.11   Filling a Simple Shape with Colour (PLOT 85)

If you need to use colour to fill a simple geometrical shape such as a triangle, a trapezium, a square or a circle, the simplest method is to use the PLOT 85 command which draws and fills a triangle. The PLOT commands were introduced briefly in section 2.3, and here we see how PLOT 85 works. The command is written in the form

PLOT 85,x-postion,y-position

i.e. PLOT 85,400,800, where x-position and y-position are measured in

Fig. 3.5 Colour filling using
the PLOT 85 command

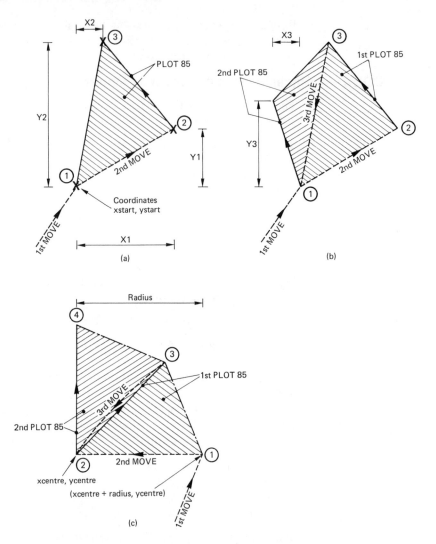

graphics units. The command fills in the triangle formed between the
coordinates given in the PLOT 85 command and the last two points visited
by the computer. That is, two MOVE instructions (or the equivalent
PLOT instructions — see section 2.3) must have been executed before the
PLOT 85 command is given.

Fig. 3.5a illustrates how a triangle is drawn and filled on the screen.
Listing 3.4 shows how this command is used to fill several shapes including
a triangle, a quadrilateral and a circle. The executive program calls for the
procedures PROC_triangle, PROC_quadrilateral and PROC_circle to fill
in the respective shapes, each procedure being separated by a time delay,
after which the screen is cleared and the new shape is drawn and filled. On
completion of the program, the RUN instruction in line 100 re-runs it; an
escape is made from the program by pressing the ESCAPE key.

Line 140 of PROC_triangle specifies the graphics value of the points
xstart, ystart, X1, Y1, X2 and Y2 illustrated in Fig. 3.5a. The next line of

Listing 3.4

```
10   REM****PROGRAM "P3.4"****
20   REM****PLOT 85 COMMAND****
30   *TV0,1
40   MODE 1
50   PROC_triangle
60   PROC_delay
70   PROC_quadrilateral
80   PROC_delay
90   PROC_circle
95   PROC_delay
100  RUN
110  :
120  DEF PROC_triangle
130  GCOL 0,1
140  xstart=300:ystart=300:X1=500:Y1=400:X2=100:Y2=600
150  MOVE xstart,ystart:MOVE xstart+X1,ystart+Y1:PLOT 85,xstart+X2,ystart
+Y2
160  ENDPROC
170  :
180  DEF PROC_delay
190  T=TIME
200  REPEAT:UNTIL TIME>T+300
210  ENDPROC
220  :
230  DEF PROC_quadrilateral
240  PROC_triangle
250  GCOL 0,2
260  X4=-100:Y4=200
270  MOVE xstart,ystart:PLOT 85,xstart+X4,ystart+Y4
280  ENDPROC
290  :
300  DEF PROC_circle
310  xcentre=640:ycentre=512:radius=500
320  MOVE xcentre+radius,ycentre:CLS
330  FOR angle=10 TO 360 STEP 10
340    GCOL 0,angle/10
350    X=radius*COS(RAD(angle)):Y=radius*SIN(RAD(angle))
360    MOVE xcentre,ycentre:PLOT 85,xcentre+X,ycentre+Y
365    NEXT angle
370  ENDPROC
```

the procedure contains two MOVE commands and the PLOT command which fix the three points between which the triangle is to be drawn and filled.

The mechanics of drawing and filling a 4-sided figure or quadrilateral are shown in Fig. 3.5*b*. The shape is drawn and filled using the triangle-fill routine twice, but only two points on the second triangle need be specified (see PROC_quadrilateral).

The final colour-fill exercise in program *P3.4* is a circle comprising thirty-six 10° sectors, drawn in the manner outlined in Fig. 3.5c. Each sector is a triangle identified by three points [say points (1), (2) and (3) in Fig. 3.5c], defined by MOVEing the graphics cursor to point (1), then to point (2), and then by executing a PLOT 85 command to point (3). This is repeated until the circle is complete. The program fills each sector in a different colour.

Shapes which are more complex then those described above, e.g. a circle containing a rectangle, can be colour-filled firstly by filling the larger shape first, and then filling the smaller (inner) shape afterwards.

Fast colour-fill for a rectangular area   A very quick method of filling a rectangular shape with colour is to define the rectangular area by means of the following sequence of instructions:

1   Define a *background* colour which is to fill the specified rectangular area either by a GCOL Ø instruction or a VDU 18 instruction.
2   Define the graphics area which is to be filled using a VDU 24 instruction.
3   Clear the graphics area (the area of the rectangle) using the CLG instruction; this colours the area to the specified background colour.
4   Restore the graphics window to its correct value (if the default window is required, use VDU 26).

Program *P3.5* (*listing 3.5*) illustrates the use of this technique. You will recall that program *P2.8* (the character-definer program) used this technique in PROC_fill and PROC_empty to produce the matrix of cells used to define a programmable character.

Listing 3.5

```
10  REM****PROGRAM "P3.5"****
20  REM****COLOUR QUICK-FILL FOR RECTANGLES****
30  *TVØ,1
40  MODE 2
50  CLS
60  REM BLUE SCREEN
70  GCOL Ø,132:CLG
80  REM GREEN AREA
90  GCOL Ø,130:VDU 24,Ø;Ø;1279;400;:CLG
100 REM RED RECTANGLE
110 GCOL Ø,129:VDU 24,300;200;700;600;:CLG
120 REM YELLOW RECTANGLES
130 GCOL Ø,131:VDU 24,450;200;550;450;:CLG
140 VDU 24,350;500;400;550;:CLG
150 VDU 24,600;500;650;550;:CLG
160 VDU 26:REM RESTORE DEFAULT WINDOWS
170 END
```

You can modify program *P3.5* to remove the cursor from the screen by including the following lines:

162 VDU 5:REM JOIN TEXT CURSOR AND GRAPHICS CUR-
SOR

164 MOVE 0, 1200:REM MOVE BOTH CURSORS OFF THE
SCREEN

To restore the cursor, simply type VDU 30⟨RETURN⟩.

3.12   Filling a Complex Shape with Colour

The triangle-fill feature of the BBC micro (PLOT 80 to 87) is convenient
for use with simple shapes, but has limitations where the shape is complex.

An alternative method of filling an area is to flood it with colour;
consequently, these methods are known as **flood-fill** methods. There are
two important requirements for the use of this method, namely that the
area to be flooded is outlined in a non-background colour (otherwise the
colour will "escape" and flood the whole screen), and that each pixel in the
enclosed area can be reached from an adjacent pixel.

Another method of colour-filling which places little demand on the
memory of the computer is introduced in the chapter on computer-aided
drawing (Chapter 8).

3.13   A Simple Animation Program

The animation program in *listing 3.6* causes a small yellow space-man like
person (called Charlie in the program) with transparent eyes to move
around the screen (see Fig. 3.6). He firstly moves between a green shape

Fig. 3.6 A scene from the
animation program

Listing 3.6

```
  10  REM****PROGRAM "P3.6"****
  20  REM****ANIMATION****
  30  *TV0,1
  40  MODE 2
  50  VDU 19,0,4;0;:REM BLUE SKY
  60  GCOL 0,3:REM YELLOW GROUND
  70  PROC_fillsquare(0,0,1279,500)
  80  GCOL 0,5:REM MAGENTA SHAPE
  90  PROC_fillsquare(500,470,50,400)
 100  PROC_fillsquare(550,820,200,50)
 110  PROC_fillsquare(700,470,50,350)
 120  GCOL 0,2:REM GREEN SHAPE
 130  PROC_fillsquare(400,370,50,400)
 140  PROC_fillsquare(450,720,200,50)
 150  PROC_fillsquare(600,370,50,350)
 160  PROC_redefine_colours
 170  VDU 5:GCOL 3,8
 180  PROC_charlie
 190  PROC_move_charlie
 200  VDU 20:MODE 2
 210  END
 220  :
 230  DEF PROC_move_charlie
 240  x=300:y=530
 250  REPEAT
 260    key$=INKEY$(0):IF key$="Q" ENDPROC
 270    VDU 19,10,2;0;:REM CHARLIE+GREEN=GREEN
 280    REPEAT:MOVE x,y:PRINT charlie$
 290      PROC_delay
 300      MOVE x,y:PRINT charlie$:x=x+8
 310      UNTIL x>=800
 320    REPEAT:MOVE x,y:PRINT charlie$
 330      PROC_delay
 340      MOVE x,y:PRINT charlie$:y=y-8
 350      UNTIL y<=450
 360    VDU 19,10,0;0;:REM CHARLIE+GREEN=BLACK
 370    REPEAT:MOVE x,y:PRINT charlie$
 380      PROC_delay
 390      MOVE x,y:PRINT charlie$:x=x-8
 400      UNTIL x<=300
 410    REPEAT:MOVE x,y:PRINT charlie$
 420      PROC_delay
 430      MOVE x,y:PRINT charlie$:y=y+8
 440      UNTIL y>=530
 450    VDU 19,10,2;0;:REM CHARLIE+GREEN=GREEN
 460    UNTIL 1=2
 470  :
```

```
480  DEF PROC_fillsquare(X1,Y1,width,height)
490  MOVE X1,Y1:MOVE X1+width,Y1:PLOT 85,X1,Y1+height:PLOT 85,X1+width,Y1
+height
500  ENDPROC
510 :
520  DEF PROC_redefine_colours
530  VDU 19,8,0;0;:REM CHARLIE+SKY=BLACK
540  VDU 19,11,0;0;:REM CHARLIE+GROUND=BLACK
550  VDU 19,13,0;0;:REM CHARLIE+MAGENTA=BLACK
560  ENDPROC
570 :
580  DEF PROC_charlie
590  VDU 23,227,0,60,126,255,90,126,60,24
600  VDU 23,228,255,189,189,189,189,189,189,60
610  VDU 23,229,36,36,36,36,36,36,231,0
620  bsp$=CHR$(8):REM BACKSPACE
630  dn$=CHR$(10):REM DOWN ONE LINE
640  charlie$=CHR$(227)+bsp$+dn$+CHR$(228)+bsp$+dn$+CHR$(229)
650  ENDPROC
660 :
670  DEF PROC_delay
680  FOR D=1 TO 100:NEXT
690  ENDPROC
```

and a magenta shape (vanishing behind the green shape and passing in front of the magenta shape), and completes his journey by passing in front of the two shapes to return to the starting position. This process is repeated continuously until you press the Q key to quit the program. Pressing the Q key while Charlie is in motion has no immediate effect, but when he reaches the starting position, control is transferred to line 200 of the program which clears the screen and restores the default screen colours. Important points relating to the program are now described.

Line 50 fills the screen with blue (to be used as the colour of the sky), and lines 60 and 70 fill the lower half of the screen (the ground) with yellow. Lines 80–110 and 120–150, respectively, draw the magenta and green shapes on the screen.

The effect of line 160 (PROC_redefine_colours) is described a little later. The VDU 5 instruction in line 170 results in the text and graphics cursors being joined together, allowing you to write text at the graphics cursor position; that is, you can control the position of the text cursor using the graphics MOVE instruction. Moreover, since Charlie is defined as a series of text characters, i.e. as several user-defined characters, Charlie is PRINTed at the current position of the graphics cursor. The instruction GCOL 3,8 in line 170 causes the colour of the character at the graphics cursor to be EXCLUSIVE-ORed with colour 8. The reasons for choosing colour 8 is quite simple when you look at Table 3.5; if you EXCLUSIVE-

OR any colour number in the range 0–7 with colour 8, the resulting actual colour number is given by

Actual colour = 8 + colour already there

Hence, if you EXCLUSIVE-OR colour 2 with colour 8, you get actual colour 10; this leads to relatively simple arithmetic in order to determine the actual colour. Let us now look at the various actual colours produced when Charlie moves around the screen.

Initially, Charlie's head is in front of both the sky and the ground; however, in line 50 the logical colour 0 is redefined as actual colour blue (colour 4). Hence, when calculating the logical colour of the combined effect of Charlie and the sky, you must use the logical colour 0 rather than the actual colour 4. That is

Charlie's head and sky [blue (or logical colour black)] $= 8 + 0 = 8$
Charlie's body and ground (yellow) $= 8 + 3 = 11$

This is where PROC_redefine_colours comes in! This procedure allows you to alter the actual colour of Charlie on the screen. When Charlie is visible on the screen he appears black, and we must therefore redefine both of the logical colours 8 and 11 as black (colour 0). This is done in lines 530 and 540. Similarly, since the logical colour number of the combination of Charlie and the magenta building is 8 + 5 = 13, we must also define the logical colour 13 as black (line 550). This ensures that the black Charlie *appears in front of the magenta shape* as he moves from left to right.

However, as Charlie moves to the right, he must appear to *move behind the green building*. How this is achieved is now described. The logical colour associated with Charlie and green is 8+2 (green) = 10. To make Charlie vanish behind the green building, it is simply necessary to make (Charlie + green = green). The VDU 19,10,2;0; instruction in line 270 does this for you.

When Charlie moves to the left, he passes in front of the green building; that is, (Charlie + green = black). The VDU 19,10,0;0; instruction in line 360 ensures that this happens.

You can change the colour of Charlie simply by altering the instructions which make him black into instructions which make him, say, red (colour 1). You get a red Charlie by altering the following lines in program *P3.7*:

```
360 VDU 19,10,1;0;
530 VDU 19,8,1;0;
540 VDU 19,11,1;0;
550 VDU 19,13,1;0;
```

You can turn him into any colour in the MODE 2 spectrum by altering the third number in the above lines.

Text Operations

4.1 Representation of a Keyboard Character on the Screen

The screen display produced by a BBC micrcomputer has 1280 graphical *addressable points*, or spots, horizontally, and 1024 vertical addressable points, as shown in Fig. 4.1*a*. A keyboard character such as a letter, or a number, or a special character such as ⟨, or =, or ? is represented on an 8 × 8 pixel pattern as shown in diagram *b*; a *pixel* is defined as the smallest point of light on the screen.

Fig. 4.1 *a*) Addressable points on the screen. *b*) A character matrix on the screen; insert (i) shows a MODE 1 pixel containing 4×4 addressable points

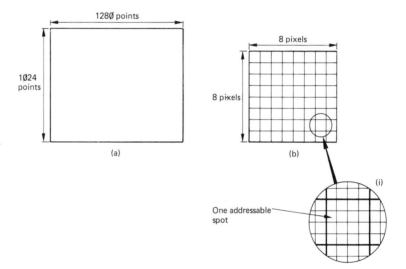

However, you will be aware that a text character in, say Mode ∅ is much smaller than the same character in Mode 5. It follows that the differing screen Modes have differing numbers of **addressable points per pixel**. It is fairly easy to work out the number of points per pixel in, for example, Mode 4 as follows.

Screen Mode 4 enables you to produce 32 lines of text, each having up to 50 characters on it. That is, one **Mode 4 printed character** contains

in the vertical direction, 1024/32 = 32 addressable points
in the horizontal direction, 1280/40 = 32 addressable points.

Thus, **each pixel in Mode 4** contains

in the vertical direction, 32/8 = 4 graphically addressable points
in the horizontal direction, 32/8 = 4 addressable points.

giving 4 × 4 = 16 addressable points per pixel (see Fig. 4.1*c*). Table 4.1

Table 4.1

Mode	0	1	2	4	5
Characters per line	80	40	20	40	20
Lines per screen	32	32	32	32	32
Horizontal graphical spots per character	16	32	64	32	64
Vertical graphical spots per character	32	32	32	32	32
Horizontal graphical spots per pixel	2	4	8	4	8
Vertical graphical spots per pixel	4	4	4	4	4

lists the details of the normally used graphical modes of the BBC micro.

When you address or communicate with a single addressable point within a pixel, you effectively address the whole pixel (this is like the situation when you write to one office in a company, you have communicated with the whole company).

Figure 4.2 illustrates how the upper-case letter G and the lower-case letter g are represented on the screen of the VDU in modes Ø to 6, each using an 8 × 8 pixel matrix. As mentioned earlier, the characters look different in differing screen Modes because of the differing number of addressable points used on the screen in the Modes.

Fig. 4.2 Upper case letter G and lower case letter g in MODEs Ø to 6

| 8 pixels | 8 pixels |

4.2   Analysing the Construction of a Character

The BASIC graphics instruction POINT can be used to identify the colour at a particular addressable point on the screen; this instruction returns a value to the computer which corresponds to the colour number at that point on the screen. Thus, the instruction POINT(X,Y) returns the colour number at the **graphics address** (X,Y) on the screen; POINT(4,30) returns the colour number at the position which is 4 addressable points from the left-hand side of the screen and 30 addressable points from the bottom. That is, the POINT instruction refers to a screen location which is relative to the **graphics origin** in the bottom left-hand corner of the screen.

In general, the colour number 0 is *black* (normal background), so that it is easy to discriminate between black and any other colour by checking to see if the colour number is zero. The POINT instruction can be used, for example, in a games program in which you are looking for a particular colour on the screen.

Program *P4.1* (*listing 4.1*) allows you to investigate the way in which a keyboard character is displayed on the screen in Mode 0. The *TV0,1 instruction in line 20 is included to eliminate screen jitter. Line 40 contains the Mode 0 character to be analysed (capital G in this case, see Fig. 4.3). The character is printed in Mode 0 by line 60 at a TAB address of (20,31), i.e. part way along the bottom line on the screen.

Two nested FOR-NEXT loops in line 70 through 120 cause the PRINTed character to be scanned commencing at its bottom left-hand corner; the graphical address of this point is

$X = 20$ TAB positions from the left-hand side of the screen
$= 20 \times 16 = 320$ graphical spots to the right of the graphical origin
$Y = 31$ TAB positions from the top of the screen
$= 0$ graphical spots above the graphical origin

Listing 4.1

```
10  REM ****PROGRAM "P4.1"****
20  *TV0,1
30  REM ***KEYBOARD CHARACTER ANALYSIS***
40  A$="G"
50  MODE 0
60  PRINT TAB(20,31);A$;
70  FOR X = 320 TO 320+15
80    FOR Y = 0 TO 31
90      C = POINT(X,Y)
100     PRINT TAB(X-320,31-Y);C;
110    NEXT Y
120   NEXT X
130 END
```

Fig. 4.3 Content of all the addressable points in the letter G in MODE 0

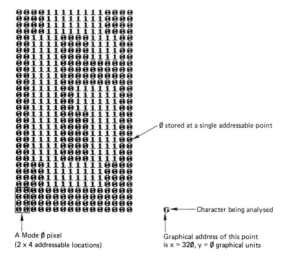

0 stored at a single addressable point

G ◄──── Character being analysed

A Mode 0 pixel
(2 x 4 addressable locations)

Graphical address of this point
is x = 320, y = 0 graphical units

Listing 4.2

```
10  REM****PROGRAM"P4.2"****
20  *TV0,1
30  MODE1
40  PROC_lineprint1(1,4,"Text",450,500)
50  END
60  :
70  DEF PROC_lineprint1(mode%,mag%,S$,XSTART%,YSTART%)
80  L%=LEN S$
90  PROC_spots
100 PROC_print
110 PROC_frame
120 PROC_string1
130 ENDPROC
140 :
150 DEF PROC_spots
160  IF mode%=0THEN K%=2
170  IF mode% = 1 THEN K%=4
180  IF mode% = 2 THEN K%=8
190  IF mode% = 4 THEN K%=4
200  IF mode% = 5 THEN K%=8
210  spots% = K%*8*L%
220 ENDPROC
230 :
240 DEF PROC_print
250  PRINT TAB(0,31);S$;
260 ENDPROC
270 :
280 DEF PROC_frame
290  H%=1023:W%=1279
300  MOVE 0,32:DRAW 0,H%:DRAW W%,H%:DRAW W%,0:DRAW (spots%+10),0
310 ENDPROC
320 :
330 DEF PROC_string1
340  FOR X% = 0 TO (spots%-1)
350    FOR Y% = 0 TO 31
360      IF POINT(X%,Y%) <> 0 THEN PROC_box1(X%,Y%,XSTART%,YSTART%,mag%)
370      NEXT Y%:NEXT X%
380 ENDPROC
390 :
400 DEF PROC_box1(X%,Y%,XSTART%,YSTART%,mag%)
410  LOCAL XPOS%,YPOS%
420  XPOS% = XSTART%+X%*mag%
430  YPOS% = YSTART%+Y%*mag%
440  MOVE XPOS%,YPOS%
450  MOVE XPOS%+(mag%-1),YPOS%
460  PLOT 85,XPOS%,YPOS%+(mag%-1)
470  PLOT 85,XPOS%+(mag%-1),YPOS%+(mag%-1)
480 ENDPROC
```

The POINT instruction in line 90 reads the screen colour at each graphical point in the PRINTed character, and the PRINT instruction in line 100 prints the colour value on the screen. The screen display for the letter G is shown in Fig. 4.3.

4.3   Changing the Size of the Character

One method of printing an enlarged character on the VDU screen is to cause the computer to scan through all the addressable points in the original (normal size) character, and magnify the content of the original point using a suitable magnification index. The program in *listing 4.2* does this.

PROCEDURES

PROC_lineprint1 is the master procedure for printing text in a straight line. The variables passed to the procedure are:
mode% – the screen mode.
mag% – the amount by which the original character is to be magnified.
S$ – the string of text to be magnified and printed.
XSTART% – the graphics position in the X-direction on the screen where the lower left-hand corner of the enlarged character is to appear.
YSTART% – as for XSTART% but in the Y-direction.
PROC_spots calculates the number of graphic spots needed in the X-direction by the enlarged text string.
PROC_print prints the normal size string of text, S$, in the bottom left-hand corner of the screen.
PROC_frame draws a frame around the screen to show the printing limits.
PROC_string1 causes the computer to scan each addressable point in the string, and where it finds a "non-zero" colour it fills an area on the screen by calling PROC_box1.
PROC_box1 uses MOVE and PLOT 85 instructions to fill a rectangular area on the screen.

Description   PROC_lineprint1 initially calls for PROC_spots to calculate the number of graphical spots in the X-direction required by the mangified version of text string S$ whose length is L% (*note:* K% is the number of addressable spots per pixel — see Table 4.1). Next, PROC_print causes the string S$ to be displayed at the foot of the screen (see Fig. 4.4). Following this, PROC_frame draws a frame around the limits of the screen; you will note from Fig. 4.4 that the frame is kept clear of the string of text for the reason given later.

PROC_string1 causes the computer to scan each addressable spot in the string S$ ("Text" in this case) and, if any spot contains a colour, PROC_box1 is called on to fill in a box at a specified point on the screen. The variables XPOS% and YPOS% give the coordinates of the lower left-hand corner of the box; the size of the box is controlled by the

Fig. 4.4 Screen display for
program P4.2

magnification parameter mag%. In this way, the enlarged string is printed
on the screen of the VDU (see Fig. 4.4).

Figure 4.5 shows the way in which the program locates the box to be
filled in. It reads the content of the screen memory at location X%,Y%
(which is in the string S$), and fills in a box at location XPOS%, YPOS%
where

$$XPOS\% = XSTART\% + X\% * mag\%$$
$$YPOS\% = YSTART\% + Y\% * mag\%$$

This process is repeated for all addressable points in the string "Text".

Fig. 4.5 This figure shows
how an enlarged character
is drawn

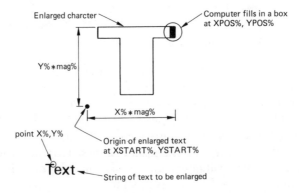

When using this technique, you must not allow anything on the screen to
overlap the string being copied. For example, if the frame around the
screen were complete so that it started and finished at the bottom left-hand
corner of the screen, then not only would the word "Text" be copied but
also the part of the frame which surrounded the word. You can check this

by changing line 300 to the following, after which you should RUN the program and observe the result:

300 MOVE 0,0:DRAW 0,H%:DRAW W%,H%:DRAW W%,0: DRAW 0,0

Making the string being copied invisible   In some cases it may be desirable to make the string ("Text") in the lower left-hand corner of the screen invisible during the screen printing operation. This is done by inserting the following line in PROC_print:

242 VDU 19,3,0,0,0,0:REM REDEFINE WHITE AS BLACK

or

242 VDU 19,3,0;0;

On its own, this has the effect of producing a blank (black) screen, and it is necessary to insert another instruction to cause the enlarged text to be visible. Since the enlarged text is written using graphics instructions, it can be "turned on" using a GCOL 0,n instruction; if n = 2, the text is printed in yellow, and if n = 1 the text is in red. Thus inserting the instruction

244 GCOL 0,2

results in both the enlarged string and the frame being displayed in yellow (the string S$ meanwhile being invisible to the eye, but not to the computer).

It is, of course, vital to restore the logical colours to their normal value at the end of the program, and this is done by inserting the following instruction at the end of the main program:

45 VDU 20

However, the latter instruction has the effect of causing the string to reappear in the bottom corner of the screen. One way of preventing this is to print a number of blank spaces at the point where the normal size string appears by inserting the following instruction at the end of the main program:

42 PRINT TAB(0,31);"   ";

You need to include as many blank spaces between the quotation marks as you have characters in the string S$ (four in the case of "Text").

Double-height characters in any screen MODE   Double-height characters can easily be obtained in any screen mode on the BBC micro using program *P4.3* (*listing 4.3*). The program prints the words Normal MODE, followed by the MODE number and the word Height (this displays print in the normal height for that mode), followed on a lower line by Double Height in its double-height size.

After the double-height text has been printed, line 100 introduces a time delay which allows you study the text. After running through all eight MODES, the program repeats itself; you can quit the program at any time

Listing 4.3

```
10  REM ****PROGRAM P.4.3****
20  REM DOUBLE HEIGHT IN ANY MODE
30  *TV0,1
40  A$="Double Height"
50  REPEAT
60    FOR M=0 TO 7
70      MODE M
80      PRINT TAB(5,6);"Normal MODE ";M;" Height"
90      IF M=7 PROC_mode7 ELSE PROC_other_modes
100     FOR T=1 TO 2000:NEXT
110     NEXT M
120   UNTIL 1=2
130 END
140 :
150 DEF PROC_mode7
160 FOR N=0 TO 1
170   PRINT TAB(5,8+N);CHR$(141);A$
180   NEXT N
190 ENDPROC
200 :
210 DEF PROC_other_modes
220 A%=&A:X%=&72:Y%=0:C=&72
230 FOR N=1 TO LEN(A$)
240   B$=MID$(A$,N,1)
250   ?C=ASC(B$):CALL(&FFF1)
260   VDU 23,224,C?1,C?1,C?2,C?2,C?3,C?3,C?4,C?4
270   VDU 23,225,C?5,C?5,C?6,C?6,C?7,C?7,C?8,C?8
280   PRINT TAB(4+N,8);CHR$224
290   PRINT TAB(4+N,9);CHR$225
300   NEXT N
310 ENDPROC
```

by pressing either the ESCAPE key or the BREAK key.

The BBC micro has a simple method of giving double-height characters in MODE 7 as follows. The effect is enabled, or turned on, by the ASCII code 141 (see line 170). The specified string of characters (string A$) to be printed in double height is printed twice (see lines 160 to 180, inclusive). The first time it prints the upper half of the text, and then it prints the lower half of the text.

The method used to print double-height text in MODEs 0–6 inclusive is a little more complex, but follows the same general principles. Line 220 passes the variables A%, X% and Y% respectively to the accumulator, the X-register and the Y-register of the microprocessor. This information is needed later when the OSWORD routine is called from address &FFF1 in line 250. When the accumulator contains &A (or decimal 10), the OSWORD routine puts the ASCII value of B$ into the memory lcoation at address &0072 [which is the address of C in line 250 (see also line 220)]; it also puts a block of eight bytes of data into the memory locations which follow address &0072. This data corresponds to the eight bytes which specify the shape of the character B$.

The data in the latter eight bytes is used for the upper-half (see line 260) and lower-half (see line 270) of the double-height character; the two halves are defined using the VDU 23 command in lines 260 and 270.

You will find that, when the program runs in MODES 3 and 6, there is a space between the upper- and the lower-half of the character on the screen. This is due to the spacing between the printed lines in the non-graphics modes (MODE 7 is also a non-graphics mode, but the CHR$(141) command overcomes this).

4.4 Using a "Negative" Magnitude Factor

When a negative value is used in line 40 of program *P4.2* for the magnitude factor mag%, it has the effect of causing the position of the filled-in box to be *turned upside down* and also moved downwards and to the left of its position when compared with the use of a positive value. This can be appreciated by an inspection of Fig. 4.5, where it is seen that a positive value of mag% causes the position of the filled-in box to be above and to the right of the origin at XSTART%, YSTART%.

Fig. 4.6 The effect of changing the mathematical sign of mag%

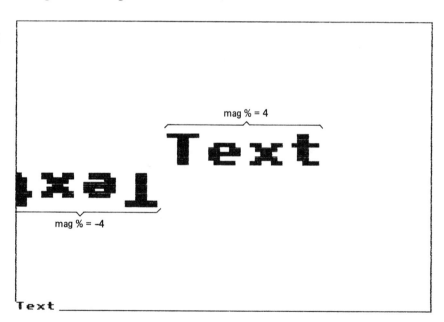

The effect of using a mag% value of both +4 and −4 is shown in Fig. 4.6. In effect,

a negative magnitude factor turns the printed character upside down

This can be used to advantage in graphics programs, as illustrated in section 4.7.

4.5 Printing Englarged Text at an Angle

A program for printing text at an angle is basically the same as that for printing text in a straight line, with the exception that a modified calculation is needed to allow for the angle at which the text is to be printed (this angle is the variable called textangle% in the program). Program *P4.4* (*listing 4.4*) lists the program.

Listing 4.4

```
10   REM****PROGRAM"P4.4"****
20   *TV0,1
30   MODE1
40   PROC_lineprint2(1,4,"Text",450,300,45)
50   END
60   :
70   DEF PROC_lineprint2(mode%,mag%,S$,XSTART%,YSTART%,textangle%)
80   L%=LEN S$
90   PROC_spots2
100  PROC_frame
110  PROC_string2
120  ENDPROC
130  :
140  :
150  DEF PROC_spots2
160  IF mode% = 0 THEN K%=2
170  IF mode% = 1 THEN K%=4
180  IF mode% = 2 THEN K%=8
190  IF mode% = 4 THEN K%=4
200  IF mode% = 5 THEN K%=8
210  spots% = K%*8
220  ENDPROC
230  :
240  DEF PROC_print2
250  PRINT TAB(0,31);MID$(S$,I,1);
260  ENDPROC
270  :
280  DEF PROC_frame
290  H%=1023:W%=1279
300  MOVE 0,32:DRAW 0,H%:DRAW W%,H%:DRAW W%,0:DRAW (spots%+10),0
310  ENDPROC
320  :
330  DEF PROC_string2
340  LOCAL XSTEP%,YSTEP%
350  XSTEP%=spots%*COS(RAD(textangle%))*mag%
360  YSTEP%=spots%*SIN(RAD(textangle%))*mag%
370  FOR I=1 TO L%
380    IF I=1 THEN XSTART%=XSTART% ELSE XSTART%=XSTART%+XSTEP%
390    IF I=1 THEN YSTART%=YSTART% ELSE YSTART%=YSTART%+YSTEP%
400    PROC_print2
410    FOR X% = 0 TO (spots%-1)
420      FOR Y% = 0 TO 31
430        IF POINT(X%,Y%) <> 0 THEN PROC_box2(X%,Y%,XSTART%,YSTART%,mag%
,textangle%)
```

```
440        NEXT Y%:NEXT X%:NEXT I
450  ENDPROC
460  :
470  DEF PROC_box2(X%,Y%,XSTART%,YSTART%,mag%,textangle%)
480  LOCAL XPOS%,YPOS%,cos,sin
490  angle=RAD(textangle%)
500  cos=COS(angle)
510  sin=SIN(angle)
520  XPOS% = XSTART%+(X%*mag%*cos-Y%*mag%*sin)
530  YPOS% = YSTART%+(X%*mag%*sin+Y%*mag%*cos)
540  MOVE XPOS%,YPOS%
550  MOVE XPOS%+(mag%-1),YPOS%
560  PLOT 85,XPOS%,YPOS%+(mag%-1)
570  PLOT 85,XPOS%+(mag%-1),YPOS%+(mag%-1)
580  ENDPROC
```

PROCEDURES

PROC_lineprint2 is the master procedure for printing text at an angle. It is
similar to PROC_lineprint1 with the exception that it does not call for
PROC_print (a modified procedure called PROC_print2 is used at
another point in the program). The variables mode%, mag%, S$,
XSTART% and YSTART% used by this procedure are as defined for
PROC_lineprint1 in section 4.3. The variable textangle% is the angle
(in degrees) from the horizontal axis at which the enlarged text is to be
printed. The convention is adopted that a positive angle represents
anticlockwise movement of the text, and a negative angle gives
clockwise movement.

PROC_spots2 calculates the number of graphic spots needed in the
X-direction for *one* enlarged character.

PROC_frame draws a frame around the screen, but does not intrude upon
the character being enlarged (see Fig. 4.7).

PROC_string2 calculates the position of XSTART% and YSTART% for
the enlarged character.

PROC_print2 displays, *one character at a time,* each character in the string
being enlarged. It retains the character in the lower left-hand corner of
the screen until it is printed.

PROC_box2 uses MOVE and PLOT 85 instructions to fill a rectangular
area on the screen. It differs from PROC_box1 in section 4.3 in that it
accounts for the angle (textangle%) at which the text is printed.

Description   The main program (lines 10 through 50) passes parameters to
PROC_lineprint2 which are used in the program. This procedure calls
upon PROC_spots2 to calculate the number of graphical spots needed in
the "forward" direction of printing for each character (the "forward"
direction cannot be called the X-direction since the text is printed at an
angle). Since only one text character at a time is displayed by PROC_
print2, PROC_spots2 only calculates the number of graphical spots needed
in one enlarged character.

Fig. 4.7 Screen display on
the completion of program
P4.3: it shows the effect of
using a magnification factor
of (i) +4 and (ii) −4

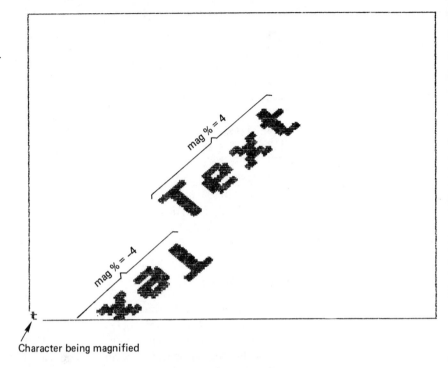

Character being magnified

PROC_frame draws a frame around the viewing area, after which
PROC_string2 is called; the latter procedure calculates the starting position of the next character in the string (which is at XSTART%,
YSTART%) before calling PROC_print2 which prints the normal size
character in the lower left-hand corner of the screen. The nested FOR-
NEXT loops commencing at line 410 scan the printed character and, at
each location containing a non-zero "colour", it calls PROC_box2. The
way in which the character is copied is illustrated in Fig. 4.8.

Fig. 4.8 Printing text at an
angle

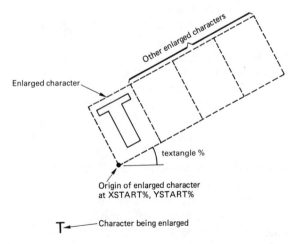

In order to print a character at any angle θ, it is necessary to "rotate"
each addressable point in the character about a centre of rotation. The

mathematics of rotating a point is fully described in Chapter 9, but it is worthwhile observing here that the new coordinates, say X2 and Y2, of a point which is rotated through θ from its original coordinates X1,Y1 (see Fig. 4.9), are given by the equations:

$$X2 = X1 \cos \theta - Y1 \sin \theta$$
$$Y2 = X1 \sin \theta + Y1 \cos \theta$$

The principle of these equations is utilized in lines 520 and 530 of PROC_box2.

Fig. 4.9 Change of coordinates by rotation

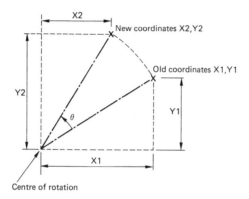

Centre of rotation

Using a negative magnitude factor   The effect of using a negative magnitude factor (mag% = −4) is illustrated in the screen display in Fig. 4.7. It generally has a similar effect to that in program *P4.2*; that is, it writes the text upside down and in the opposite direction.

4.6   Printing Enlarged Text around an Arc or a Circle

The techniques of printing enlarged text around an arc or a circle of radius rad% is generally similar to printing enlarged text at any angle, with the exception that additional calculations need to be carried out to determine the angle and position at which each character is printed. Program *P4.5* (*listing 4.5*) does this, the text being proportionally spaced around the arc or circle.

PROCEDURES

PROC_circleprint is the master procedure for printing characters around an arc or circle. The variables mode%, mag% and S$ are as described for PROC_lineprint1 in section 4.3. The variables xcentre% and ycentre% give the centre of the arc or circle (in graphics units). Variables startangle% and arcangle% give the basic starting angle (in degrees) and arc angle (in degrees) through which the text is to be written — see Fig. 4.10. (You should note that positive angles are measured in the anticlockwise direction.) Variable rad% gives the radius of the circle in graphics units.

PROC_spots2 and PROC_frame are as described in section 4.5.

PROC_curvemessage not only calculates the angle (textangle%) at which

Listing 4.5

```
10  REM****PROGRAM"P4.5"****
20  *TV0,1
30  MODE 1
40  PROC_circleprint(1,4,"Text",640,500,180,-180,200)
50  END
60  :
70  DEF PROC_circleprint(mode%,mag%,S$,xcentre%,ycentre%,startangle%,arc
angle%,rad%)
80  PROC_spots2
90  PROC_frame
100  PROC_curvemessage(mag%,S$,xcentre%,ycentre%,startangle%,arcangle%,ra
d%)
110  ENDPROC
120  :
130  :
140  :
150  DEF PROC_spots2
160  IF mode% = 0 THEN K%=2
170  IF mode% = 1 THEN K%=4
180  IF mode% = 2 THEN K%=8
190  IF mode% = 4 THEN K%=4
200  IF mode% = 5 THEN K%=8
210    spots% = K%*8
220  ENDPROC
230  :
240  DEF PROC_print2
250    PRINT TAB(0,31);MID$(S$,I,1);
260  ENDPROC
270  :
280  DEF PROC_frame
290  H%=1023:W%=1279
300  MOVE 0,32:DRAW 0,H%:DRAW W%,H%:DRAW W%,0:DRAW (spots%+10),0
310  ENDPROC
320  :
330  DEF PROC_curvemessage(mag%,S$,xcentre%,ycentre%,startangle%,arcangle
%,rad%)
340  LOCAL I,stepangle,printangle
350  arcangle=RAD(arcangle%)
360  startangle=RAD(startangle%)
370  L%=LEN S$
380  stepangle=arcangle/(L%-1)
390  FOR I=1 TO L%
400    printangle=startangle+stepangle*(I-1)
410    textangle=printangle-PI/2
420    printangle=printangle+((-1)*(arcangle/ABS(arcangle))*ATN(K%*4*ABS(
mag%)/rad%))
430    XSTART%=xcentre%+rad%*COS(printangle)
440    YSTART%=ycentre%+rad%*SIN(printangle)
450    PROC_print2
```

```
460     PROC_string3
470     NEXT I
480  ENDPROC
490 :

500  DEF PROC_string3
510  FOR X% = 0 TO (spots%-1)
520    FOR Y% = 0 TO 31
530      IF POINT(X%,Y%) <> 0 THEN PROC_box3(X%,Y%,XSTART%,YSTART%,mag%,t
extangle)
540      NEXT Y%:NEXT X%
550  ENDPROC
560 :
570  DEF PROC_box3(X%,Y%,XSTART%,YSTART%,mag%,textangle)
580  LOCAL XPOS%,YPOS%,cos,sin
590  angle=textangle
600  cos=COS(angle)
610  sin=SIN(angle)
620  XPOS% = XSTART%+(X%*mag%*cos-Y%*mag%*sin)
630  YPOS% = YSTART%+(X%*mag%*sin+Y%*mag%*cos)
640  MOVE XPOS%,YPOS%
650  MOVE XPOS%+(mag%-1),YPOS%
660  PLOT 85,XPOS%,YPOS%+(mag%-1)
670  PLOT 85,XPOS%+(mag%-1),YPOS%+(mag%-1)
680  ENDPROC
```

Fig. 4.10 a) The coordinates of the starting point of the first character in a string, and b) the final character in the string after moving through an angle of arcangle%

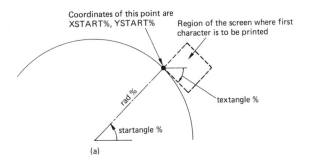

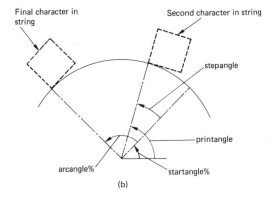

the text is to be printed but also the starting position (XSTART%, YSTART%) of the enlarged character.

PROC_print2 prints one character of the string S$ in the lower left-hand corner of the screen.

PROC_string3 scans each addressable spot in the character printed by PROC_print2 and calls for PROC_box3 if a spot contains a non-zero "colour".

PROC_box3 is generally similar to PROC_box2, and uses MOVE and PLOT 85 instructions to fill in a box on the screen.

Description The master procedure, PROC_circleprint, firstly calls PROC_spots2 to calculate the number of graphical spots in the forward direction in the enlarged character to be printed, and then calls PROC_frame to draw a frame around the limits of the viewing area.

Next PROC_curvemessage calculates not only the angle (textangle%) at which the text is to be printed, but the starting point of the enlarged character (XSTART%, YSTART%), and also the angle which must be stepped through (stepangle) in order to give proportional spacing — see Fig. 4.10. In the program line 420, PROC_curvemessage uses a novel technique to calculate the printing angle (printangle) which prints the text perpendicular to the radius; we will return to this later.

Having done the preliminary calculations, PROC_curvemessage transfers program control firstly to PROC_print2 to print a character in the lower left-hand corner of the screen and, secondly, transfers control to PROC_string3 to print the enlarged character (this procedure also calls on PROC_box3). The display on the screen at the completion of the program is shown in Fig. 4.11.

Determination of the value of textangle and printangle To obtain proportional spacing of the text, it is necessary to determine the angular step between each character. This is obtained in line 380 by dividing the arcangle by (length of string *minus* 1). Line 400 calculates the correct printing angle [printangle (see Fig. 4.10b)] by adding the angular step (stepangle) for each character to the starting angle.

The standard mathematical notation that a "positive" angular change is an anticlockwise movement has been adopted, so that a positive arc angle causes the characters to be printed from right to left. This is overcome in practice by using a negative value for the arc angle (see lines 40 and 70 of program *P4.4*), causing the text to be printed from left to right.

Inspection of Fig. 4.10 shows that for a character to be printed at a tangent to the curve, it must be turned clockwise through 90° or PI/2 radian. The resulting angle (textangle) is calculated in line 410 as follows:

Textangle = printangle − PI/2

Text printed at the textangle calculated above with the printangle calculated above looks rather peculiar on the screen because the point of tangency with the curve is the starting point of the character, i.e. the lower left-hand corner of the character; the character appears to jut out from the curve. This is shown in character (i) in Fig. 4.12.

Fig. 4.11 Display produced
by program P4.4

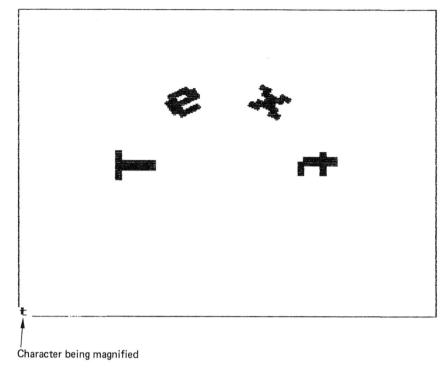

Character being magnified

Fig. 4.12 Improving the
presentation of a character
printed on the arc of a circle

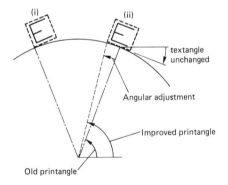

The presentation of the character is improved by altering the "print-angle" from the "old printangle" value to the "improved printangle" as shown in Fig. 4.12. The net result is that the centre of the character is tangential to the curve as shown in character (ii). This change is effected in the program *P4.4* in line 420.

Following line 420, the XSTART% and YSTART% positions of the character are calculated and passed to PROC_string3 which produces the enlarged screen display.

4.7 A Combined Text Printing Program

A useful facility in any graphics routine is the ability to call up procedures allowing you to write text of any size either at any angle or around any curve. The procedures described in this chapter can be linked together to do this. Program *P4.6* (*listing 4.6*) shows a typical executive program which does this, the resulting display being shown in Fig. 4.13. The procedures used are not listed here, and have been described earlier.

The program uses PROC_lineprint2 once (see section 4.5 for details) and PROC_circleprint four times (see section 4.6). Other procedures involved are PROC_spots2, PROC_string2, PROC_box2, PROC_curvemessage, PROC_string3 and PROC_box3.

Listing 4.6

```
 60  PROC_circleprint(1,2,"LINEAR and",640,0,120,-60,750)
 70  PROC_circleprint(1,2,"CURVED",640,0,110,-40,650)
 80  PROC_lineprint2(1,2,"text",485,450,0)
 90  PROC_circleprint(1,-2,"on the",600,1023,250,40,750)
100  PROC_circleprint(1,-3,"SCREEN",600,1023,250,40,885)
110  END
```

Fig. 4.13 The display produced by program P4.6

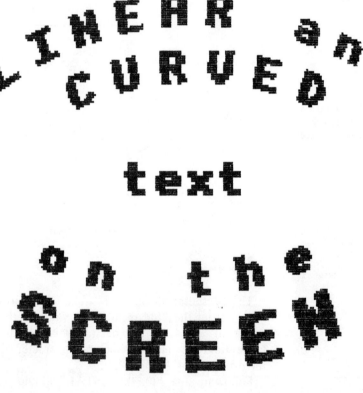

A few points are worth noting and are discussed below. The two upper curved strings. ("LINEAR and" and "CURVED") are printed around an arc having its centre at the middle of the bottom line of the screen. The characters are twice the normal Mode 1 size and are proportionally spaced along an arc of −60° from the starting angle of 120°. That is, the text is printed upright and from left to right (which is clockwise around the arc).

The two lower curved strings ("on the" and "SCREEN") are printed around an arc having its centre at the middle of the top line of the screen. The string "on the" is twice normal Mode 1 size and "SCREEN" is three times the normal size, and is proportionally spaced along its arc. That is, the text is printed from left to right (which is anticlockwise around the arc). The interesting point about line 90 of *listing 4.6* is that the "magnitude" factor of the text is -2, and in line 100 it is -3. The reason for doing this is that a positive magnitude would print the text upside down around the bottom of the arc. A negative magnitude has the effect of turning the printed text uside down, that is, it appears the correct way up on the screen.

The presentation of the display is improved by the following modifications. By inserting the following line as the first instruction in the PROC_print2 procedure, the normal-size character in the bottom left-hand corner of the screen becomes invisible:

VDU 19,3,0;0;

This, of course, has the disadvantage that all the printed text also becomes invisible to the eye! You must therefore insert instructions elsewhere to cause the enlarged characters printed on the screen to be visible. You can take advantage here of printing the enlarged characters in colour. To cause every string printed by PROC_lineprint2 to be yellow, you need to add the following instruction in PROC_string2 immediately after calling for PROC_print2:

GCOL 0,2

To cause every string printed by PROC_circleprint to appear in red, add the following instruction in PROC_curvemessage immediately after calling for PROC_print2:

GCOL 0,1

You also need to add the following instructions in the main program:

```
102 REM CLEAR DISPLAYED CHARACTER
104 PRINT TAB(0,31);" ";
106 REM RESTORE LOGICAL COLOURS
108 VDU 20
```

Graphs, Histograms and Pie Charts

5.1 The Basic Requirements of a Graph Drawing Program

One of the more serious uses of a computer is to produce a graph relating one variable, say the temperature of a hospital patient, to another variable, say time. Certain requirements must be satisfied in order to draw a graph of any kind, some of which are listed below:

1 *The graph must have axes.* Most graphs have two axes (X and Y), but three-dimensional graphs have three axes (the third usually being labelled Z).
2 *The axes must be scaled.* The maximum and minimum values should not exceed the size of the monitor screen.
3 *The graph may have a grid.* This is useful for estimating values on the monitor screen.
4 *The axes should be labelled and the graph may need a title.*
5 *The graph needs to be plotted.*

Not all graphs need a grid, but most graphs need 1, 2, 4 and 5 above (although item 5 depends on whether you need only to plot the points).

The value of mathematical and scientific functions, such as the sine function, can be predicted by calculation, whilst the graph of a random function such as the rainfall in your home town cannot be predicted. The form that the graph takes therefore depends on the data. For this reason, it is difficult to produce a completely general-purpose graph-plotting program.

In some cases, you may have plotted a set of points which are supposed to represent a straight line graph, but these are randomly distributed around the "straight line". This occurs in many scienfitic experiments, and the problem may be to estimate the equation for the "best" straight line through the points. There are a number of statistical methods for doing this, one of the most popular being known as the *least squares method*. This method is used later in the chapter, and the theory is discussed in more detail in the final chapter.

5.2 A Graph-plotting Program (program P5.1)

When writing any graphics program, you must give serious consideration to the screen MODE used in the program. Computer graphics programs can consume a vast amount of memory, and you need to consider the trade-off between the number of colours, the size of text on the screen, and the amount of memory used by the computer to display the graphics.

If you select a Mode needing more than one of these factors, then there is a reduction in either or both of the other factors. The graph-plotting programs in this chapter use screen MODE 1 because it provides 4 colours and up to 40 text characters on one line; however, the computer itself needs 20 Kbytes of memory, which is two-thirds of the total memory of the model B computer! Other graphic Modes take up less memory, but provide you either with a smaller number of colours, or with fewer text characters per line, or both.

Suppose that you wish to plot a graph using the X- and Y-axes in Fig. 5.1. The first step is to write down an executive program which establishes a series of PROCedures, each dealing with one stage of the operation. Such an executive program is given in lines 10–190 of *listing 5.1*.

Fig. 5.1 Scaling and titling a graph

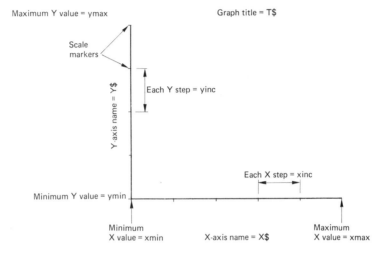

Lines 10–40 inclusive deal with the program title and general "house-keeping". Line 50 handles the important aspect of reporting errors. Additionally, since the procedure PROC_scales contains a VDU 5 instruction (which has the effect of switching the text cursor OFF), the line which causes the errors to be reported (line 1560) contains a VDU 4 command which restores the text cursor.

Line 60 DIMensions a 2-dimensional array entitled "points" which is used to store the X- and Y-value of each point on the graph; a limit of 20 points is chosen in *P5.1*, but you can increase the limit merely by increasing the first value in the array definition (be careful, arrays can consume a lot of memory!).

The program written here is as near-universal as can be made within the limits of the memory capacity of the computer. (Improvements are, of course, always possible and the author would be pleased to hear any suggestions.) The program will deal with almost any value or mathematical sign of variable.

5.3   Gathering Information about the Axes

The procedure PROC_basic_information (see *listing 5.2*) asks you to provide data relating to the axes in the form given in Fig. 5.1; a typical computer display and user response is shown in Fig. 5.2. You will notice in

Listing 5.1

```
  10  REM****PROGRAM "P5.1"****
  20  REM****GRAPH DRAWING PROGRAM****
  30  *TV0,1
  40  MODE 1
  50  ON ERROR GOTO 1560
  60  DIM points(20,1):REM ARRAY TO STORE X AND Y VALUES
  70  PROC_basic_information:REM GRAPH SPECIFICATION
  80  PROC_data:REM GET DATA FROM KEYBOARD
  90  PROC_select:REM CHOOSE TYPE OF DISPLAY
 100  PROC_axes:REM DRAW AXES IN YELLOW
 110  PROC_scales:REM MARK SCALES ON AXES
 120  PROC_grid:REM DRAW GRID ON GRAPH IN RED
 130  PROC_title:REM TITLE GRAPH
 140  PROC_axis_names:REM PRINT NAMES OF AXES
 150  PROC_points:REM PRINT POINTS ON GRAPH
 160  IF graph_select=2 THEN PROC_graph1:REM JOIN POINTS WITH STRAIGHT LIN
ES
 170  IF graph_select=3 THEN PROC_graph2:REM DRAW BEST STRAIGHT LINE THROU
GH POINTS
 180  VDU4:REM RESTORE TEXT CURSOR
 190  END
 200  :

1560  VDU 4:REPORT:PRINT " AT LINE ";ERL:END
```

Listing 5.2

```
 210  DEF PROC_basic_information
 220  CLS:COLOUR 1
 230  PRINT TAB(6,4)"GRAPH SCALE SPECIFICATION";TAB(0,6)"TITLE OF GRAPH"
 240  PRINT TAB(0,8)"X-AXIS NAME";TAB(0,10)"MAXIMUM VALUE OF X"
 250  PRINT TAB(0,12)"MINIMUM VALUE OF X";TAB(0,14)"X-AXIS INCREMENT SIZE"
 260  PRINT TAB(0,16)"Y-AXIS NAME";TAB(0,18)"MAXIMUM VALUE OF Y"
 270  PRINT TAB(0,20)"MINIMUM VALUE OF Y";TAB(0,22)"Y-AXIS INCREMENT SIZE"
 280  PRINT TAB(0,24)"Is the X-origin (X=0) of the graph on"
 290  PRINT TAB(0,25)"the screen? Answer Y or N"
 300  PRINT TAB(0,27)"Is the Y-origin (Y=0) of the graph on"
 310  PRINT TAB(0,28)"the screen? Answer Y or N"
 320  COLOUR 2:REM YELLOW TEXT
 330  INPUT TAB(16,6)T$,TAB(16,8)X$,TAB(23,10)xmax$,TAB(23,12)xmin,TAB(23,
14)xinc
 340  INPUT TAB(16,16)Y$,TAB(23,18)ymax$,TAB(23,20)ymin,TAB(23,22)yinc
 350  INPUT TAB(30,25)true_x$,TAB(30,28)true_y$
 360  xmax=EVAL(xmax$)
 370  ymax=EVAL(ymax$)
 380  ylength=LEN(Y$)
 390  ENDPROC
 400  :
```

listing 5.2 that both the maximum value of the X-scale (line 330) and of the Y-scale (line 340) are read by the computer as a string, namely xmax$ and ymax$. The reason for this is that the length of the string, i.e. the number of characters in the string, is needed later to determine the printed position of the string on the screen. The numeric value of xmax and ymax is EVALuated in lines 360 and 370, respectively.

In some cases you may need to use very large X- and Y-values. For example, you may be plotting the population of various areas of the world, which means that you need to display values of several million on the screen. In this case it is advisable to include a multiplying factor (say, x millions) with the (say) X-axis name.

Fig. 5.2

```
GRAPH SCALE SPECIFICATION

TITLE OF GRAPH     RESISTANCE-TEMPERATURE

X-AXIS NAME        TEMP

MAXIMUM VALUE OF X        90

MINIMUM VALUE OF X        0

X-AXIS INCREMENT SIZE     10

Y-AXIS NAME        RES

MAXIMUM VALUE OF Y        16

MINIMUM VALUE OF Y        0

Y-AXIS INCREMENT SIZE     2

Is the X-origin (X=0) of the graph on
the screen? Answer Y or N         Y

Is the Y-origin (Y=0) of the graph on
the screen? Answer Y or N         Y
```

The two sentences printed at the foot of the screen (see Fig. 5.2) by PROC_basic_information ask if the X-origin and Y-origin, respectively, are on the screen. This request enables the computer to decide whether a "true origin" or a "false origin" is to be displayed. This information is read in line 350 of the program as true_x$ and true_y$. If either of these is N (No), the computer must calculate where to draw the axes. This is discussed in section 5.6.

5.4 Getting the Data Relating to the Graph

The procedure PROC_data in *listing 5.3* collects data for each point in the graph via the keyboard. After asking you for the number of points (see Fig. 5.3), the computer enables you to input the data into an array named "points". You will find it an interesting exercise to modify the program to read the data from a DATA list contained in the program.

Listing 5.3

```
410  DEF PROC_data
420  CLS:COLOUR 1
430  PRINT TAB(11,2)"DATA FOR GRAPH"
440  COLOUR 2
450  INPUT TAB(5,4)"NUMBER OF POINTS ON GRAPH = "N
460  FOR row=1 TO N
470    COLOUR 1:PRINT TAB(5,5+row)"X";row;" = ",TAB(20,5+row)"Y";row;" =
"
480    COLOUR 2:INPUT TAB(10,5+row)points(row,0),TAB(25,5+row)points(row,
1)
490    NEXT row
500  ENDPROC
510 :
```

Fig. 5.3

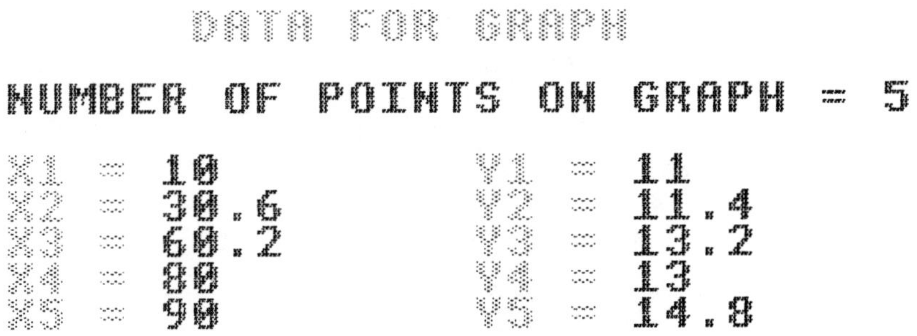

```
DATA FOR GRAPH

NUMBER OF POINTS ON GRAPH = 5

X1 = 10        Y1 = 11
X2 = 30.6      Y2 = 11.4
X3 = 60.2      Y3 = 13.2
X4 = 80        Y4 = 13
X5 = 90        Y5 = 14.8
```

5.5   Choosing the Type of Display

PROC_select in *listing 5.4* offers you the three options shown in Fig. 5.4; you simply type in the required option (option 3 being chosen in Fig. 5.4). The variable graph_select (see line 590) stores your answer.

Listing 5.4

```
520  DEF PROC_select
530  CLS:COLOUR 1
540  PRINT TAB(8,2)"CHOOSE TYPE OF DISPLAY"
550  COLOUR 2:PRINT TAB(0,4)"1. PLOT POINTS ONLY"
560  PRINT TAB(0,6)"2. JOINT THE POINTS WITH STRAIGHT LINES"
570  PRINT TAB(0,8)"3. DRAW THE BEST STRAIGHT LINE"
580  PRINT TAB(0,10)"TYPE YOUR SELECTION (1, 2 OR 3)"
590  COLOUR 1:INPUT TAB(36,10)graph_select
600  IF graph_select<1 OR graph_select>3 THEN PRINT TAB(36,10)"  ":GOTO
590
610  ENDPROC
620 :
```

If you only need to plot the points on the graph, you can enter the X- and Y-values (see section 5.4) in any order. The computer will simply plot the points in the order in which they are given.

Fig. 5.4

CHOOSE TYPE OF DISPLAY

1. PLOT POINTS ONLY

2. JOINT THE POINTS WITH STRAIGHT LINES

3. DRAW THE BEST STRAIGHT LINE

TYPE YOUR SELECTION (1, 2 OR 3)   3

However, if you need to join the points by a series of straight lines, you must ensure that the values are entered in the order in which they are to be joined together.

Option 3, DRAW THE BEST STRAIGHT LINE, invokes a least squares routine, which is briefly touched on in section 5.11, and is discussed in more detail in Chapter 9.

5.6 Drawing the Axes

Having gathered the data relating to the scales, to the graph points, and to the display format, the computer can proceed to draw the axes.

PROC_axes in *listing 5.5* calculates the scale to be used on the X-axis (the variable *xscale*) and on the Y-axis (the variable *yscale*); the scale factors convert your real values into screen graphics units. In lines 670 and 680, the computer calculates the position of the X-origin (the variable *xorg*) and the Y-origin (the variable *yorg*); it also makes allowance for the room needed to print the title of the graph together with the axis names and scales. The VDU 29 instruction in line 690 uses the value of xorg and of yorg to determine the graphics origin.

Listing 5.5

```
630  DEF PROC_axes:REM DRAW AXES
640  CLS:GCOL 0,2
650  xscale=(1279-(7+LEN(ymax$))*32)/(xmax-xmin)
660  yscale=(1024-148-128)/(ymax-ymin)
670  xorg=84+LEN(ymax$)*32-xmin*xscale:REM LEAVE ROOM FOR Y SCALE DATA
680  yorg=200-ymin*yscale:REM LEAVE ROOM FOR X SCALE DATA
690  VDU29,xorg;yorg;:REM DEFINE GRAPHICS ORIGIN
700  x_move=0:y_move=0
710  IF true_x$="N" THEN y_move=xmin*xscale
720  IF true_y$="N" THEN x_move=ymin*yscale
730  MOVE xmin*xscale,x_move:DRAW xmax*xscale,x_move:REM DRAW X AXIS
740  MOVE y_move,ymin*yscale:DRAW y_move,ymax*yscale:REM DRAW Y AXIS
750  ENDPROC
760  :
```

The variables x_move and y_move in lines 700–740 inclusive are used to determine the position of the axes (remember, if true_x$="N" then the X-axis does not have a true zero, and the y-axis does not have a true zero if true_y$="N".

5.7 Marking the Scales on the Axes

PROC_scales in *listing 5.6* positions markers on the X- and Y-axes (see

Listing 5.6

```
770  DEF PROC_scales
780  MOVE 0,0:VDU 5
790  REM DRAW MARKERS AND VALUES ON X-AXIS
800  FOR xval=xmin TO xmax STEP xinc
810    MOVE xval*xscale,-10+x_move:DRAW xval*xscale,x_move
820    MOVE xval*xscale-(LEN(xmax$)*32)DIV 2,-20+x_move:PRINT;xval:REM CE
NTRE LARGEST X VALUE ON MARKER
830    NEXT xval
840  REM DRAW MARKERS AND VALUES ON Y-AXIS
850  FOR yval=ymin TO ymax STEP yinc
860    MOVE -10+y_move,yval*yscale:DRAW y_move,yval*yscale
870    MOVE -((LEN(ymax$)*32)+20)+y_move,(yval*yscale)+16:PRINT;yval:REM
CENTRE Y VALUE ON MARKER
880    NEXT yval
890  ENDPROC
900  :
```

lines 810 and 860 respectively) corresponding to the X- and Y-increments you have chosen.

Also, after drawing the X-marker, it prints the X-value against it, the X-value being centred under the marker. The program is written so that the maximum value is centred below its marker (see line 820). If other X-values do not contain the same number of digits as the largest value, they are printed slightly to the left of the marker. You will find it an interesting exercise to modify the program to cause all X-values to be centred on their markers. (*Hint:* you will need to change the array "points" to the string array "points$", and use the length of each value in a calculation.)

The computer then draws the Y-markers and centres the Y-values against them (see line 870). The first part of the MOVE instruction in this line makes allowance for the length of the maximum value of Y.

5.8   Drawing a Grid on the Graph

The procedure PROC_grid in *listing 5.7* draws a series of red horizontal lines from the minimum value of X to the maximum value of Y (see lines

Listing 5.7

```
910   DEF PROC_grid:GCOL 0,1
920   REM DRAW HORIZONTAL LINES
930   FOR yline=ymin TO ymax STEP yinc
940     IF yline=0 AND ymax=0 THEN 970 ELSE IF yline=0 NEXT yline
950   MOVE xmin*xscale,yline*yscale:DRAW xmax*xscale,yline*yscale
960   NEXT yline
970   REM DRAW VERTICAL LINES
980   FOR xline=xmin TO xmax STEP xinc
990     IF xline=0 AND xmax=0 THEN ENDPROC ELSE IF xline=0 NEXT xline
1000  MOVE xline*xscale,ymin*yscale:DRAW xline*xscale,ymax*yscale
1010  NEXT xline
1020  ENDPROC
1030  :
```

930 to 960 inclusive) for each Y-increment (except Y=0). It also draws vertical red lines to give X-increment values (except X=0).

The grid lines are missing for X=0 and Y=0 so that the grid does not obscure the true origin of the graph.

5.9   Printing the Title and Axis Names

PROC_title in *listing 5.8* uses the length of the name of the title you have selected (see line 1060) to calculate the starting point on the screen of your title. Line 1070 causes the title to be printed at the centre of the screen. You should not use a title length greater than one screen width (40 characters), otherwise wrap-around of the title occurs on the screen.

Listing 5.8

```
1040  DEF PROC_title
1050  GCOL 0,2
1060  title_start=640-((LEN(T$)DIV 2)*32)-xorg:REM CALCULATE TITLE STARTIN
G POINT
1070  MOVE title_start,ymax*yscale+50:PRINT T$
1080  ENDPROC
1090 :
1100  DEF PROC_axis_names
1110  REM PRINT X-AXIS NAME
1120  tab=xmax*xscale-(LEN(X$)*32)
1130  MOVE tab,-70+x_move:PRINT X$
1140  REM PRINT Y-AXIS NAME
1150  tab=ymax*yscale
1160  FOR no=1 TO LEN(Y$)
1170    MOVE -(LEN(ymax$)*32+70)+y_move,tab:PRINT MID$(Y$,no,1)
1180    tab=tab-32
1190    NEXT no
1200  ENDPROC
1210 :
```

The names of the X-axis and the Y-axis are printed by PROC_axis_ names (also in *listing 5.8*). Once again, the computer calculates the starting position of the name on the axis by using the length of the string containing the axis name [LEN(X$) and LEN(Y$) respectively]. For printing purposes, the X-axis name should not contain more than 34 characters (including spaces), and the Y-axis name should not be longer than 25 characters.

However, if you use the best-straight-line option (see section 5.11), you should keep the axis name down to not more than three characters.

5.10   Plotting Points on the Graph

PROC_points in *listing 5.9* reads the X- and Y-value of each point stored in the array named "points", and draws a cross on the screen at each point.

5.11   Graph Options

The final menu offered before the computer plots the graph asks you for the display format (see Fig. 5.4). If you select option 1 (plot points only),

Listing 5.9

```
1220  DEF PROC_points
1230  GCOL 0,3
1240  FOR spot=1 TO N
1250    xp=points(spot,0)*xscale:yp=points(spot,1)*yscale
1260    MOVE xp+12,yp:DRAW xp-12,yp
1270    MOVE xp,yp+12:DRAW xp,yp-12
1280    NEXT spot
1290  ENDPROC
1300  :
```

the computer merely executes the procedures up to and including PROC_
points.

However, if you select option 2 (join the points with straight lines), the
computer also executes PROC_graph1 in *listing 5.10*; this determines the
position of adjacent pairs of points and, having MOVEd to the first point,
it DRAWs a line to the second point; this process is repeated until every
point has been dealt with.

Listing 5.10

```
1310  DEF PROC_graph1
1320  MOVE points(1,0)*xscale,points(1,1)*yscale
1330  FOR spot=2 TO N
1340    DRAW points(spot,0)*xscale,points(spot,1)*yscale
1350    NEXT spot
1360  ENDPROC
1370  :
1380  DEF PROC_graph2
1390  a=0:b=0:c=0:d=0:e=0
1400  FOR row=1 TO N
1410    x=points(row,0):y=points(row,1)
1420    a=a+x:b=b+y:c=c+x*y:d=d+x*x:e=e+y*y
1430    NEXT row
1440  num=N*c-a*b:denom1=N*d-a^2:denom2=N*e-b^2
1450  IF denom2=0 GOTO 1500
1460  M=num/denom2:I=(a-M*b)/N
1470  GCOL 0,2:MOVE -xorg,-yorg+64:PRINT X$;" = ";M;"*";Y$;:IF SGN(I) =-1
PRINT" ";SGN(I)*ABS(I) ELSE PRINT" + ";I
1480  MOVE (M*ymin+I)*xscale,ymin*yscale:DRAW(M*ymax+I)*xscale,ymax*yscale
1490  IF denom1=0 GOTO 1530
1500  m=num/denom1:i=(b-m*a)/N
1510  GCOL 0,3:MOVE -xorg,-yorg+96:PRINT Y$;" = ";m;"*";X$;:IF SGN(i) =-1
PRINT" ";SGN(i*ABS(i)) ELSE PRINT" + ";i
1520  MOVE xmin*xscale,(m*xmin+i)*yscale:DRAW xmax*xscale,(m*xmax+i)*yscal
e
1530  MOVE -xorg,-yorg+32:PRINT"CORRELATION COEFFICIENT = ";(c-a*b/N)/SQR(
(d-a^2/N)*(e-b^2/N))
1540  ENDPROC
1550  :
```

Figure 5.5 shows one application of the point-joining program by plotting the share value of the BLUE SKY company over a number of years. In this case, the graph is plotted with a "false zero".

Should you choose option 3, the computer executes PROC_graph2 in which the procedure is a little more complex, and is described in the following. To understand what is happening, we must digress a little and discuss the statistical meaning of the relationship between two variables.

Fig. 5.5 A graph which is drawn using the point-joining option

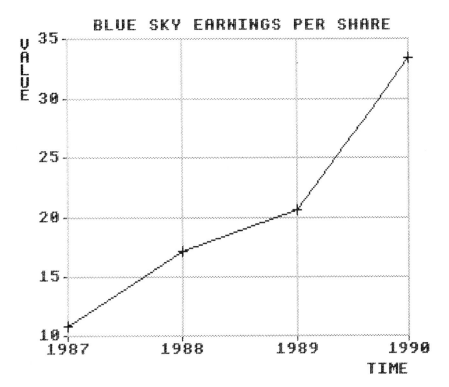

Suppose that you were to investigate the statistics relating, say, the number of serious accidents which occur in a building to the size of the building. Clearly, the result from one building is not statistically reliable, and you must consider the results from many buildings. The net result will give a graph which indicates the relationship between the number of accidents and the size of the building. Such a graph may be as shown in Fig. 5.6.

Depending on your point of view, any one of several lines drawn through the points can be considered to be the "best" graph. You may consider, on the one hand, that it is the size of the building which fixes the number of accidents; on the other hand, you may think that it is the number of accidents which indicates the size of the building. Depending on your choice, there are at least two possible best graphs, shown as graph A and graph B in Fig. 5.6. The equations for the two graphs in this case they are assumed to be straight-line graphs) are, if you decide that X causes Y to happen, i.e. X is the *independent variable*:

$$Y = mX + c$$

Fig. 5.6 A graph relating
the number of accidents in
a building to the size of the
building in which they occur

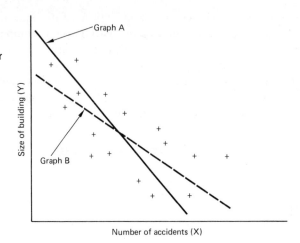

where m is the *slope* of the graph (change-in-Y/change-in-X) and c is the *intercept* of the graph on the Y-axis. If, on the other hand, you decide that Y is the independent variable, and causes X to happen, then the equation is

$$X = MY + C$$

where M is the slope of the graph (change-in-X/change-in-Y) and C is the intercept of the graph on the X-axis.

If the points are scattered, as shown in Fig. 5.6, there will be two best graphs, one assuming that X is the independent variable and the other assuming that Y is the independent variable.

Fig. 5.7 Correlation
coefficient of *a*) +1, *b*) less
than +1, *c*) between zero
and −1, *d*) zero

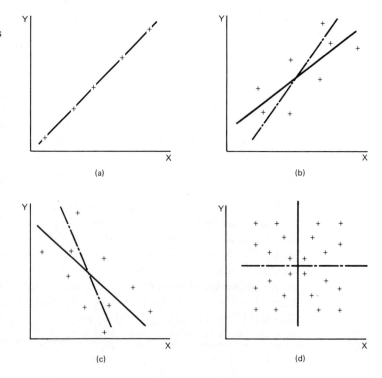

A factor known as the **correlation coefficient** gives an indication of how closely the graphs agree with one another. If all the points lie on a straight line (see Fig. 5.7a) which has a positive slope, the correlation coefficient is +1. However, if the points are scattered around a positive slope (see Fig. 5.7b), the correlation coefficient has a value of less than +1. If the points are scattered around a line of negative slope (see Fig. 5.7c), the correlation coefficient has a value between zero and −1. (A correlation coefficient of −1 corresponds to the case where all the points lie on the same line, but having a negative slope.) Finally, should all the points be completely randomly scattered (see Fig. 5.7d), the two best graphs are at right-angles to one another, and the correlation coefficient is zero.

When a choice of option 3 is selected, the computer draws the two best straight lines, one in white and the other in yellow, and prints the equation for each graph together with the correlation coefficient between the graphs. (The least squares method for predicting the graphs is dicussed in Chapter 9.)

Figure 5.8 shows a set of values for the resistance of a length of wire plotted to a base of temperature drawn using option 3. The computer draws the two best graphs and prints the equations for them together with the correlation coefficient. The graph is plotted to a true zero of resistance and a true zero of temperature (in deg. C). However, you can take a look at the graph in more detail (see Fig. 5.9) simply by entering the same details, but altering the minimum value on each scale. This technique allows you to "zoom" into any part of the graph.

Fig. 5.8 A graph drawn using the "best" straight-line option

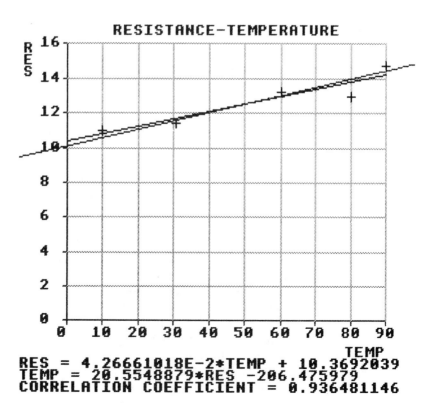

$$RES = 4.26661018E{-}2{*}TEMP + 10.3692039$$
$$TEMP = 20.5548879{*}RES - 206.475979$$
$$CORRELATION\ COEFFICIENT = 0.936481146$$

Fig. 5.9 An enlarged part of
the graph in Fig. 5.8

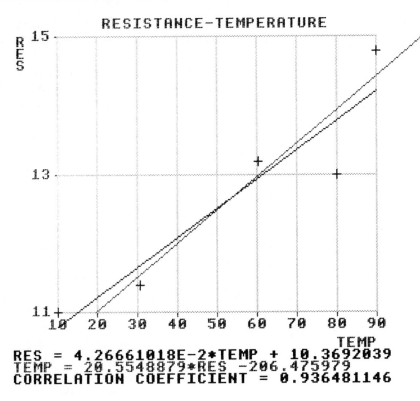

RESISTANCE-TEMPERATURE

RES = 4.26661018E-2*TEMP + 10.3692039
TEMP = 20.5548879*RES -206.475979
CORRELATION COEFFICIENT = 0.936481146

5.12 Drawing the Graph of a Scientific Equation

The techniques involved here are generally similar to those for the general graph-drawing equation program (*P5.1*), with the exception that you need to provide the equation rather than the data relating to the points on the graph.

The equation-plotting program (program *P5.2*) in *listing 5.11* is a modified version of program *P5.1*. You simply need to load program *P5.1* into the memory of the computer and modify the lines in *listing 5.11*. The program should then be SAVEd as "P5.2".

The change in line 20 merely explains the purpose of the program. Line 80 calls on PROC_equation, which asks you to type in the equation of the curve *in the BASIC language* (this is input to the computer as eqn$ in line 480). Line 150 of the executive program calls on PROC_draw_graph, whose function it is to plot the graph of the equation.

PROC_equation is inserted in lines 410 to 500 of the program, and replaces PROC_data in *listing 5.3*. PROC_draw_graph commences at line 1220 and replaces PROC_points in *listing 5.9*. The graph-drawing procedure simply divides the full range of X-values into 100 steps and calculates the value of Y for each X-value. Line 1260 of the program causes the computer to join the resulting Y-values with straight lines to give the complete X-Y graph.

Figure 5.10 shows a plot of the angular movement of the output of a control system, such as the movement of the dish of a radar system which is

Listing 5.11

```
10   REM****PROGRAM "P5.2"****
20   REM****EQUATION PLOTTING PROGRAM****

80   PROC_equation:REM SPECIFY THE EQUATION
90  :

150  PROC_draw_graph:REM PLOT THE GRAPH OF THE EQUATION
160  :
170  :

410  DEF PROC_equation
420  CLS:COLOUR 1:PRINT TAB(0,2)"The computer will draw the curve"
430  PRINT"corresponding to your own equation."
440  COLOUR 2:PRINT TAB(0,5)"The equation must be expressed in BASIC"
450  PRINT"For example Y = 3.5*X^2/SIN(X)"
460  PRINT"Remember: use X and Y as the variables"
470  PRINT TAB(0,9)"Please type your equation"
480  COLOUR 1:INPUT TAB(2,11)"Y = "eqn$
490  ENDPROC
500  :

940  IF yline=0 NEXT yline

990  IF xline=0 NEXT xline

1220  DEF PROC_draw_graph
1230  GCOL 0,3:X=xmin:xstep=(xmax-xmin)/100
1240  MOVE X*xscale,EVAL(eqn$)*yscale
1250  FOR X=xmin TO xmax STEP xstep
1260    DRAW X*xscale,EVAL(eqn$)*yscale
1270    NEXT X
1280  MOVE -xorg,-yorg+32:PRINT TAB(0,33)"Y = "eqn$
1290  ENDPROC
1300  :
```

following a change of command signal. The equation relating X and Y is printed at the foot of the screen. Once again, you can enlarge a part of the graph merely by providing the same equation to the computer, but altering the origin of the graph.

5.13 Plotting Bar Charts

Bar charts are particularly useful when comparing events or the frequency of occurence of a range of factors, and are widely used by financial, scientific and commercial organizations.

The procedure for plotting a bar chart generally follows that for a graph with the exception that some of them need a little alteration when compared with X-Y graphs. The executive for program *P5.3* is shown in

Fig. 5.10 The graph of a
scientific equation

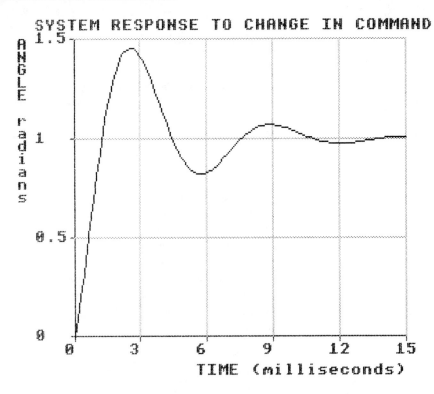

$$Y = 1-EXP(-0.3*X)*(COS(X)-.28*SIN(X))$$

listing 5.12. Since the X-data on a bar chart is ofen a series of names rather than numbers, the array (points$) in line 60 which stores the X- and Y-data is a string array. In contrast to the graph-plotting program, *the grid is drawn after the chart*; this is done so that the broad bars do not obscure the

Listing 5.12

```
10  REM****PROGRAM "P5.3"****
20  REM****BAR CHART PROGRAM****
30  *TV0,1
40  MODE 1
50  ON ERROR GOTO 1230
60  DIM points$(20,1):REM ARRAY TO STORE X AND Y VALUES
70  PROC_basic_information2:REM CHART SPECIFICATION
80  PROC_data2:REM GET DATA FROM KEYBOARD
90  PROC_axes2:REM DRAW AXES IN YELLOW
100 PROC_scales2:REM MARK SCALES ON AXES
110 PROC_title:REM TITLE GRAPH
120 PROC_axis_names2:REM PRINT NAMES OF AXES
130 PROC_bars:REM DRAW BARS ON CHART
140 PROC_grid2:REM DRAW GRID
150 VDU4:REM RESTORE TEXT CURSOR
160 END
170 :
```

grid lines (see also section 5.15). The operation of the program is described below.

5.14 Collecting the Bar Chart Information

The procedure PROC_basic_information2 (see *listing 5.13*) simply asks you to provide the title of the chart together with the X-axis name and the Y-axis increment size. You will note that lines 250 to 270 inclusive and line 300 are left blank; *they are needed later for program development.*

PROC_data2 (line 360) asks you to provide data relating to the number of bars on the chart, the name of each bar, and its frequency of occurence. The last two items of data are stored as a pair of X and Y values in the array points$.

Listing 5.13

```
180  DEF PROC_basic_information2
190  CLS:COLOUR 1
200  PRINT TAB(6,4)"BAR CHART SCALE SPECIFICATION";TAB(0,6)"TITLE OF CHAR
T"
210  PRINT TAB(0,8)"X-AXIS NAME"
220  PRINT TAB(0,10)"Y-AXIS NAME";TAB(0,12)"MAXIMUM VALUE OF Y"
230  PRINT TAB(0,14)"Y-AXIS INCREMENT SIZE"
240  COLOUR 2:REM YELLOW TEXT
250  :
260  :
270  :
280  INPUT TAB(23,6)T$,TAB(23,8)X$
290  INPUT TAB(23,10)Y$,TAB(23,12)ymax$,TAB(23,14)yinc$
300  :
310  ymax=EVAL(ymax$)
320  ylength=LEN(Y$)
330  yinc=EVAL(yinc$)
340  ENDPROC
350  :
360  DEF PROC_data2
370  CLS:COLOUR 1:REM RED TEXT
380  PRINT TAB(9,2)"DATA FOR BAR CHART"
390  :
400  :
410  :
420  INPUT TAB(5,4)"NUMBER OF BARS ON CHART = "N
430  FOR row=1 TO N
440     PRINT:COLOUR 1:PRINT "NAME OF BAR ";row;" = ";:COLOUR 2:INPUT TAB(
17)points$(row,0)
450     COLOUR 1:PRINT"FREQUENCY ";row;" = ";:COLOUR 2:INPUT TAB(15)points
$(row,1)
460     NEXT row
470  ENDPROC
480  :
```

5.15   Drawing the Bar Chart Axes, Sales and Grid

Listing 5.14 contains the three procedures PROC_axes2, PROC_scales2 and PROC_grid2, which are used respectively for drawing the axes, scales and grid on the chart.

The method of drawing the axes (see PROC_axes2) is generally similar to that used in the graph-plotting program with the exception that negative X- and Y-axes are not allowed (you can allow for these by modifying

Listing 5.14

```
490  DEF PROC_axes2:REM DRAW AXES
500  CLS:GCOL 0,2:REM YELLOW AXES
510  xscale=(1279-(7+LEN(ymax$))*32)/N
520  yscale=(1024-295)/ymax
530  xorg=130+LEN(ymax$)*32:REM LEAVE ROOM FOR Y SCALE DATA
540  yorg=148:REM LEAVE ROOM FOR X SCALE DATA
550  VDU29,xorg;yorg;:REM DEFINE GRAPHICS ORIGIN
560  :
570  :
580  :
590  MOVE 0,0:DRAW N*xscale,0:REM DRAW X AXIS
600  MOVE 0,0:DRAW 0,ymax*yscale:REM DRAW Y AXIS
610  ENDPROC
620  :
630  DEF PROC_scales2:REM MARK SCALES ON AXES
640  MOVE 0,0:VDU 5:REM WRITE TEXT AT GRAPHICS CURSOR
650  REM DRAW MARKERS AND VALUES ON X-AXIS
660  start=-(xscale)DIV 2-16
670  FOR xval=1 TO N
680    xstep=xscale*xval
690    MOVE (start+xstep-LEN(points$(xval,0))DIV 2*32),-20
700    PRINT;points$(xval,0):REM CENTRE X VALUE ON BAR
710    NEXT xval
720  REM DRAW MARKERS AND VALUES ON Y-AXIS
730  FOR yval=0 TO ymax STEP yinc
740    MOVE -10,yval*yscale:DRAW 0,yval*yscale
750    MOVE -((LEN(ymax$)*32)+20),(yval*yscale)+16:PRINT;yval:REM CENTRE
Y VALUE ON MARKER
760    NEXT yval
770  ENDPROC
780  :
790  DEF PROC_grid2:GCOL 0,1:REM DRAW RED GRID
800  REM DRAW HORIZONTAL LINES
810  FOR yline=0 TO ymax STEP yinc
820    IF yline=0 NEXT yline
830  MOVE 0,yline*yscale:DRAW N*xscale,yline*yscale
840  NEXT yline
850  ENDPROC
860  :
```

PROC_axes2 in line with the axes procedure in program P5.1).

PROC_scales2 marks the scales on the X- and Y-axes. In the case of the X-axis, the "scales" are the names of the bars (which could either be a number, such as a year, or an alphabetical character or a word). The procedure centres the X-axis scale below the centre of the bar (see line 690). Lines 730 to 760 inclusive puts markers on the Y-axis and prints the value of the Y-axis variable (which is centred on the marker).

Finally, PROC_grid2 draws red horizontal grid lines on the chart (vertical lines are meaningless on this form of bar chart). The grid lines are drawn after the bar chart in order that they are not obscured by the chart itself.

5.16 Titling the Bar Chart and Printing the Axis Names

The procedure which prints the title of the bar chart (PROC_title) is unchanged from the graph-titling program (see *listing 5.15*). There is, however, a minor variation in the procedure which prints the X-axis name (see PROC_axis_names2) because the length of the X-axis is

Number of bars (N) * xscale

with the result that line 950 in PROC_axis_names2 differs from the corresponding line (line 1120) in PROC_axis_names in *listing 5.8*. The part of the procedure which prints the Y-axis name is unchanged in this program.

Listing 5.15

```
 870  DEF PROC_title:REM TITLE GRAPH
 880  GCOL 0,2:REM YELLOW TITLE
 890  title_start=640-((LEN(T$)DIV 2)*32)-xorg:REM CALCULATE TITLE STARTIN
G POINT
 900  MOVE title_start,ymax*yscale+100:PRINT T$
 910  ENDPROC
 920  :
 930  DEF PROC_axis_names2
 940  REM PRINT X-AXIS NAME
 950  tab=N*xscale-(LEN(X$)*32)
 960  MOVE tab,-70:PRINT X$
 970  REM PRINT Y-AXIS NAME
 980  tab=ymax*yscale
 990  FOR no=1 TO LEN(Y$)
1000     MOVE -(LEN(ymax$)*32+70),tab:PRINT MID$(Y$,no,1)
1010     tab=tab-32
1020     NEXT no
1030  ENDPROC
1040  :
```

5.17 Drawing the Bars

The procedure in *listing 5.16* draws the bars on the screen, and is coloured alternately in yellow and white; the procedure also includes the facility for

Listing 5.16

```
1050  DEF PROC_bars
1060  :
1070  colour=2:REM FIRST BAR IN YELLOW
1080  n=60:REM SET GAP BETWEEN BARS
1090  x1=n/2
1100  FOR bar=1 TO N
1110    x2=x1+(xscale-n)
1120    y2=EVAL(points$(bar,1))*yscale
1130    GCOL 0,colour
1140    colour=colour+1:IF colour>3 THEN colour=2
1150    MOVE x2,0:MOVE x1,0:PLOT 85,x2,y2:PLOT 85,x1,y2
1160    :
1170    :
1180    :
1190    x1=x2+n
1200  NEXT bar
1210  ENDPROC
1220  :
1230  VDU 4:REPORT:PRINT " AT LINE ";ERL:END
```

including a gap between the bars. The default gap is 60 graphics units (set by the value of the variable n in line 1080). If you change n to zero, adjacent bars just touch one another.

The method adopted for drawing the bars is shown in Fig. 5.11, each bar being n graphics units narrower than the maximum allowable width. The procedure automatically adjusts the width the bars to accommodate the number of bars you need in the chart. A print-out of a bar chart using program *P5.3* is shown in Fig. 5.12.

Fig. 5.11 Bar chart plotting

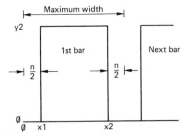

5.18   A Three-dimensional Bar Chart

A 3-D bar chart is often much more impressive than a 2-D bar chart; program *P5.3* is easily modified to accommodate the 3-D facility using an "oil painters" algorithm. (As you are probably aware, oil paints are so dense that one colour is completely obliterated when you paint over it with another colour; this technique is used here.) In program *P5.3D* (which is a modified version of program *P5.3*), given in *listing 5.17,* the bar which is farthest away from you is painted first of all, then the next most remote bar

Fig. 5.12 An example of a
flat or 2-D bar chart or
histogram

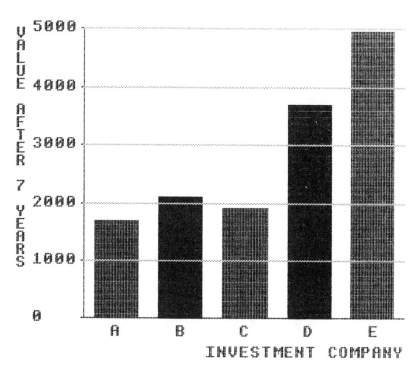

is painted; where the latter 3-D bar overlaps the first bar, it obliterates it. This program is repeated until all the bars have been painted.

At this stage you should load program *P5.3* into the memory of the computer, and modify it as shown in *listing 5.17*; afterwards you should save it as program *P5.3D*. The changes are as follows.

Listing 5.17

```
 10  REM****PROGRAM "P5.3D"****
 20  REM****BAR CHART PROGRAM WITH 3-D OPTION%***

 80  PROC_data3:REM GET DATA FROM KEYBOARD
 90  PROC_axes3:REM DRAW 3-D AXES

130  PROC_bars2:REM DRAW BARS ON CHART

360  DEF PROC_data3

390  PRINT TAB(0,4)"You have a choice of a 2-D or a 3-D"
400  PRINT"display. Do you want a 3-D display?":PRINT
410  PRINT"Answer Y (Yes) or N (No)":COLOUR 2:INPUT TAB(30,7)ans$:COLOUR
1:CLS

490  DEF PROC_axes3:REM DRAW AXES
```

```
560  xa=N*xscale:xb=xa+80:ya=ymax*yscale:yb=ya+50
570  REM IF  ans$=Y DRAW 3-D SCALES
580  IF ans$="Y" THEN MOVE xa,0:MOVE 0,0:PLOT 85,xb,50:PLOT 85,80,50:MOVE
80,yb:PLOT 85,0,0:PLOT 85,0,ya:MOVE 0,0:GCOL 0,0:DRAW 80,50:GCOL 0,2:ENDPR
OC

1050  DEF PROC_bars2

1160  REM DRAW 3-D SHAPE
1170  IF ans$="Y" THEN MOVE x2,0:MOVE x2+80,50:PLOT 85,x2,y2:PLOT 85,x2+80
,y2+50:PLOT 85,x1,y2:PLOT 85,x1+80,y2+50
1180  IF ans$="Y" THEN GCOL 0,0:MOVE x1,0:DRAW x1,y2:DRAW x2,y2:DRAW x2,0:
MOVE x1,y2:DRAW x1+80,y2+50:MOVE x2,y2:DRAW x2+80,y2+50:MOVE x2+4,0:DRAW x2
+84,50
```

PROC_data3 gives you the option of selecting either a 2-D or a 3-D display. Should you choose a 3-D display, lines 560–580 inclusive draw 3-D axes on the chart; lines 1160–1180 inclusive draw the 3-D bar chart, the edges of each of the bars being outlined for clarity. A typical screen display is shown in Fig. 5.13.

Fig. 5.13 A 3-D bar chart

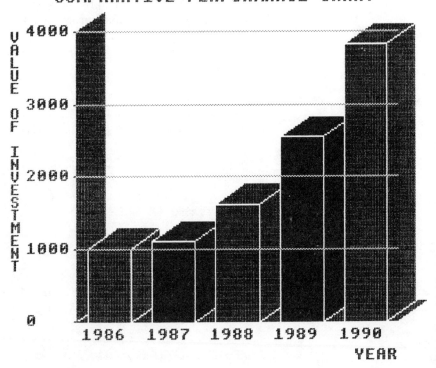

5.19 A Bar Chart which Indicates when a Limiting Value is Reached

Many industrial systems monitor variables such as temperature, pressure, gas percentage, etc. whose value is indicated on a bar chart on a monitor screen. In these cases, it is of value to be able to change the colour of the bar when the value of the variable exceeds some predetermined "safety" limit. Program *P5.3D* can be modified to incorporate this feature as shown in *listing 5.18*.

You should now load *P5.3D* into the memory of the computer and modify it as shown in *listing 5.18*, saving the resulting program as program *P5.3LIM*.

Listing 5.18

```
10  REM****PROGRAM "P5.3LIM"****
20  REM****BAR CHART PROGRAM INDICATING A LMITING VALUE****

70  PROC_basic_information3:REM CHART SPECIFICATION

130  PROC_bars3:REM DRAW BARS ON CHART
140  PROC_grid3:REM DRAW GRID

180  DEF PROC_basic_information3

250  PRINT TAB(0,16)"The bars are coloured";:COLOUR 1:PRINT" RED ";:COLOU
R 2:PRINT"above some"
260  PRINT"limiting value.":PRINT
270  PRINT TAB(0,19)"Your selected limiting value = "

300  INPUT TAB(31,19)ylimit

790  DEF PROC_grid3:GCOL 3,3:REM DRAW GRID (EX-OR)

1050  DEF PROC_bars3
1060  ylimit=ylimit*yscale:REM A "SAFETY" LIMIT ON y

1080  n=30:REM SET GAP BETWEEN BARS

1130  IF y2>=ylimit THEN GCOL 0,1 ELSE GCOL 0,colour
```

PROC_basic_information3 gives you the option of including a limiting value, beyond which the colour of the bar will change to red; if, in reply, you simply press the RETURN key, the computer assumes that *any value* is in excess of the limit. If you type in a limiting value which is greater than the maximum value of Y, the program runs in the same way as program *P5.3D*. The decision to change the colour of the line when the limit is exceeded is taken in line 1130.

5.20 Pie Charts

A pie chart is used to show how the whole of a "cake" is cut up into its constituent parts. Pie charts are widely used, for example, to display how the total assets of a company or club are divided; another example in, say, science is to show how different forms of aquatic life are apportioned in a pond.

In a pie chart, the whole (or 100 per cent) of item you are considering (for example, the assets of a company) are contained within a circle. The circle is then divided into a number of sectors of different size and colour, each sector representing some aspect of the whole. For example, the pie chart in Fig. 5.14 may represent the hypothetical world-wide distribution of the assets of an international company.

Fig. 5.14 A pie chart

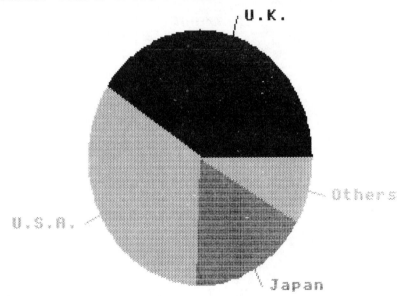

WORLD-WIDE INVESTMENTS (total assets)

U.K. = 49 (40.5%)
U.S.A. = 41 (33.88%)
Japan = 21 (17.36%)
Others = 10 (8.26%)
TOTAL = 121 (100%)

The executive program for the pie chart is shown in *listing 5.19* (program *P5.4*). Line 60 DIMensions the two arrays sector_size and name$; sector_size is a numeric array for storing the size of each sector, and name$ is a string array which stores the name of each sector. The three procedures called for in lines 70–90 are described below.

5.21 Collecting the Pie Chart Data

The procedure PROC_data4 (*listing 5.20*) asks you for the title of the chart and for the number of sectors in the chart; after this it asks for the name of each sector and its size. The data is stored in the arrays mentioned in section 5.20. You will notice that the VDU 19 instruction in line 140 changes the yellow colour of MODE 4 to green; this is to give a better contrast on the screen between adjacent sectors.

Listing 5.19

```
  10  REM****PROGRAM "P5.4"****
  20  REM****PIE CHART****
  30  *TV0,1
  40  MODE 1
  50  ON ERROR GOTO 870
  60  DIM sector_size(10),name$(10):REM ARRAYS FOR SECTOR DATA AND NAME
  70  PROC_data4:REM GET DATA FROM KEYBOARD
  80  PROC_title2:REM PRINT TITLE AND PROPORTIONS
  90  PROC_pie:REM DRAW PIE CHART
 100  VDU 4:REM RESTORE TEXT CURSOR
 110  END
 120  :
```

Listing 5.20

```
 130  DEF PROC_data4
 140  CLS:COLOUR 1:VDU 19,2,2,0,0,0
 150  PRINT TAB(8,4)"CHART SPECIFICATION"
 160  PRINT TAB(0,6)"TITLE OF CHART";TAB(0,8)"NUMBER OF SECTORS (LIMIT 10)
"
 170  :
 180  :
 190  COLOUR 2:INPUT TAB(20,6)name$(0)
 200  INPUT TAB(31,8)sector_size(0):PRINT
 210  IF sector_size(0)>10 PRINT TAB(31,8)"     ":GOTO 200
 220  :
 230  total=0
 240  FOR sector=1 TO sector_size(0)
 250    COLOUR 1:PRINT"NAME OF SECTOR ";sector;:COLOUR 2:INPUT TAB(20)name
$(sector)
 260    COLOUR 1:PRINT"SIZE OF SECTOR ";sector;:COLOUR 2:INPUT TAB(20)sect
or_size(sector):PRINT
 270    total=total+sector_size(sector):REM CALCULATE TOTAL SIZE
 280    NEXT sector
 290  :
 300  :
 310  :
 320  :
 330  ENDPROC
 340  :
```

5.22   Printing the Pie Chart Title and Sector Sizes

Listing 5.21 shows PROC_title2, which prints the title of the bar chart centrally at the top of the screen. Following this, it calculates the per cent proportion of each sector and prints it at the foot of the screen.

Listing 5.21

```
350  DEF PROC_title2
360  CLS:VDU 5:REM WRITE TEXT AT GRAPHICS CURSOR
370  title_start=624-((LEN(name$(0))DIV 2)*32):REM CALCULATE TITLE STARTI
NG POINT
380  MOVE title_start,1000:PRINT name$(0)
390  FOR sector=1 TO sector_size(0)
400    IF sector=1 THEN colour=3
410    GCOL 0,colour
420    MOVE 0,(sector_size(0)+2-sector)*32
430    PRINT name$(sector);" = ";sector_size(sector);" (";(INT(0.5+sector
_size(sector)*10000/total)/100);"%)"
440    colour=colour+1:IF colour>2 THEN colour=1
450    NEXT sector
460  MOVE 0,32:GCOL 0,3:PRINT"TOTAL = ";total;" (100%)"
470  ENDPROC
480  :
```

5.23   Drawing the Pie Chart

PROC_pie in *listing 5.22* calculates the radius of the pie chart; it automatically makes the radius smaller if there are large number of sectors (this is to make allowance for the larger number of printed lines at the foot of the screen — see section 5.22).

Listing 5.22

```
490  DEF PROC_pie
500  rad=(1024-256-sector_size(0)*32)DIV 2
510  ycentre1=rad+96+32+sector_size(0)*32:xcentre1=640
520  :
530  VDU 29,xcentre1;ycentre1;:REM DEFINE GRAPHICS ORIGIN
540  REM DRAW SECTORS
550  angle=0
560  FOR sector=1 TO sector_size(0)
570    IF sector=1 THEN colour=3
580    sector_angle=sector_size(sector)*360/total:REM sector_angle IN DEG
REES
590    half_angle=sector_angle/2
600    centre_angle=angle+half_angle:REM CENTRE OF SECTOR
610    MOVE rad*COS(angle*PI/180),rad*SIN(angle*PI/180)
620    steps=INT(sector_angle/2):REM CALCULATE NUMBER OF 2 DEGREE steps
630    cos=50*COS(centre_angle*PI/180):sin=50*SIN(centre_angle*PI/180)
640    :
650    FOR fill =1 TO steps
660      angle=angle+2
670      GCOL 0,colour
680      MOVE 0,0:PLOT 85,rad*COS(angle*PI/180),rad*SIN(angle*PI/180)
690      NEXT fill
700    REM COMPLETE SECTOR
```

```
710    remainder=sector_angle-steps*2:REM CALCULATE remainder ANGLE
720    angle=angle+remainder
730    MOVE 0,0:PLOT 85,rad*COS(angle*PI/180),rad*SIN(angle*PI/180)
740    PROC_names
750    colour=colour+1:IF colour>2 THEN colour=1
760    :
770    IF sector=sector_size(0)-1 THEN VDU 29,xcentre1;ycentre1-4;
780    NEXT sector
790  ENDPROC
800  :
810  DEF PROC_names:REM LABEL PIE CHART
820  MOVE 0,0:DRAW (rad+50)*COS(centre_angle*PI/180),(rad+50)*SIN(centre_
angle*PI/180)
830  IF centre_angle>=270 OR centre_angle<=90THEN PLOT 0,20,16:PRINT name
$(sector):ENDPROC
840  PLOT 0,(-20-LEN(name$(sector))*32),16:PRINT name$(sector)
850  ENDPROC
860  :
870  VDU4:REPORT:PRINT" AT LINE ";ERL:END
```

The VDU 29 command in line 530 uses the radius to define the graphics origin of the chart, and lines 560–780 inclusive calculate the angle (in degrees) subtended by each sector at the centre of the circle (which is stored in the variable sector_angle); the sector is then filled in with colour in steps of 2°. Any remaining angle at the end of the sector which is less than 2° is filled in by lines 700–720, inclusive. The first sector is coloured white, the remaining sectors being alternately yellow and red.

PROC_pie also determines the total angle turned through in degrees (this is stored as the variable angle) and, at the same time, it calculates the angle which bisects the sector (stored as the variable half_angle). The sum of angle and half_angle giving the angle (stored as the variable centre_angle) between origin and the line which bisects the sector currently being drawn on the screen. The need for this is outlined below.

Having drawn and filled the sector with colour, control is transferred to PROC_names (see line 810), which commences by drawing a radial line at angle centre_angle to a point just beyond the pie chart. It then prints the name of the sector on the screen at the end of the line. This process is repeated until the pie chart is complete.

5.24 Drawing a Pie Chart with a Displaced Slice

To highlight a feature of the pie chart, it is helpful to be able to displace a sector from the main body of the pie chart. An example of a display of this kind is shown in Fig. 5.15. This feature can be added by amending program *P5.4* as shown in *listing 5.23* (the resulting program being called *P5.4CUT*).

The program gives you the options of selecting the sector to be displaced (you merely type in the name of the sector to be displaced) — see line 220. If your answer to line 180 is anything other than Y, the program gives the

Fig. 5.15 A pie chart with a
displaced slice

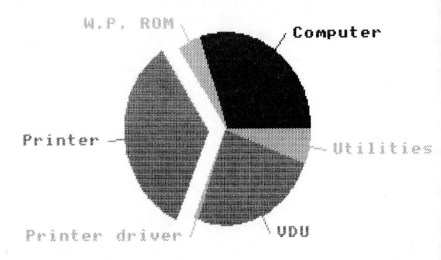

WORD PROCESSOR COST

Computer = 350 (30.04%)
W.P. ROM = 50 (4.29%)
Printer = 400 (34.33%)
Printer driver = 10 (0.86%)
VDU = 290 (24.89%)
Utilities = 65 (5.58%)
TOTAL = 1165 (100%)

Listing 5.23

```
 10  REM****PROGRAM "P5.4CUT"****
 20  REM****PIE CHART WITH SLICE DISPLACED****

 70  PROC_data5:REM GET DATA FROM KEYBOARD

130  DEF PROC_data5

170  PRINT TAB(0,10)"Do you wish to take a slice out of the"
180  PRINT"pie? Type Y (Yes) or N (No)"

220  INPUT TAB(31,11)ans$:PRINT

290  IF ans$<>"Y" THEN name_sector$="ZZZZZZZZZZZZZZ":ENDPROC
300  CLS:COLOUR 1:PRINT TAB(0,4)"Type the name of the sector to be"
310  PRINT"moved away from the PIE chart"
320  COLOUR 2:INPUT TAB(7,10)name_sector$

490  DEF PROC_pie2

520  IF ans$="Y" THEN rad=rad-50
```

```
 640  IF name_sector$=name$(sector) THEN xcentre=xcentre1+cos:ycentre=ycen
tre1+sin:VDU 29,xcentre;ycentre;:GCOL 0,0:MOVE rad*COS(angle*PI/180),rad*SI
N(angle*PI/180):REM REDIFINE GRAPHICS ORIGIN
```

```
 760  IF name_sector$=name$(sector) THEN VDU 29,xcentre-cos;ycentre-sin;:G
COL 0,0:MOVE 0,0:REM RESET GRAPHICS ORIGIN
```

selected sector a name which is so artificial that you are unlikely to use it (see line 290).

PROC_pie2 (see line 490) causes the computer to compare each sector name with the selected sector to be displaced. When it reaches this sector name, it simply changes the graphics origin so that the sector is displaced by 50 graphics units radially outwards at an angle of centre_angle.

5.25   Drawing Several Charts or Graphs on the Screen

In some applications, you may wish to display several graphs or charts simultaneously on the screen. A method of doing this is described here using a bar chart procedure to illustrate the process (see Fig. 5.16).

The program in *listing 5.24* (program *P5.5*) calls on PROC_multiple_histogram in line 60 in the executive program. In turn, this used PROC_histogram four times; you will notice that each time the latter procedure is

Fig. 5.16 Plotting several bar charts on the screen

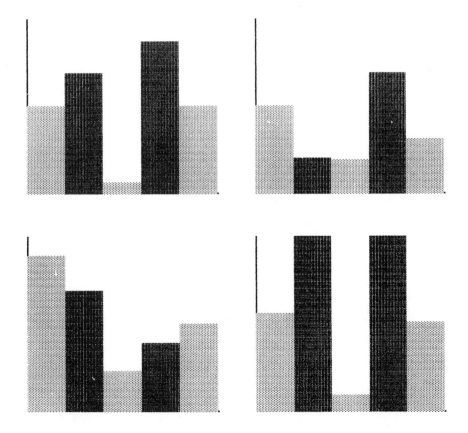

Listing 5.24

```
10  REM****PROGRAM "P5.5"****
20  REM****MULTIPLE BAR CHARTS****
30  *TV0,1
40  MODE 1
50  ON ERROR GOTO 310
60  PROC_multiple_histogram
70  END
80  :
90  DEF PROC_multiple_histogram
100 PROC_histogram(100,100)
110 PROC_histogram(700,100)
120 PROC_histogram(100,600)
130 PROC_histogram(700,600)
140 ENDPROC
150 :
160 DEF PROC_histogram(orgx,orgy)
170 VDU 29,orgx;orgy;:REM SET GRAPHICS ORIGIN
180 GCOL 0,3:REM DRAW WHITE AXES
190 MOVE 0,400:DRAW 0,0:DRAW 500,0
200 colour=1:REM FIRST BAR IN RED
210 x=0:y=0:REM SET CURSOR TO GRAPHICS ORIGIN
220 FOR N=0 TO 4
230   h=RND(400):REM BAR HAS RANDOM HEIGHT
240   GCOL 0,colour
250   MOVE x,y:MOVE x+96,y:PLOT 85,x,y+h:PLOT 85,x+96,y+h
260   colour=colour+1:IF colour>2 THEN colour=1
270   x=x+100
280   NEXT N
290 ENDPROC
300 :
310 REPORT:PRINT" AT LINE ";ERL:END
```

called, it transfers two parameters to the procedure. These values are the X- and Y-values to be assumed in the VDU 29 command in line 170 for setting the graphics origin of the histogram currently being drawn. This causes each bar chart to be drawn from a different graphics origin.

The technique can be amended to include titling, scaling, etc., and can be extended to include graphs and pie charts. You may like to use this technique to display different types of diagram simultaneously on the screen.

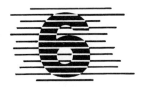

Line Diagrams — the Basis of Computer-aided Drawing

6.1 Man-Machine Interaction

Computer graphics is perhaps the most exciting area of computer applications, and calls for a wide variety of intefacing devices and techniques. Graphics enable complex problems and diagrams to be presented in a straightforward manner, and the software enables you to present information in a clear and concise manner. In this chapter we will develop a program for drawing a wide variety of diagrams.

Many hardware devices have been developed which enable you to communicate with the computer and include the *keyboard, thumbwheels, joysticks, digitizers, graphics tablets, light pens, tracker balls, mice*, etc. The program developed in this chapter uses the keyboard as the interface device, but a word at this time about the principle of operation of other devices is not out of place.

6.2 Direct Digital Input to the Computer

A number of the devices mentioned above generate a digital code pattern (either in the American Standard Code for Information Interchange ASCII, pronounced askey, or in pure binary) which controls the position of the cursor on the screen. This information can be input directly to the BBC micro via the user port.

Fig. 6.1 Thumbwheel control of the cursor using direct digital input

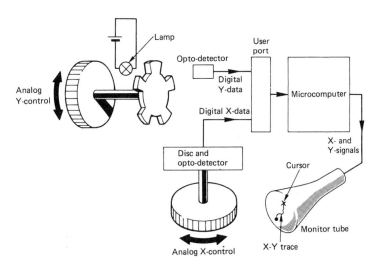

The basis of a typical digital thumbwheel control system is shown in Fig. 6.1. The X- and Y-position controls are manipulated by the user, each

thumbwheel control giving **direct digital control** (DDC) over the movement of the screen cursor. A range of other hardware devices using the user port of the BBC micro also generate digital signals.

6.3 Analog Input to the Computer

The basis of one system using analog input signals is shown in Fig. 6.2. The control lever of the joystick is mechanically connected to two potentiometers. One potentiometer produces a voltage which corresponds to the X movement of the cursor on the screen of the monitor, and the other produces a voltage which gives rise to the Y movement of the cursor.

Each analog voltage is converted into its equivalent digital signal inside the computer by means of an **analog-to-digital converter (ADC)**. The two digital signals are then used to control the movement of the cursor on the screen.

Fig. 6.2 Cursor control using a joystick

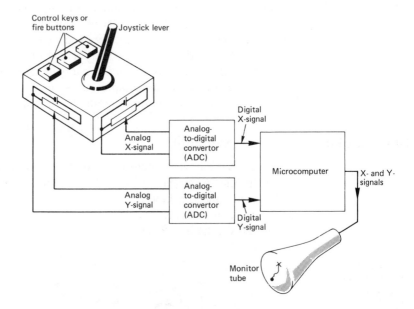

A joystick usually has one or more control buttons on it for the purpose of sending digital (ON/OFF) signals to the computer. For games applications, they are used as "fire" buttons.

A **bit-stick** is a 3-dimensional joystick which allows you to control a third dimension by rotating the control lever, which has the effect of controlling a third potentiometer.

6.4 Other Input Devices

A **digitizer** (see Fig. 6.3) is a device widely used in engineering and surveying for tracing a drawing. The drawing is placed on a surface or **tablet**, and the hand-held cursor or **puck** is moved over the drawing. The movement of the cursor on the screen mirrors the movement of the stylus. The information from the puck can be used, for example, to determine the area of a shape on the drawing.

Fig. 6.3 A digitizer

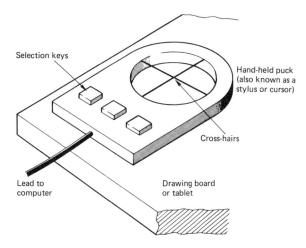

A typical low-cost **graphics tablet** is shown in Fig. 6.4. It uses two potentiometers, the voltage from them representing the two angles θ_1 and θ_2. The graphics tablet software uses these angles together with the arm lengths r_1 and r_2 to determine the position of the stylus at the end of the arm.

Fig. 6.4 A low-cost graphics tablet

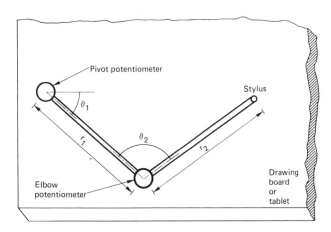

A **lightpen** (see Fig. 6.5) is a hand-held device which is held against the face of the monitor screen, and is connected to the computer by a cable which carries a stream of data. When the electron beam passes the lightpen, a photo-detector in its tip generates a pulse which is passed to the computer.

Fig. 6.5 A light pen

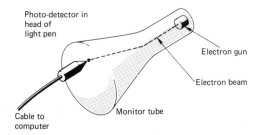

A **tracker ball** (see Fig. 6.6) comprises a small box with a ball protuding from it. The ball is mechanically linked with two potentiometers to give control of the cursor in the X- and Y-direction. The movement of the ball is controlled either by the fingers or by the palm of the hand; additionally, the box housing the tracker ball has several control keys on it which provide digital (ON/OFF) signals.

Fig. 6.6 A tracker ball

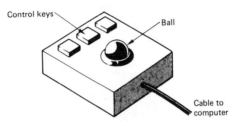

A **mouse** can be thought of as a tracker ball which is turned over so that the ball runs on the surface of a desk. Moving the mouse about on the desk provides signals (either digital or analog) which are used to control the position of the cursor on the screen. As with the tracker ball, the mouse has several control keys on it which can be programmed, either by the mouse software or by the user, to perform special functions.

Other devices including sonic graphics tablets and wire-mesh tablets; you may like to undertake a project to survey not only the types of graphic devices in use, but also why they are used in preference to other devices.

6.5 The Requirement of a Drawing Program

The principal requirements of a drawing program fall into two broad areas:

1 Drawing and deleting line drawings
2 Drawing and deleting icons (images or pictures)

Program *P6* (*listing 6.1*) builds up the above features, beginning with a simple line-drawing program. These techniques are extended later in the book.

The program is written in modular form, each module being usable in any further programs you may develop. As each module is developed, it is added to the existing program to extend it facilities. When typing the program into the computer, you should take great care to enter the line numbers listed in the book; the "missing" lines are needed to accommodate further program lines at a later stage. You are also reminded that the full program is available on disc.

As the program develops, an increasing number of keys on the keyboard are employed to call in the extra features. The function of each key is described in the appropriate section but, for your convenience, a summary of the keys together with their function in this program are given in section 6.13.

6.6 A Line-drawing Program

The executive program of *P6* is given in lines 10-90, respectively of *listing 6.1*. It calls for only two procedures: PROC_initialize (which initializes the computer) and PROC_keys (which causes the computer to read the state of the keyboard). You can exit from the program by pressing the Q (Quit) key (see line 910); this also has the effect of clearing the screen and returning all keys to their normal function (see line 80).

PROC_initializes starts by drawing a frame around the part of the screen which is available to you for drawing or graphics purposes (see line 130). The area is limited by virtue of later developments in the program.

During the program you will use the four cursor control keys in the upper right-hand corner of the keyboard to control the movement of a cursor on the screen. The ∗FX 4,1 command in line 230 has the effect of causing these keys to return ASCII values to the computer; these ASCII values are in the range 136 to 139, inclusive (for details of ASCII values, see Appendix 1).

Lines 240 to 270, inclusive cause information to be printed at the top of the screen; we will return to this information later. Line 280 sets up some variables or flags used in the program, each having zero value; the function of the variables is to flag when a particular condition occurs. Lines 290 and 300 initialize a number of other variables used in connection with the movement of the cursor on the screen. In particular, you should note that all the measurements in this program are in screen graphics units (remember, the screen size is 1024 graphics units high and 1280 graphics units wide). The variables xstart and ystart correspond to the X- and Y-centre of your drawing frame.

PROC_keys simply contains a REPEAT-UNTIL loop which scans the keyboard to see if selected keys have been pressed. The ∗FX 15,0 command in line 610 causes the internal buffers of the computer to be "flushed" or emptied. Its purpose is to ensure that, when you release any key, the computer stops responding to that key. [If the ∗FX 15,0 command is not included, the computer forms a queue of requests in its input buffer, and will continue to execute the keyboard request for a short time even after the key is released (try deleting the instruction, and press one of the cursor control keys down for a short time, and see what happens when you release it).]

When you RUN the program, a small flashing cross-wire cursor appears at the centre of the graphics area. This is drawn by PROC_cursor, which is called at the end of practically every line in PROC_keys. If you inspect PROC_cursor, you will see that in line 950 the cursor is drawn using a PLOT 6 instruction, which DRAWs a line in the logical inverse colour; this is repeated in line 960. The net effect is that line 950 draws the cursor in white (which is the logical inverse of the black background colour), and line 960 draws the cursor in black (which is the logical inverse of the white cursor already on the screen!). This routine has three effects:

1   The cursor flashes on and off.
2   After PROC_cursor is completed, the cursor vanishes from the screen (the second cursor "rubs out" the first).
3   The cursor can pass over any line which is already on the screen without rubbing it out.

Lines 620 to 650 test to see if a cursor control key has been pressed. If

Listing 6.1

```
10  REM****PROGRAM "P6"****
20  REM****DRAWING PROGRAM****
30  *TV0,1
40  MODE4:CLS
50  ON ERROR GOTO 1560
60  PROC_initialize:REM INITIALIZE COMPUTER
70  PROC_keys:REM READ KEYBOARD
80  MODE4:*FX4,0
90  END
100 :
110 DEF PROC_initialize
120 REM DRAWING FRAME
130 MOVE 0,0:DRAW 0,840:DRAW 890,840:DRAW 890,0:DRAW 0,0

200 VDU 24,6;6;884;836;:REM GRAPHICS WINDOW
210 VDU 23;8202;0;0;0;:REM TURN TEXT CURSOR OFF
220 REM MAKE KEYS RETURN ASCII NUMBERS
230 *FX4,1
240 PRINT TAB(0,0)"LINE (L,F)="
250 PRINT TAB(17,0)"RUBBER/DRAW (R,W,O)="
260 PRINT TAB(0,1)"STEP SIZE (S,N,M) ="
270 PRINT TAB(0,2)"X =";TAB(15,2)"Y =";TAB(24,2)"LENGTH ="
280 line=0:rub=0:draw=0:escape=0:REM SET UP PROGRAM FLAGS
290 step=4:size=6
300 xstart=445:ystart=450:x=xstart:y=ystart
310 ENDPROC
320 :

570 DEF PROC_keys
580 REPEAT
590   K=INKEY(0)
600   REM FLUSH BUFFERS
610   *FX 15,0
620   IF K=136 x=x-size*step:PROC_cursor
630   IF K=137 x=x+size*step:PROC_cursor
640   IF K=138 y=y-size*step:PROC_cursor
650   IF K=139 y=y+size*step:PROC_cursor
660   IF (K=76 OR line=1) PROC_line:PROC_cursor:REM L (draw Line) KEY
670   IF K=70 PROC_fix:PROC_cursor:REM F (fix line) KEY

740  IF line=1 PRINT TAB(12,0)"ON "ELSE PRINT TAB(12,0)"OFF":PROC_cursor

790  PRINT TAB(4,2);"    ";TAB(19,2);"    ":PROC_cursor
800  PRINT TAB(4,2);x;TAB(19,2);y:PROC_cursor
810  length=SQR((x-xstart)^2+(y-ystart)^2)
820  IF line=1 PRINT TAB(33,2);"      ":PRINT TAB(33,2);(INT(length*100))
/100:PROC_cursor
```

```
910   UNTIL K=81:REM Q (Quit) KEY
920   ENDPROC
930 :
940   DEF PROC_cursor:REM DRAW CURSOR
950   MOVE x,y+12:PLOT 6,x,y-12:MOVE x-12,y:PLOT 6,x+12,y
960   MOVE x,y+12:PLOT 6,x,y-12:MOVE x-12,y:PLOT 6,x+12,y
970   ENDPROC
980 :
990   DEF PROC_line
1000  line=1:REM SET line FLAG
1010  IF K=76 THEN xstart=x:ystart=y:REM ESTABLISH STARTING POINT
1020  MOVE xstart,ystart:PLOT 6,x,y:FOR T=1 TO 200:NEXT T:MOVE xstart,ysta
rt:PLOT 6,x,y:REM DRAW FLASHING LINE
1030  ENDPROC
1040 :
1050  DEF PROC_fix
1060  line=0:REM RESET line DRAWING FLAG
1070  MOVE xstart,ystart:DRAW x,y
1080  ENDPROC
1090 :

1560  MODE4:*FX4,0
1570  REPORT:PRINT" AT LINE ";ERL:END
```

one of them has been pressed, the computer updates the value of x or y and moves the cursor to the new position by transferring control to PROC_ cursor. The latter procedure draws a + at the current cursor position; you will see from this that the cursor movement is controlled by the cursor keys.

Each cursor key-press moves the cursor in either the X- or Y-direction by an amount size*step (see lines 620-650), where "step" is 4 graphics units (see line 290) — which is one pixel in MODE 4 — and "size" is a multiplying factor. Initially, size = 6, so that each time a cursor control key is pressed, the cursor moves by $4 \times 6 = 24$ graphics units or six MODE 4 pixels (which is equal to the width of the cursor). A method of altering the size of the cursor movement is discussed later.

You will notice that, if you continue to move the cursor in one direction, it vanishes off the screen. This can be an advantage if you want to view a diagram you have drawn without the cursor on the screen.

Program lines 790 and 800 cause the computer to continually report the current position of the cursor *in graphics units* at the top of the screen. You may like to undertake a scaling modification to the program so that the computer prints the cursor position in real units such as millimetres or metres. You will also note that the X and Y values at the top of the screen flicker continuosly; this is because the computer reports the position of the cursor during every pass of the REPEAT-UNTIL loop in PROC_keys.

At this stage we have not asked the computer to draw anything, and you will see that the computer's response to the statement LINE (L,F) at the top of the screen is OFF. The letters L and F are prompts to remind you which keys control the LINE drawing program. When you press key L (which produces the ASCII code 76 — see program line 660), control is transferred to the line drawing procedure PROC_line.

The first instruction in this procedure causes the flag called "line" to be set to logic 1. The purpose of this flag is to remind the computer that is is currently drawing a LINE (this technique is used several times in this program). Also, at the instant of pressing the L-key (see program line 1010), it establishes the starting location (xstart, ystart) of the line.

You will also observe that, at the instant the L-key is pressed, the LENGTH of the line is reported on the screen. Initially the LENGTH is zero (its value is calculated to two decimal places by program line 810). Whilst you are drawing the line, the length of the current line is continuously updated on the screen. The status of LINE at the top of the screen now becomes ON, telling you that a line is being drawn.

The program line 1020 contains two MOVE and DRAW instructions (the latter is, more accurately, a PLOT 6 instruction). This technique is similar to that used when drawing the cursor: the first MOVE and PLOT 6 instructions draw a white line on the screen, and the second MOVE and PLOT 6 instructions rub the line out. Thus, program line 1020 produces a flashing white line drawn between the origin of the line, i.e. X = xstart, Y = ystart, and the current position of the cursor (X = x, Y = y).

Once again, PLOT 6 is used rather than DRAW because it allows the line currently being drawn to cross another line without affecting the first line. When dawing a line by this method you will immediately observe its primary limitation, namely it is difficult to pinpoint the starting position of the line. There are several ways of overcoming this, and we shall introduce one of them later.

When you have moved the cursor to the point where the line is to end, you *finish the line or fix it by pressing the F-key*. This transfers control (see program line 670) to PROC_fix. This procedure resets the line flag to logic 0 and permanently draws the line (see program line 1070). It also fixes the LENGTH of the current line at the top of the screen, and causes the computer to print the status of LINE as OFF.

You can think of the L-key as an instruction to "lower" the pen on to the paper to draw a line, and the F-key as an instruction to "raise" it off the paper.

When you draw your next line, you will notice that the previous line LENGTH is cancelled as soon as you press the L-key.

We are now in a position to discuss one method of overcoming the drawback mentioned earlier, that is the difficulty in determining the starting position of the line on a completely blank screen. The problem can be solved by marking the position of the starting point on the screen by printing a white dot at that point; with the facility at your disposal at the moment, it can be done as follows:

1   Move the cursor to the starting point of the line.
2   Press the L key to commence drawing a line.

3 *Without moving the cursor*, press the F-key. This draws a "line" of zero length, i.e. a dot.

4 Press the L-key and draw the line as described above (you will clearly see the "starting dot" on the screen).

5 Fix the end of the line by pressing the F-key.

Figure 6.7 shows a number of shapes and lines drawn using the procedures outlined so far.

Fig. 6.7 Typical display obtained by using program P6

```
LINE (L,F)= OFF  RUBBER/DRAW (R,W,O)=OFF
STEP SIZE (S,N,M) = N
X = 109        Y = 402   LENGTH = 122.37
```

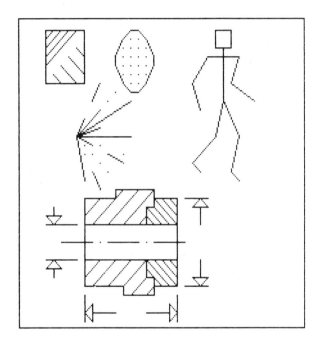

6.7   Rubbing out Errors

So far we have described a simple method for drawing lines. However, anyone can make an error, and our program needs a means of rubbing out any errors. If you add the program lines in *listing 6.2* to *listing 6.1*, you will be provided with two methods of eliminating lines on the diagram.

This first of these methods allows you to *eliminate a line you are currently drawing, but have not yet fixed*. To do this whilst drawing a line, simply press the U-key (Undraw a line) – see program line 680. The latter line calls on PROC_unline which, in turn, calls on PROC_fix but using a GCOL 4,1 instruction. That is, it fixes the line in complementary logical colour.

If you have *already drawn and fixed a line*, you can undraw it simply by moving the cursor to one end of the line and pressing the L-key to

Listing 6.2

```
 680  IF K=85 PROC_unline:PROC_cursor:REM U (Undraw line) KEY
 690  IF (K=82 OR rub=1) PROC_rubber:PROC_cursor:REM R (Rubout) KEY
 700  IF K=79 PROC_rubber_off:PROC_cursor:REM O (rubber Off) KEY

 750  IF rub=1 OR draw=1 PRINT TAB(37,0)"ON "ELSE PRINT TAB(37,0)"OFF":PRO
C_cursor

1100  DEF PROC_unline
1110  GCOL 4,1:PROC_fix:GCOL 0,1:REM RUB line OUT
1120  ENDPROC
1130  :
1140  DEF PROC_rubber
1150  rub=1:REM SET rubout FLAG
1160  MOVE x-12,y-12:DRAW x-12,y+12:DRAW x+12,y+12:DRAW x+12,y-12:DRAW x-1
2,y-12:REM DRAW RUBBER
1170  VDU 24,x-12;y-12;x+12;y+12;:REM GRAPHICS WINDOW=RUBBER
1180  VDU 16:REM RUB OUT GRAPHICS WINDOW
1190  VDU 24,6;6;884;836;:REM OPEN UP GRAPHICS WINDOW
1200  ENDPROC
1210  :
1220  DEF PROC_rubber_off
1230  rub=0:draw=0:size=6:REM TURN rubber AND draw FLAGS OFF
1240  ENDPROC
1250  :
```

commence drawing the line once more, and then move the cursor to the other end of the line.

If you have very accurately positioned the second line over the first, the line will vanish when you press the U-key. If you have not positioned the line too accurately, you will be left with a few dots on the screen.

It is worth pointing out at this stage that the undraw, U, key acts as a **toggle**. That is, if you have deleted a line by pressing the U-key, the line can be restored by pressing the U-key once again. This allows you to have second thoughts about deleting the line. However, do not be misled into thinking that you can use the U-key both to fix and delete a line; the procedure involved is specifically written for line deletion. Be warned: should you use the U-key to fix a line, you will find that, wherever the new line crosses or intersects with another line, the point of intersection will be in black, that is it disappears!

To remove these dots (and any other marks) you can use a **general-purpose rubber** defined in PROC_rubber. To put the rubber on the screen, you position the cursor at the point where it is needed and press the R-key (Rubber key) – see line 690.

This turns the RUBBER ON by transferring control to PROC_rubber. The first instruction in this procedure sets the rub flag to 1, and line 1160 draws the shape of the rubber on the screen (which is a rectangle having the same size as the cursor). The instructions in lines 1170 and 1180 perform the rubbing-out procedure, and line 1190 restores the graphics window to its normal size.

Since the outline of the rubber comes within the rubbout area, the outline is also rubbed out – which eliminates all trace of the rubber. So long as the rub flag is set to 1, the status of the RUBBER/DRAW condition at the top of the screen is given as ON (the DRAW aspect is dealt with later). The rubber remains ON just so long as you need it, and you simply use the cursor control keys to move the rubber around the screen to continue the process of rubbing out.

With this version, you are warned that if you take the rubber off the screen, it will rub out the border around the graphics area of the screen where it leaves the screen.

A version of the rubber used later in the book does not do this, and you will find it an interesting exercise to modify this program so that it does not happen here!

To turn the rubber OFF, you merely press the O key (see line 700).

This transfers program control to PROC_rubber_off, which resets the rub flag and restores the cursor to its normal state. It also causes the RUBBER/DRAW status to be in the OFF state.

6.8 Changing the Size of the Cursor Movement

Up to this point, you have only been able to move the cursor and rubber in steps of 24 graphics units. In a number of cases, this movement may be either too small or too large. If you include the instructions in *listing 6.3* in program *P6*, you are given the option of three values of the variable size.

Listing 6.3

```
710  IF K=78 size=6:PROC_cursor:REM N (Normal step size) KEY
720  IF K=77 size=18:PROC_cursor:REM M (Magnified step) KEY
730  IF K=83 size=1:PROC_cursor:REM S (Small step) KEY

760  IF size=1 PRINT TAB(20,1)"S":PROC_cursor
770  IF size=6 PRINT TAB(20,1)"N":PROC_cursor
780  IF size=18 PRINT TAB(20,1)"M":PROC_cursor
```

If you press key N, you will get the Normal step size (6 pixels or 24 graphics units, which is the default value); key S gives the Small step size (1 pixel or 4 graphics units); key M gives a Magnified step of 18 pixels or 72 graphics units. The step size which is currently being used (S, N, M) is displayed on the second line of the screen.

6.9 Centring the Cursor and Global Erasure

It is sometimes convenient to be able to move the cursor from a remote point to the centre of the screen, and on other occasions you may need to completely clear the graphics drawing area of the screen. If you add the

Listing 6.4

```
830  IF K=67 x=445:y=450:PROC_cursor:REM C (Centre) KEY
840  IF K=71 CLG:PROC_cursor:REM G (clear Graphics) KEY
```

two instructions in *listing 6.4* to program *P6*, both features are added to your program.

When you press the **C-key** (Centre cursor), the current values of the variables x and y are changed to x = 445 and y = 450, corresponding to the centre of the graphics area. This causes the cursor to move to the centre of the graphics area when PROC_cursor is executed.

When you press the **G-key** (clear Graphics), the computer executes a CLG instruction, which clears the graphics area and deletes the diagram currently on the screen.

6.10 Sketching using Dots

So far you have only dealt with line drawing and with a crude method of filling a pixel (drawing a dot). If you add the program lines in *listing 6.5* to program *P6*, you will be able to sketch awkward parts of diagrams using a **point-plotting** method.

Listing 6.5

```
 850 IF K=84 PROC_dot:PROC_cursor:REM T (doT) KEY
 860 IF (K=87 OR draw=1) PROC_draw:PROC_cursor:REM W (draW) KEY

1260 DEF PROC_dot
1270 MOVE x,y:DRAW x,y:REM DRAW A dot
1280 ENDPROC
1290:
1300 DEF PROC_draw
1310 draw=1:size=1:REM SET draw FLAG TO '1' AND size=S
1320 PROC_dot
1330 ENDPROC
1340:
```

When you press the **T-key** (doT), the computer illuminates a dot or point at the centre of the current cursor position. This action calls on PROC_dot to draw a "line" of zero length; when in the dot mode, you can use any of the step sizes (S, N or M) when moving the cursor.

If you press the **W-key** (draW), control is transferred to PROC_draw which, after setting the draw flag to 1 and the step size to 1 (thereby forcing the cursor to step by one pixel at a time), it calls on PROC_dot to illuminate a pixel. So long as you remain in the draw mode, the computer continues to illuminate every pixel it meets. Also, to remind you that you are in the draw mode, the RUBBER/DRAW status is given as ON by line 750. A diagram produced by the draw and other features of the program is shown in Fig. 6.8.

You escape from the draw mode by pressing the **O-key** (OFF). This resets the draw flag and restores the cursor step size to its default value.

6.11 Adding Icons to the Program

A useful feature of any drawing program is the ability to call on a range of ready-made drwings or **icons** (images). If you add the instructions in *listing*

Fig. 6.8 Diagram obtained
using the line and draw
facility

```
LINE (L,F)= OFF   RUBBER/DRAW (R,W,O)=OFF
STEP SIZE (S,N,M) = N
X = 205        Y = 582   LENGTH = 48.16
```

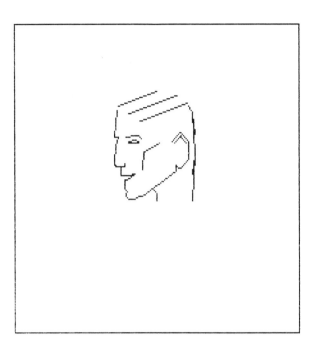

6.6 to your program, four icons are drawn in frames by the side of your drawing area.

Program lines 150–180 inclusive draw the frames within which the icons are drawn, and line 190 calls on PROC_icons which initiates the drawing process.

PROC_icons in lines 330–390 inclusive calls on four other procedures called PROC_icon1 to PROC_icon4 to draw the individual icons; these are, in this case, a shell, a roof, a door, and a window of a house. The program passes an X- and a Y-starting point to the procedure (see lines 340–370 inclusive) which is initially inside one of the icon frames. Later values passed to the procedures correspond to the current X- and Y-position of the cursor.

To select an icon, you press the **I-key** (Icon select) – see line 870 which causes program control to be transferred to PROC_select. Ths procedure asks you to select one of the icons by typing the number of the icon (1–4); at the same time, the cursor vanishes from the screen (this prompts you to make the selection). When you press one of the keys in the range 1–4, the cursor reappears on the screen. You are now free to continue moving the cursor around the screen until the cursor reaches the position where you need to draw the icon. The icon is drawn on the screen when you press the **D-key** (Draw icon) – see line 890. Unless you choose another icon, the same shape is printed whenever you press the D-key. To draw another icon, you simply go through the above procedure, but select another icon number.

The technique of picking an icon and placing it at a point on the screen is described as **picking and placing.**

If, whilst being given the choice of icons, you need to escape from the

Listing 6.6

```
140  REM icon FRAME
150  MOVE 890,840:DRAW 1240,840:DRAW 1240,0:DRAW 890,0
160  FOR N=1 TO 3
170    MOVE 890,N*210:DRAW 1240,N*210
180    NEXT N
190  PROC_icons:REM DRAW icons

330  DEF PROC_icons
340  PROC_icon1(910,640)
350  PROC_icon2(910,450)
360  PROC_icon3(1040,260)
370  PROC_icon4(1040,100)
380  PRINT TAB(39,8);"1";TAB(39,15);"2";TAB(39,22);"3";TAB(39,28);"4";TAB
(0,0)
390  ENDPROC
400  :
410  DEF PROC_icon1(x,y)
420  MOVE x,y:PLOT 1,296,0:PLOT 0,4,0:PLOT 1,0,180:PLOT 0,0,4:PLOT 1,-296
,0:PLOT 0,-4,0:PLOT 1,0,-180:REM HOUSE SHELL
430  ENDPROC
440  :
450  DEF PROC_icon2(x,y)
460  MOVE x,y:PLOT 1,296,0:PLOT 0,4,0:PLOT 1,-50,96:PLOT 0,-4,4:PLOT 1,-1
92,0:PLOT 0,-4,0:PLOT 1,-50,-96:PLOT 0,138,100:PLOT 1,0,46:PLOT 0,0,4:PLOT
1,21,0:PLOT 0,4,0:PLOT 1,0,-50:REM ROOF
470  ENDPROC
480  :
490  DEF PROC_icon3(x,y)
500  MOVE x,y:PLOT 1,36,0:PLOT 0,4,0:PLOT 1,0,76:PLOT 0,0,4:PLOT 1,-36,0:
PLOT 0,-4,0:PLOT 1,0,-76:REM DOOR
510  ENDPROC
520  :
530  DEF PROC_icon4(x,y)
540  MOVE x,y:PLOT 1,46,0:PLOT 0,4,0:PLOT 1,0,46:PLOT 0,0,4:PLOT 1,-46,0:
PLOT 0,-4,0:PLOT 1,0,-46:PLOT 0,4,30:PLOT 1,42,0:PLOT 0,-20,-30:PLOT 1,0,26
:PLOT 0,0,8:PLOT 1,0,8:REM WINDOW
550  ENDPROC
560  :

870  IF K=73 PROC_select:REM I (Icon select) KEY
880  IF escape=1 ENDPROC
890  IF K=68 PROC_draw_icon(select$):PROC_cursor:REM D (Draw icon) KEY
900  IF K=69 PROC_eliminate_icon(select$):PROC_cursor:REM E (Eliminate ic
on) KEY
```

```
1350  DEF PROC_select
1360  PRINT TAB(0,4)"Select icon (1,2,3,4)"
1370  PRINT TAB(22,4);" "
1380  REPEAT
1390    select$=GET$
1400    UNTIL INSTR("12340",select$)>0
1410  IF select$="Q" escape=1:ENDPROC
1420  PRINT TAB(22,4);select$
1430  ENDPROC
1440  :
1450  DEF PROC_draw_icon(select$)
1460  IF select$="1" PROC_icon1(x,y)
1470  IF select$="2" PROC_icon2(x,y)
1480  IF select$="3" PROC_icon3(x,y)
1490  IF select$="4" PROC_icon4(x,y)
1500  ENDPROC
1510  :
1520  DEF PROC_eliminate_icon(select$)
1530  GCOL 4,1:PROC_draw_icon(select$):GCOL 0,1
1540  ENDPROC
1550  :
```

program, you can do so by pressing the **Q-key** (Quit); this sets the escape flag to 1, which ensures that all the computer controls are returned to normal when you quit the program.

As in life itself, we can all make mistakes either when selecting an icon or when positioning it on the screen. The instructions in *listing 6.6* provide a means of elminating the icon just drawn on the screen. You do so by pressing the **E-key** (Eliminate icon) – see line 900. This transfers control to PROC_eliminate_icon, which draws the icon in inverse colour, which makes it vanish!

A diagram obtained using the icons in the program together with other features is shown in Fig. 6.9.

An alternative method of handling icons is known as **picking and dragging** in which, after picking the icon, you "drag" it across the screen using the cursor control keys. This method is illustrated in Chapter 8.

6.12 Suggested Extensions to the Program

With this program, it is only possible to make a selection from the four icons displayed. You may like to modify the program to increase the number of icons on offer to include, say, electrical and electronic circuit symbols, or architectural symbols (see, for example, Chapter 8).

Another feature which would be useful is to provide the facility to rotate the icons through an angle, or to enlarge the icon, or to reduce it in size. Although we have not yet considered the basic principles of these techniques, it would be helpful for you to anticipate ways of dealing with these features.

Fig. 6.9 The addition of "house" icons to the program; the icons are positioned by a method known as picking and placing

```
LINE (L,F)= OFF   RUBBER/DRAW (R,W,O)=OFF
STEP SIZE (S,N,M) = N
X = 421          Y = 758   LENGTH = 24

Select icon (1,2,3,4) 4
```

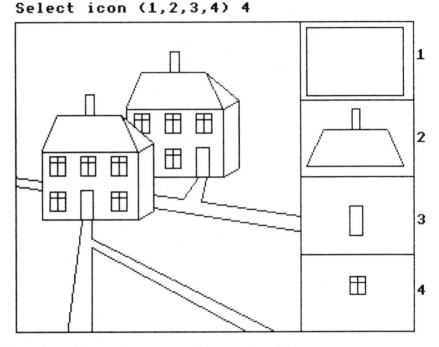

The program in this chapter does not enable you to print any text in the drawing area. A feature of any drawing program is the ability to position text on the diagram. You may like to consider how the program can be modified to include text handling (see also Chapter 8).

6.13   Summary of the Keyboard Controls in Program P6

Cursor control keys – cursor, rubber and icon positioning.

C – centre cursor.

D – draw icon at cursor position.

E – eliminate icon at cursor position.

F – fix line on screen.

G – clear graphics area.

I – select icon.

L – enter line-drawing mode.

M – magnified (large) cursor step size.

N – normal cursor step size.

O – turn rubber off and drawing mode off.

Q – quit program.

R – enter rubout mode.

S – small cursor step size.

T – draw a dot at the cursor position.

U – undraw (remove) a line.

W – enter the draw (sketching) mode.

Three-dimensional Shapes

7.1 Specifying a Three-dimensional Wire-frame Shape

This chapter introduces one of the most fascinating areas of computer graphics, namely three-dimensional displays. The simplest method of drawing a 3-D shape is in the form of a wire-frame, in which the corners or vertices of the shape are joined together by lines or "wires". Provided that enough detail is included, the resulting shape on the screen is realistic.

Consider the simple wire-frame cube in Fig. 7.1. For the computer to be able to draw the shape, it must know not only the number of corners involved and their position in space, but also the number of lines or wires in the drawing together with the corners which are to be joined by the wires. In this book we adopt the following measuring notation:

Positive values of X are to the right of the graphics origin.
Negative values of X are to the left of the graphics origin.
Positive values of Y are above the graphics origin.
Negative values of Y are below the graphics origin.
Positive values of Z are out of the page (or VDU screen).
Negative values of Z are into the page (or VDU screen).

Fig. 7.1 A simple wire-frame cube

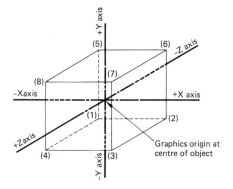

These coordinates are known mathematically as **right-handed coordinates** because (see Fig. 7.2) if the thumb, first finger and second finger of the right hand are held mutually perpendicular to one another they point, respectively, in the positive directions of the X, Y and Z axes. These coordinates are widely used in *vector algebra* (although it should be pointed out that *left-handed coordinates* can also be used, in which the positive direction of Z is reversed). The programs in this book are all written using right-handed coordinates.

Fig. 7.2 Illustrating right-
handed coordinates

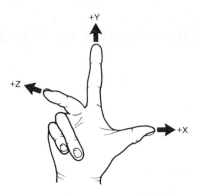

Fig. 7.2 Illustrating right-handed coordinates

When specifying a drawing, the first step is to sketch the object and give
each corner or vertex a number; these are shown in parenthesis in Fig. 7.1.
Next, you must write down a table (see Table 7.1). listing the X, Y and Z
coordinates of each corner. The dimensions of the corners of the cube in
Fig. 7.1 are measured from the *graphics origin* which, in this case, is
positioned at the centre of the cube.

Table 7.1   Coordinates of the corners of Fig. 7.1

Corner number	Coordinates		
	X	Y	Z
1	-0.5	-0.5	0.5
2	0.5	-0.5	0.5
3	0.5	0.5	0.5
4	-0.5	0.5	0.5
5	-0.5	-0.5	-0.5
6	0.5	-0.5	-0.5
7	0.5	0.5	-0.5
8	-0.5	0.5	-0.5

At this stage a decision must be made whether to work in abstract
graphic units of the screen size or in the real units used in practice. The
latter is selected here because it allows us to think in real dimensions. It is
therefore necessary to include a scaling factor in the executive program
which scales the screen measurements in terms of real units. Since the
screen dimensions are approximately 1200×1000 graphics units (g.u.), we
can scale the largest (L) dimension of the object to take up about 1000 g.u.
on the screen. The equation used to calculate the scale is

$$1000 \text{ g.u.} = \text{scale} \times \text{L (metres)}$$

hence

$$\text{Scale} = 1000/\text{L g.u. per metre}$$

Since the length of each side of the cube in Fig. 8.1 is 1 m, the scale used in
the program is $1000/1 = 1000$ g.u. per metre. Hence, to determine the
graphical position of a corner in, say, the X-direction, the computer needs
to perform the calculation:

$$\text{X coordinates in g.u.} = \text{real X coordinate} * \text{scale}$$

The scale factor calculated above applies equally to the X, Y and Z directions of the shape. If you are concerned with the process of designing shapes, you may need a different scale factor for each axis. This is an interesting problem you may like to investigate as a project.

Having specified the position of each corner of the object, you must also list the number of lines to be drawn together with the corners to be joined by the lines, the latter being listed for Fig. 7.1 in Table 7.2.

Table 7.2 Corners to be joined to draw Fig. 7.1

Line number	1	2	3	4	5	6	7	8	9	10	11	12
Corners to be joined	1-2	2-3	3-4	4-1	5-6	6-7	7-8	8-5	1-5	2-6	3-7	4-8

7.2 The Three-dimensional World

In this chapter we will build up a program for drawing three-dimensional objects. Initially the program will simply draw the cube viewed from the Z-direction, that is looking towards the X-Y plane. However, the limitations of this simple program are quickly revealed. Later, we look at methods of dealing with perspective (vital in any 3-D drawing) and also methods of "moving" the shape around in a three-dimensional space. We will also investigate methods of zooming and shrinking the object.

Using standard mathematical techniques such as basic trigonometry, the above techniques are discussed in this chapter. Readers interested in developing the subject to a greater depth will find relevant advanced methods such as matrices in Chapter 9. These techniques are known as **linear transformations.**

Later in the chapter we will look at methods of presenting solid 3-D shapes. This involves programs needing vector algebra; however, if you are not mathematically inclined, you simply type in the appropropriate procedures and use them. Details of the approach used are described in Chapter 9.

7.3 A Simple Program for Handling Three-dimensional Data

The program described in this section is fairly simple and is extended as the chapter proceeds; it is for this reason that the data relating to the shape is introduced at an early point in the executive program. At a later stage (when the program is more fully developed) you may wish to accommodate your own 3-D shapes; lines 70 to 340 are available for this purpose.

Program *P7.1A* is a simple program which handles the data in Tables 7.1 and 7.2. If you copy program *P7.1A* (*listing 7.1*) into the computer, *you must take care to use the line numbers specified;* the reason is that gaps in the line numbers are used in more advanced versions of the program which are developed as the chapter unfolds. Program *P7.1A* calls on three procedures as follows.

PROC_corners reads the number of corners (given by corner_no in line 80), after which it reads the coordinates of each corner (given in blocks

Listing 7.1

```
10  REM****PROGRAM "P7.1A"****
20  REM****WIRE FRAME 3-D DRAWING WITHOUT PERSPECTIVE****
30  ON ERROR GOTO 1880
40  *TV0.1
50  MODE 4
60  :
70  REM NUMBER OF CORNERS
80  DATA 8
90  REM COORDINATES OF CORNERS
100 DATA -0.5,-0.5,-0.5,  0.5,-0.5,-0.5,  0.5,-0.5,0.5,  -0.5,-0.5,0.5
110 DATA -0.5,0.5,-0.5,  0.5,0.5,-0.5,  0.5,0.5,0.5,  -0.5,0.5,0.5
120 :
130 REM NUMBER OF LINES
140 DATA 12
150 REM CORNERS TO BE JOINED
160 DATA 1,2,  2,3,  3,4,  4,1,  5,6,  6,7
170 DATA 7,8,  8,5,  1,5,  2,6,  3,7,  4,8
180 :

350 REM REDEFINE GRAPHICS ORIGIN AND ELIMINATE CURSOR
360 VDU 29,640;512;23;8202;0;0;0;
370 scale=1000

450 PROC_corners
460 PROC_lines
470 :

500 PROC_draw

550 END
560 :
570 DEF PROC_corners
580 REM DIMENSION ARRAYS AND READ COORDINATES
590 READ corner_no
600 DIM X(corner_no),Y(corner_no),Z(corner_no)
610 FOR corner=1 TO corner_no
620   READ X(corner),Y(corner),Z(corner)
630   NEXT corner
640 ENDPROC
650 :
660 DEF PROC_lines
670 REM DIMENSION ARRAYS AND READ CORNERS TO BE JOINED
680 READ line_no
690 DIM start(line_no),end(line_no)
700 FOR line=1 TO line_no
710   READ start(line),end(line)
720   NEXT line
730 ENDPROC
740 :
```

```
780  DEF PROC_draw
790  REM DRAW SHAPE
800  CLS
810  FOR line=1 TO line_no
820     MOVE scale*X(start(line)),scale*Y(start(line)):DRAW scale*X(end(li
ne)),scale*Y(end(line))
830     NEXT line
840  ENDPROC
850  :

1880  MODE 1:*FX4,0
1890  REPORT:PRINT" AT LINE ";ERL:END
```

of three items, corresponding to the X, Y and Z coordinate of each corner) in lines 100 and 110.

Thus element $X(1)$ of array X stores the X value of corner number 1, i.e. $X(1) = 0.5$ m, and element $Y(5)$ stores the Y value of corner 5, i.e. $Y(5) = 0.5$ m, etc.

PROC_lines reads the number of wires or lines to be drawn (given by line_no in line 140), after which it reads the starting corner and ending corner of each line (given in pairs in lines 160 and 170) which it stores in arrays "start" and "end".

Thus elements start(1) and end(1) store corner numbers 1 and 2 respectively, elements start(3) and end(3) store corner numbers 3 and 4 respectively, etc.

PROC_draw causes line_no lines (12 in Fig. 7.1) to be drawn, each line commencing at the X- and Y-coordinates stored in the X and Y start array, and terminating at the X- and Y-coordinates stored in the X and Y end array.

On the first pass through PROC_draw, the variable line has the value 1, so that the graphics cursor initially MOVES to

$$X(start(line)), Y(start(line)) = X(start(1)), Y(start(1)$$
$$= X(1), Y(1)$$

where $X(1) = -0.5$ and $Y(1) = -0.5$. You will also see that in line 820 these values are multiplied by the scale factor of 1000. That is, the graphics cursor moves to a point which is 500 g.u. to the left of the graphics origin (which is set at the centre of the screen by line 360) and 500 graphics units below the graphics origin. Next the computer DRAWs a line from that point to the point whose coordinates are

$$X(end(line)), Y(end(line)) = X(end(1)), Y(end(2))$$
$$= X(2), Y(2)$$

corresponding to $X = 0.5$ m = 500 g.u., $Y = -0.5$ m $-$ 500 g.u. This procedure is repeated until every line has been drawn.

When you run the program, you will see that the monitor simply displays a rectangular shape on the screen. The reason is that the program does not allow for perspective; that is, the size of all sides of the cube are the same. Consequently, program *P.1A* produces a front elevation as one might expect in an engineering **orthographic drawing**. Perspective is introduced in section 7.4.

It is of interest here to point out a number of practical features incorporated in program *P7.1A*. The first of these is the error trap in lines 30, 1880 and 1890. The second of these is screen jitter elimination instruction in line 40, and the third is the elimination of the text cursor using the VDU 23,8202;0;0;0; instruction in line 360. Having RUN the program, you will need to type MODE followed by a screen MODE number, i.e. MODE 4 followed by ⟨RETURN⟩ in order to return the text cursor to the screen; this also has the effect of clearing the screen. The series of operations described in the last sentence are not needed in many of the programs listed later in this chapter.

7.4 Perspective

When you look at a real 3-D object, parts which are further away from you appear smaller than parts which are close to you. To handle this situation, the computer must calculate the perspective "screen" coordinates for each actual 3-D corner in the object. That is, it converts the 3-D dimension in Table 7.1 into 2-D screen dimensions. The method of doing this is illustrated in Fig. 7.3a.

The graphics origin of the object (the cube in this case) can be thought of as being positioned behind the monitor screen. The "front" of the object is displaced distance Z in front of the graphics origin, so that the distance between the eye and the front face of the object is

origin_distance − Z

where the length origin_distance is specified in Fig. 7.3a. Angle θ is the angle seen by the eye between the centre of the object and top. We can now determine the Y-ordinate transformation which transforms the actual (3-D) dimension into the screen (2-D) dimension. The tangent of angle θ is given by

$$\tan \theta = \frac{Y}{(\text{origin\_distance} - Z)} = \frac{YS}{\text{screen\_distance}}$$

where Y is the actual Y-value of the object, YS is the Y-value of the shape on the screen, and screen_distance is the distance from the imaginary eye to the screen. From this we see that the Y-ordinate transformation is given by

$$YS = Y * \text{screen\_distance}/(\text{origin\_distance} - Z)$$

We will now attempt to put some values into the equation for the purpose of scaling it. It has been suggested by some authorities that the most pleasing effect is obtained when the viewing distance is about two to three times the height of an object. Since the height of the screen is about 1000 g.u. (equivalent to about 1 m using our scale), a suitable screen_distance is 2000 to 3000 g.u.; we will use a figure of 2500 g.u. or 2.5 m. That is

Fig. 7.3 Perspective
calculations

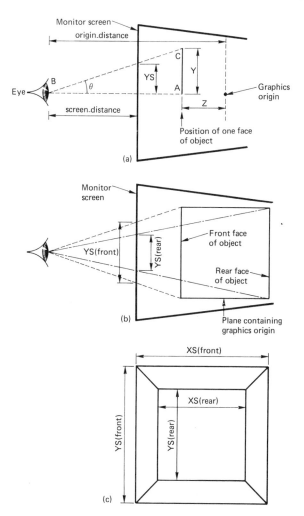

$$YS = Y*screen\_distance*scale/((origin\_distance - Z)*scale)$$

The length of screen_distance and origin_distance are inserted as variables in *listing 7.2* (see *P7.1B*) so that you can, if you wish, alter them at a later stage. The origin_distance has been chosen as 5 m in the program.

The analysis for the screen X-dimensions (XS) follows the same pattern, and the screen X-ordinate transformation is given by the equation

$$XS = X*screen\_distance*scale/((origin\_distance - Z)*scale)$$

where X is the X-dimension of a corner on the 3-D object, and Z is the Z-axis measurement of the corner from the graphics origin.

You should now load program *P7.1A* into the computer and amend it as shown in *listing P7.1B*; the listing, of course, only contains amendments to *P7.1A*. You should then save the program and run it. The relative positions of the eye and the monitor are shown in Fig. 7.3*b*, and the view seen on the screen is shown in Fig. 7.3*c*. The rear surface of the cube is furthest away from you so that XS(rear) is smaller than XS(front), and

Listing 7.2

```
 10  REM****PROGRAM "P7.1B"****
 20  REM****WIRE FRAME 3-D DRAWING WITH PERSPECTIVE****

380  origin_distance=5:screen_distance=2.5

490  PROC_perspective

600  DIM X(corner_no),Y(corner_no),Z(corner_no),XS(corner_no),YS(corner_n
o)

820  MOVE scale*XS(start(line)),scale*YS(start(line)):DRAW scale*XS(end(l
ine)),scale*YS(end(line))

890  DEF PROC_perspective
900  REM PERSPECTIVE TRANSFORMATION
910  FOR corner=1 TO corner_no
920    XS(corner)=X(corner)*screen_distance/(origin_distance - Z(corner))
930    YS(corner)=Y(corner)*screen_distance/(origin_distance - Z(corner))
940    NEXT corner
950  ENDPROC
960  :
```

YS(rear) is smaller than YS(front). The procedure PROC_perspective called by the executive program calculates the perspective of each corner in the cube; the equations in lines 920 and 930 are generally similar to the equations developed above for the perspective calculations.

The program modifications introduce two further arrays, XS and YS, which respectively handle the perspective measurements in the X- and Y-directions; PROC_draw is modified as shown in line 820 to use the perspective coordinates.

Once again, after RUNning the program, you will need to type MODE followed by a mode number and ⟨RETURN⟩ to restore the cursor to the screen.

7.5 Enlarging and Reducing the Image — Zooming

So far you have not had hands-on control over the dispaly on the screen; you have merely RUN the program and seen the result. You now enter the world in which you begin to control what is happening on the screen, commencing by enlarging and reducing the image on the screen, i.e. respectively, zooming towards or away from the object.

An understanding of the technique involved is obtained by studying Fig. 7.3*a*. If you reduce the length origin_distance, the object is brought "closer" to you and is enlarged, i.e. you appear to zoom into the object. On the other hand, if origin_distance is increased, the object moves away from you and gets smaller. At this point you should LOAD program *P7.1B* into the micro and amend it as shown in *listing 7.3*.

We will use the DELETE and COPY keys to reduce and enlarge, respectively, the size of the image on the screen. Each time the DELETE

Listing 7.3

```
10   REM****PROGRAM "P7.1C"****
20   REM****WIRE FRAME 3-D DRAWING WITH ZOOMING****

390  origin_step=0.5

440  *FX4,1

480  REPEAT

520  PROC_keys
530  UNTIL key=81:REM Q (QUIT) KEY
540  MODE 4:*FX4,0

1070 DEF PROC_keys
1080 REM READ KEYBOARD
1090 REPEAT
1100   *FX 15,0
1110   key=GET
1120   UNTIL key=127 OR key=135 OR key=81
1130 IF key=127 THEN origin_distance=origin_distance+origin_step:REM DELE
TE KEY
1140 IF key=135 THEN origin_distance=origin_distance-origin_step:REM COPY
KEY
1150 ENDPROC
1160 :
```

key is pressed, the object is moved 0.5 m (500 g.u.) away from you (this is
called origin_step in program *P8.1C*), and is moved 0.5 m towards you
each time the COPY key is pressed. The program provides both perspective and zooming.

The use of the keys to control the on-screen operations is enabled by
means of the *FX 4,1 instruction in line 440. This has the effect of
disabling the cursor and COPY keys, and making them return ASCII
codes. In fact we shall be using the ASCII values returned by a number of
keys during this chapter for control purposes. The keys together with the
ASCII values used in this chapter are listed in Table 7.3; full information
on the ASCII code generated by the keys is given in Appendix 1.

Table 7.3 ASCII codes generated by keys used in this chapter

Key	ASCII value	Key	ASCII value
RETURN	13	]	93
C	67	DELETE	127
D	68	COPY	135
L	76	←	136
Q	81	→	137
R	82	↓	138
U	85	↑	139

The procedure which handles the ASCII values is called PROC_keys. This causes the computer to wait for the COPY key or DELETE key to be pressed, after which it amends the origin_distance. This, in turn, has the effect of modifying the size of the image on the screen. PROC_keys also gives you the opportunity of escaping from the program by pressing the Q (quit) key. When you press the Q-key, line 540 of the program has the effect of clearing the screen and restoring the text cursor to the screen.

7.6 Moving the Image around the Screen

The process of moving the image around the screen without altering its size is known as **translation**. In this section of the book we develop a **translation transformation** (contained in PROC_move in program *P8.1D*) which enables you to move the cube to the left (using the L-key), or to the right (using the R-key), or up the screen (using the U-key), or down the screen (using the D-key). Each time you press one of these keys, the image is moved 0.1 m (or 100 g.u.). The effect of PROC_move is to add (or to subtract) 0.1 m to either the X-measurement or the Y-measurement of all corners.

Since PROC_move is contained within the REPEAT-UNTIL loop containing PROC_perspective, the perspective of the object on the screen is maintained as it is moved. You should now load *P7.1C* into the computer and add the instructions in *listing 7.4*.

Listing 7.4

```
10  REM****PROGRAM "P7.1D"****
20  REM****WIRE FRAME 3-D DRAWING WITH TRANSLATION****

400  move=0.1
410  movex=0:movey=0

1120 UNTIL key=127 OR key=135 OR key=81 OR key=76 OR key=82 OR key=85 OR
key=68

1150 IF key=76 OR key=82 OR key=85 OR key=68 THEN PROC_move
1160 ENDPROC
1170 :

1250 DEF PROC_move
1260 REM TRANSLATION TRANSFORMATION
1270 IF key=76 THEN movex=-move:REM L KEY
1280 IF key=82 THEN movex=move:REM R KEY
1290 IF key=85 THEN movey=move:REM U KEY
1300 IF key=68 THEN movey=-move:REM D KEY
1310 FOR corner=1 TO corner_no
1320   x=X(corner):y=Y(corner)
1330   X(corner)=x+movex:Y(corner)=y+movey
1340   NEXT corner
1350 movex=0:movey=0
1360 ENDPROC
1370 :
```

7.7   Returning the Image to its Original Position

After moving the object around the screen, you may need to quickly return it to its original position in the centre of the screen. A modification to program *P7.1D*, this is contained in *listing 7.5*. When you press key C (ASCII code 67), the program is re-run, causing the image to appear in its original position.

Listing 7.5

```
10  REM****PROGRAM "P7.1E"****
20  REM****WIRE FRAME 3-D DRAWING WITH CENTERING****

1120  UNTIL key=127 OR key=135 OR key=81 OR key=76 OR key=82 OR key=85 OR
key=68 OR key=67

1160  IF key=67 THEN RUN:REM C KEY
1170  ENDPROC
```

7.8   Rotation about the X, Y and Z Axes — the Rotation Transformation

When defining rotation in a 3-axis system, i.e. rotation about the X, Y and Z axes, the **positive direction of rotation** about the axis is taken as **anticlockwise** when **looking towards the origin from the positive direction** along the axis.

For example, in Fig. 7.4*a*, positive rotation around the Z-axis is taken as angle θ in the clockwise direction in the X-Y plane. Similarly, positive rotation around the X-axis (Fig. 7.4*b*) is taken as angle α in the anticlockwise direction in the Y-Z plane. Positive rotation around the Y-axis (Fig. 7.4*c*) is taken as angle β in the anticlockwise direction in the Z-X plane.

Fig. 7.4 The positive direction of rotation about a) the Z-axis, b) the X-axis, c) the Y-axis

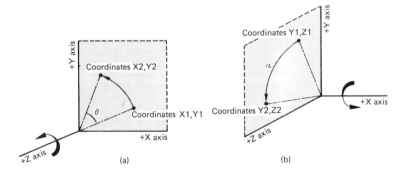

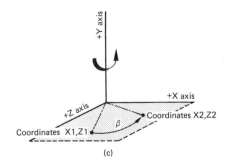

The new coordinates X2,Y2 of a point X1,Y1 in the X-Y plane after it has been rotated through angle θ are

$$X2 = X1 \cos(\text{theta}) - Y1 \sin(\text{theta})$$
$$Y2 = Y1 \cos(\text{theta}) + X1 \sin(\text{theta})$$

Details of these equations are described in Chapter 9. Similarly, the coordinates Y2,Z2 of a point Y1,Z1 which has been rotated through α about the X-axis (see Fig. 7.4b) are

$$Y2 = Y1 \cos(\text{alpha}) - Z1 \sin(\text{alpha})$$
$$Z2 = Z1 \cos(\text{alpha}) + Y1 \sin(\text{alpha})$$

Also, the coordinates of a point Z2,X2 of a point Z1,X1 which has been rotated through angle β about the Y-axis (see Fig. 7.4c) are

$$Z2 = Z1 \cos(\text{beta}) - X1 \sin(\text{beta})$$
$$X2 = X1 \cos(\text{beta}) + Z1 \sin(\text{beta})$$

Each pair of the above equations is used to produce a rotational transformation about one axis of the 3-D shape, the three rotational transformations effectively combining to form a **3-D rotational transformation**.

To incorporate rotation into your program, modify program *P7.1E* to include the program lines in *listing 7.6* (program *P7.1F*). This is the final form of the development program and, later, we will produce other versions to deal with several applications. The ultimate use of the program (and of its development) is restricted only by your own imagination!

Listing 7.6

```
10   REM****PROGRAM "P7.1F"****
20   REM****WIRE FRAME 3-D DRAWING WITH ROTATION****

420  theta=0:alpha=0:beta=0:angle_step=PI/18
430 :

1120  UNTIL key=127 OR key=135 OR key=81 OR key=76 OR key=82 OR key=85 OR
key=68 OR key=67 OR (key>135 AND key<140) OR key=13 OR key=93

1170  IF key=136 THEN beta=beta-angle_step:PROC_yrotate:REM LEFT (<) CONTR
OL KEY
1180  IF key=137 THEN beta=beta+angle_step:PROC_yrotate:REM RIGHT (>) CONT
ROL KEY
1190  IF key=138 THEN alpha=alpha+angle_step:PROC_xrotate:REM DOWN CONTROL
KEY
1200  IF key=139 THEN alpha=alpha-angle_step:PROC_xrotate:REM UP (^) CONTR
OL KEY
1210  IF key=13 THEN theta=theta+angle_step:PROC_zrotate:REM RETURN KEY
1220  IF key=93 THEN theta=theta-angle_step:PROC_zrotate:REM ] KEY
1230  ENDPROC
1240 :

1380  DEF PROC_yrotate
```

```
1390  REM Y-ROTATION TRANSFORMATION
1400  FOR corner=1 TO corner_no
1410    Z=Z(corner):X=X(corner)
1420    Z(corner)=Z*COS(beta)-X*SIN(beta)
1430    X(corner)=X*COS(beta)+Z*SIN(beta)
1440    NEXT corner
1450  beta=0
1460  ENDPROC
1470  :
1480  DEF PROC_xrotate
1490  REM X-ROTATION TRANSFORMATION
1500  FOR corner=1 TO corner_no
1510    Y=Y(corner):Z=Z(corner)
1520    Y(corner)=Y*COS(alpha)-Z*SIN(alpha)
1530    Z(corner)=Z*COS(alpha)+Y*SIN(alpha)
1540    NEXT corner
1550  alpha=0
1560  ENDPROC
1570  :
1580  DEF PROC_zrotate
1590  REM Z-ROTATION TRANSFORMATION
1600  FOR corner=1 TO corner_no
1610    X=X(corner):Y=Y(corner)
1620    X(corner)=X*COS(theta)-Y*SIN(theta)
1630    Y(corner)=Y*COS(theta)+X*SIN(theta)
1640    NEXT corner
1650  theta=0
1660  ENDPROC
1670  :
```

PROC_keys is modified in *P7.1F* to allow you to use the ← and the → keys to control rotation of the image about its Y-axis (PROC_yrotate), to use the ↓ and the ↑ keys to control rotation about the X-axis (PROC_xrotate), and the RETURN and] keys to control rotation about the Z-axis (PROC_zrotate). The image is rotated in steps of PI/18 radian or 10° (controlled by the variable angle-step in line 420).

When running the program, you should imagine that you are holding the cube in your hands and turning it around. That is, *your own position is fixed and the object is being moved* and you are looking at it along the Z-axis (*do not* imagine that the object is fixed in space and that you are "flying" around it – because this is not the case). This concept is particularly important when we consider solid 3-D shapes which have "hidden" surfaces.

A typical view of the cube on the monitor screen is illustrated in Fig. 7.5.

Summary of the use of keys in program P8.1F
L, R, U, D – movement of the image Left, Right, Up an Down the screen.
←, →, ↑, ↓,], RETURN – rotation control of the image.

COPY, DELETE – enlarge and reduce the image, respectively.
C – return the image to the Centre of the screen.
Q – Quit the program.

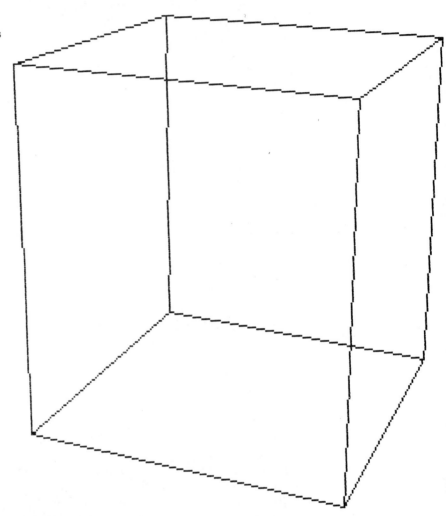

Fig. 7.5 An illustration of a
wire-frame cube which has
been rotated in the X-, Y-
and Z-directions

7.9 Other Transformations

So far we have dealt with important 3-D transformations relating to
viewing and movement. There are other transformations you may like to
implement yourself, such as altering the scaling factors along the three
viewing axes; this enables you to alter the shape of the object as you view
it.

Two other transformations which you can usefully implement are
reflection and shear. A **reflection transformation** causes the image to be
reflected about a selected axis; this causes the axis to appear as though it
were a mirror. A **shear transformation** results in the image being twisted or
sheared. These are discussed further in chapter 9.

7.10   Displaying Three-dimensional Alphabetical Characters

Having developed a general-purpose 3-D program, we will use it for a variety of applications. The first of these enables you to display 3-D wire-frame alphabetical characters (it can, of course, be modified to draw other characters such as numbers, etc.).

The first step is to draw the character on a piece of paper. Let us assume that you want to display the letter A (see Fig. 7.6). Having drawn the character, you must write down the corner numbers associated with the front face and the rear face of the character (shown in parenthesis in Fig. 7.6).

Fig. 7.6 The method of programming a 3-D letter A

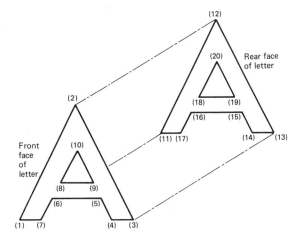

Next you need to modify the DATA section of the 3-D wire-frame program to handle the data (the remainder of the program *P7.1F* remains unchanged). At this point you must load program *P7.1F* into the memory of the computer, and modify in the way listed in program *P7.1LET* (see *listing 7.7*).

The letter A shown in Fig. 7.6 has twenty corners; the Z coordinates of points on the front face are specified in the executive program in association with variable $z1$, and those on the rear face in association with $z2$. The values of $z1$ and $z2$ are included in line 72 of the program; this facility enables you to quickly modify the depth of the letter on the screen. A typical screen image is shown in Fig. 7.7; the program enables you to rotate, move and zoom the shape under keyboard control in the manner described for program *P7.1F*.

7.11   Transferring a Character onto the Face of an Object

Once you have drawn an image (say a wire-frame cube), you can then impress any other shape on any (or all!) of the faces of the image. For example, you may wish to transfer the capital letter A onto the front face of the wire-frame cube.

In this case, you need to draw the letter A directly onto the surface of the cube as though it were painted on the face, i.e. it does not protrude out of the face (later, as an exercise, you may like to modify the program to give a protruding letter A on the face).

Listing 7.7

```
10  REM****PROGRAM "P7.1LET"****
20  REM****3-D LETTER****

70  REM NUMBER OF CORNERS
72  z1=0:z2=-0.1
80  DATA 20
90  REM COORDINATES OF CORNERS
100 DATA -0.4,-0.4,z1,  0,0.4,z1,  0.4,-0.4,z1,  0.3,-0.4,z1
110 DATA 0.2,-0.2,z1,  -0.2,-0.2,z1,  -0.3,-0.4,z1,  -0.15,-0.1,z1
120 DATA 0.15,-0.1,z1,  0,0.2,z1,  -0.4,-0.4,z2,  0,0.4,z2
130 DATA 0.4,-0.4,z2,  0.3,-0.4,z2,  0.2,-0.2,z2,  -0.2,-0.2,z2
140 DATA -0.3,-0.4,z2,  -0.15,-0.1,z2,  0.15,-0.1,z2,  0,0.2,z2
150 :
160 REM NUMBER OF LINES
170 DATA 30
180 REM CORNERS TO BE JOINED
190 DATA 1,2,  2,3,  3,4,  4,5,  5,6
200 DATA 6,7,  7,1,  8,9,  9,10,  10,8
210 DATA 11,12,  12,13,  13,14,  14,15,  15,16
220 DATA 16,17,  17,11,  18,19,  19,20,  20,18
230 DATA 1,11,  2,12,  3,13,  4,14,  5,15
240 DATA 6,16,  7,17,  8,18,  9,19,  10,20
250 :
```

Load program *P7.1F* into the computer and modify it as listed in program *P7.1LC* (see *listing 7.8*). The total number of corners involved is 18 (8 for the cube and 10 for one face of letter A); the data in lines 112-116 inclusive refer to the letter A. There are 22 lines to be joined (12 for the cube and 10 for the letter A); the data in lines 180 and 190 refer to letter A. One form of display is shown in Fig. 7.8; once again you may move the image, or rotate it or zoom into it.

7.12 A Wire-frame Space Rocket

Using a suitably modified set of data in program *P7.1F,* you can construct any wire-frame model you like. Suppose that you want to draw a space rocket on the monitor screen. Firstly you must draw the shape on a piece of paper, then number its corners and write down the X, Y and Z coordinates of each corner. Having done this, you simply have to type the data relating to the corners and to the lines which join the corners into the program.

To make the rocket a realistic size, the total height is assumed to be 100 m and, to make other sizes in proportion, it is necessary to change the size of the variables scale, origin_distance, screen_distance, origin_step, and move, when compared with program *P7.1F* (see lines 370 to 400 in program *P7.1ROC*).

Program *P7.1ROC* (see *listing 7.9*) is a modified version of *P7.1F,* and reproduces a space rocket on the screen of the monitor. Once again, you have full control over the movement of the rocket; Fig. 7.9 shows one view of the rocket.

Fig. 7.7 A rotated 3-D letter
A on the screen

7.13 Introduction to Stereoscopic Effects — the Stereoscopic Transformation

When viewing an image each eye has its own perspective but, since one eye is positioned a little way from the other eye, each has its own view of the image. It is this difference in perspective which gives humans a "true" mental 3-D image.

This situation is illustrated in Fig. 7.10*a*. To obtain a stereoscopic view of a shape, each eye must be presented with its own image; to produce this effect, each eye must "see" only its own image. One technique used to achieve this effect is to display two images on the monitor screen on a white background; one image (in, say, green) is for the left eye only and the

Listing 7.8

```
10   REM****PROGRAM "P7.1LC"****
20   REM****WIRE FRAME 3-D CUBE WITH LETTER ON ONE SIDE****

70   REM NUMBER OF CORNERS
80   DATA 18
90   REM COORDINATES OF CORNERS
100  DATA -0.5,-0.5,-0.5,  0.5,-0.5,-0.5,  0.5,-0.5,0.5,  -0.5,-0.5,0.5
110  DATA -0.5,0.5,-0.5,  0.5,0.5,-0.5,  0.5,0.5,0.5,  -0.5,0.5,0.5
112  DATA -0.4,-0.4,0.5,  0,0.4,0.5,  0.4,-0.4,0.5,  0.3,-0.4,0.5
114  DATA 0.2,-0.2,0.5,  -0.2,-0.2,0.5,  -0.3,-0.4,0.5,  -0.15,-0.1,0.5
116  DATA 0.15,-0.1,0.5,  0,0.2,0.5
120  :
130  REM NUMBER OF LINES
140  DATA 22
150  REM CORNERS TO BE JOINED
160  DATA 1,2,  2,3,  3,4,  4,1,  5,6,  6,7
170  DATA 7,8,  8,5,  1,5,  2,6,  3,7,  4,8
180  DATA 9,10,  10,11,  11,12,  12,13,  13,14
190  DATA 14,15,  15,9,  16,17,  17,18,  18,16
200  :
```

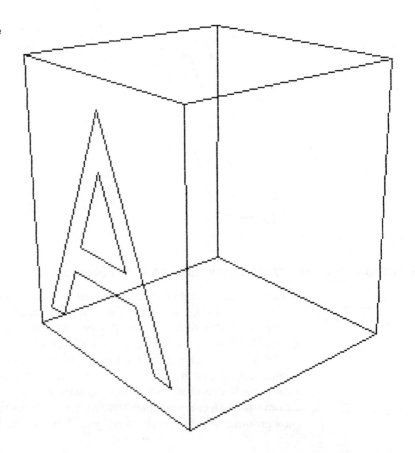

Fig. 7.8 A wire-frame cube which has the letter A embossed on one face

Listing 7.9

```
10   REM****PROGRAM "P7.1ROC"****
20   REM****WIRE FRAME 3-D ROCKET****

70   REM NUMBER OF CORNERS
80   DATA 33
90   REM COORDINATES OF CORNERS
100  DATA 5,-50,-10,  10,-50,-5,  10,-50,5,  5,-50,10
110  DATA -5,-50,10,  -10,-50,5,  -10,-50,-5,  -5,-50,-10
120  DATA 2.5,-50,-10,  0,-50,-20,  -2.5,-50,-10,  -10,-50,-2.5
130  DATA -20,-50,0,  -10,-50,2.5,  -2.5,-50,10,  0,-50,20
140  DATA 2.5,-50,10,  10,-50,2.5,  20,-50,0,  10,-50,-2.5
150  DATA 0,-20,-10,  -10,-20,0,  0,-20,10,  10,-20,0
160  DATA 5,20,-10,  -5,20,-10,  -10,20,-5,  -10,20,5
170  DATA -5,20,10,  5,20,10,  10,20,5,  10,20,-5
180  DATA 0,50,0
190  :
200  REM NUMBER OF LINES
210  DATA 52
220  REM CORNERS TO BE JOINED
230  DATA 1,2,  2,3,  3,4,  4,5
240  DATA 5,6,  6,7,  7,8,  8,1
250  DATA 9,10,  10,11,  12,13,  13,14
260  DATA 15,16,  16,17,  18,19,  19,20
270  DATA 25,26,  26,27,  27,28,  28,29
280  DATA 29,30,  30,31,  31,32,  32,25
290  DATA 8,21,  9,21,  10,21,  12,22
300  DATA 13,22,  14,22,  15,23,  16,23
310  DATA 17,23,  18,24,  19,24,  20,24
320  DATA 1,25,  2,32,  3,31,  4,30
330  DATA 5,29,  6,28,  7,27,  8,26
332  DATA 25,33,  26,33,  27,33,  28,33
334  DATA 29,33,  30,33,  31,33,  32,33
340  :

370  scale=10
380  origin_distance=200:screen distance=100
390  origin_step=5
400  move=10
```

other (in, say, red) for the right eye. You must wear a pair of stereoscopic glasses having a red lens in the left eye and a green lens in the right eye. (You can easily make up a pair of these glasses by using coloured Cellophane over an old pair of spectacle frames; however, you must experiment with the density of the colour of the lens to ensure that the red lens completely obliterates the red shape, and the green lens obliterates the green shape. This is achieved by adding more layers of Cellophane.)

The coloured lens has the effect of logically ANDing the *actual colour* on the screen with the colour of the lens. Since the red and green images are

Fig. 7.9 A rocket which is
displayed using program
P7.1ROC

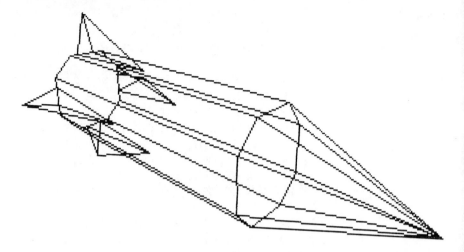

drawn on a white background, the effect on the left eye (which has a red lens) is as follows (from the chapter on colour you will remember that red has the logical value 001, green has the value 010, white has the value 111, and black has the value 000):

```
Red line      = 001
Red lens      = 001
Result (AND) = 001 = red
```

```
White screen  = 111
Red lens      = 001
Result (AND) = 001 = red
```

```
Green line    = 010
Red lens      = 001
Result (AND) = 000 = black
```

That is, both the red image and the white background appear to the left eye as red, so that the left eye cannot see the red image. However, the green image appears as a black image to the left eye, and is clearly visible against the red background. Similarly, the right eye sees a separate black image (derived from the red image on the screen) on a green background. The green image on the screen is invisible to the right eye.

Provided that the computer has calculated separate perspective views for each image, the mind focusses the two black lines at a point behind the screen, giving a mental 3-D image of the shape.

Using a technique similar to that outlined in section 7.4 (Perspective), the X position of the point being viewed in Fig. 8.10a on the screen for the left eye is

$$XS(left) = ((X+eye\_span/2)*screen\_distance/(origin\_distance - Z)) - eye\_span/2$$

and for the right is

$$XS(right) = ((X-eye\_span/2)*screen\_distance/(origin\_distance - Z)) + eye\_span/2$$

Fig. 7.10 *a*) The principle of stereoscopic viewing. *b*) Stereoscopic display of a wire-frame cube (see text for details about the stereoscopic viewing glasses)

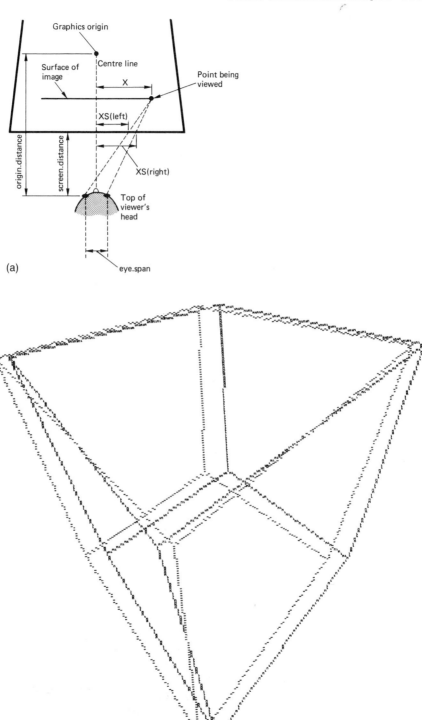

(a)

(b)

Since the upward or downward movement of the eye when looking at any corner of the object is the same for both eyes, the Y-perspective calculation for both eyes is the same as in program *P7.1F*.

Listing 7.10

```
  10  REM****PROGRAM "P7.2"****
  20  REM****WIRE FRAME 3-D DRAWING (STEREOSCOPIC)****

  50  MODE 1

 380  origin_distance=1.2:screen_distance=0.5

 430  eye_span=0.06

 470  GCOL 0,131:CLG:REM WHITE BACKGROUND
 480  REPEAT
 490    PROC_perspective_right:PROC_draw
 500    PROC_perspective_left:PROC_draw

 890  DEF PROC_perspective_right
 900  REM RIGHT EYE PERSPECTIVE
 910  CLG
 920  FOR corner=1 TO corner_no
 930    XS(corner)=((X(corner)-eye_span/2)*screen_distance/(origin_distanc
e-Z(corner)))+eye_span/2
 940    YS(corner)=Y(corner)*screen_distance/(origin_distance-Z(corner))
 950    NEXT corner
 960  GCOL 0,1:REM RED DRAWING
 970  ENDPROC
 980  :
 990  DEF PROC_perspective_left
1000  REM LEFT EYE PERSPECTIVE
1010  FOR corner=1 TO corner_no
1020    XS(corner)=((X(corner)+eye_span/2)*screen_distance/(origin_distanc
e-Z(corner)))-eye_span/2
1030    NEXT corner
1040  VDU 19,2,2;0;:GCOL 0,2:REM GREEN DRAWING
1050  ENDPROC
1060  :
```

If you load *P7.1F* into the computer and modify it in the manner listed in program *P7.2* (*listing 7.10*), you will see the stereoscopic image which, when viewed through coloured lenses, gives a realistic 3-D wire-frame image. The program contains a perspective procedure for each eye (PROC_perspective_right and PROC_perspective_left).

Figure 7.10*b* shows the two images produced on the screen after the cube has been rotated a little way. When viewed through stereoscopic glasses, the impression is very realistic.

An interesting feature of the stereoscopic display is that, when you move your head whilst wearing the glasses, the image also appears to move!

7.14 A Simple Solid Three-dimensional Shape

So far we have dealt with wire-frame objects. If you wish to display a solid 3-D shape on the screen, either you must use techniques which eliminate

Fig. 7.11 A simple solid 3-D shape: *a*) method of specifying the corners and the faces; *b*) display on the monitor

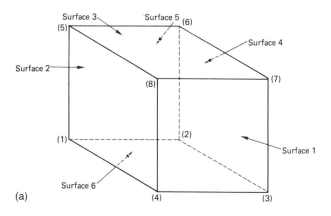

(a)

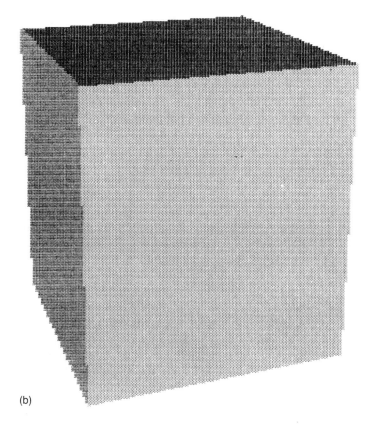

(b)

unwanted surfaces and lines, such as the back faces of the wire-frame object, or you must fill the faces of the object with colour in such a way that hidden surfaces disappear. The former is introduced in section 7.15; the mathematics associated with this type of projection involve a small amount of vector algebra, which is briefly introduced in section 7.15 and is discussed further in Chapter 9. The latter method of colour-filling the faces is much simpler and is described below; this method has its limitations, which become apparent when you run the program.

Suppose that you wish to view the cube in Fig. 7.11*a* in a solid form. It has six surfaces and, when viewing the cube, you can see up to three surfaces at any time (depending on the viewing position). When you have decided which of the three faces are most important to you, you need to provide the computer with data so that it colours each of the six faces, commencing with the three faces you do not wish to see and finishing with the three faces you do wish to see. In this way (and provided that you are looking at the cube from the correct position), the three faces you wish to see obliterate those you do not wish to see.

Since you look at the cube along the Z-axis (see Fig. 7.1), surface 1 in Fig. 7.11*b* must be the final face to be coloured in (since you always see it when the program is first run). Assuming that you wish to rotate the cube in the positive direction of rotation about the X, Y and Z axes respectively, you will see surfaces 1, 2 and 3, with surfaces 4, 5 and 6 being hidden from you. In this event, the program should colour the faces in the following sequence:

6, 5, 4, 3, 2, 1

You can modify program *P7.1F* to accommodate the colour-fill routine by typing in the changes listed in program *P7.3* (*listing 7. 11*).

In this case, Mode 2 has been selected so that you use a different colour for each surface. The DATA in lines 130 onwards is presented in a different format than in program *P7.1F*. To colour-fill a rectangular face, four operations are necessary:

MOVE to the first corner
MOVE to the second corner
PLOT 85 to the third corner
PLOT 85 to the fourth corner

Since the cube has six faces, you need six sets of information relating to four corners, i.e. twenty-four sets of data. This data is provided in lines 160 to 210 inclusive.

The drawing procedure is changed in program *P7.3* to PROC_draw2, which colours in the faces using PLOT instructions; it is therefore necessary for the data relating to each corner to include the value of the PLOT number (PLOT 4 = MOVE, PLOT 85 = fill a triangle with colour). The data for each corner must also include the corner_number and the colour number to be used. Thus the first item of data in line 160 (DATA 4,1,6) means PLOT 4 (MOVE) to corner 1 using colour 6 (cyan). The faces are coloured in the following sequence:

face 6   colour 6 (cyan)
face 5   colour 5 (magenta)
face 4   colour 4 (blue)
face 3   colour 3 (yellow)
face 2   colour 2 (green)
face 1   colour 1 (red)

Line 160 therefore reads as follows
MOVE to corner 1
MOVE to corner 2
PLOT 85 (cyan) to corner 4
PLOT 85 (cyan) to corner 3

Listing 7.11

```
10   REM****PROGRAM "P7.3"****
20   REM****PSEUDO-SOLID 3-D DRAWING****

50   MODE 2

130  REM NUMBER OF PLOT OPERATIONS
140  DATA 24
150  REM PLOT NUMBER,CORNER,COLOUR NUMBER DATA
160  DATA 4,1,6,  4,2,6,  85,4,6,  85,3,6
170  DATA 4,1,5,  4,2,5,  85,5,5,  85,6,5
180  DATA 4,2,4,  4,3,4,  85,6,4,  85,7,4
190  DATA 4,5,3,  4,6,3,  85,8,3,  85,7,3
200  DATA 4,1,2,  4,4,2,  85,5,2,  85,8,2
210  DATA 4,3,1,  4,4,1,  85,7,1,  85,8,1
220  :

460  PROC_plot_ops

500  PROC_draw2

660  DEF PROC_plot_ops
670  REM DIMENSION ARRAYS AND READ PLOT-OP DATA
680  READ plot
690  DIM plot_no(plot),corner(plot),colour_no(plot)
700  FOR line=1 TO plot
710    READ plot_no(line),corner(line),colour_no(line)
720    NEXT line
730  ENDPROC
740  :

780  DEF PROC_draw2
790  CLS
800  FOR line=1 TO plot
810    GCOL 0,colour_no(line)
820    PLOT plot_no(line),scale*XS(corner(line)),scale*YS(corner(line))
830    NEXT line
840  ENDPROC
850  :
```

The effect is quite impressive, and one view of the cube is shown in Fig. 7.11*b*. However, should you rotate the cube either in the "wrong" direction or too far in the "right" direction, the illusion of a solid shape is destroyed because the obscured surfaces appear on the screen.

7.15   Eliminating Hidden Faces from a Wire-frame Object

Hitherto, programs have been based on the simple wire-frame model in program *P7.1F.* We now enter the real world of 3-D modelling in which the hidden faces of simple structures such as the cube are removed from the screen.

To understand the principle involved, you must begin to appreciate (from a mathematical standpoint) which of the faces you can and cannot 'see'. At this point you are briefly introduced to the fascinating area of mathematics known as **vectors** .We mentioned at the beginning of the chapter that we were using a right-handed coordinate system, and a feature of this sytem is that it enables us to mathematically predict which surface of an object is facing you.

The concept of a vector is simple. It is something which has both **magnitude** (size) and **direction**. One example of this is the velocity of an aeroplane, another is the length of an object such as the side of a cube. (*Note:* anything which only has magnitude, such as temperature, is known as a **scalar**.) Hence, the length of each edge of the cube used in earlier programs is a vector since each side has a length of 1 m, and is in a particular direction, i.e. in the X-direction, or the Y-direction, or the Z-direction.

Imagine that you are looking towards the cube in program *P7.1F* in the direction shown in Fig. 7.12. Using right-handed coordinates, the vectors around an **outward-facing surface** can be thought of as pointing in an anticlockwise direction. If a woodscrew is placed so that it points outwards

Fig. 7.12 The normal vector to a surface using right-handed coordinates

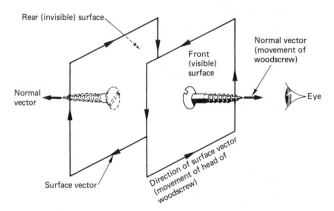

from the surface then, if the screw-head is turned in the direction of the vectors, it would be propelled *towards you*. The direction of movement of the screw is known as the **normal vector**; that is, it is *another vector* which is perpendicularly outwards from the surface.

> *If the screw (the normal vector) moves towards you, then you can see the surface.* It follows from this that, *if the screw moves away from you, then you cannot see the surface.*

For example, a woodscrew with its head placed flat on the rear surface of the cube, whose head is rotated in the direction of the vectors on that surface (see Fig. 7.12) moves away from you; that is the surface is mathematically invisible.

To decide the direction in which the normal vectors point, simply visualize yourself looking at the outward face of the surface in question and imagine the vectors around the edges pointing in an anticlockwise direction. This topic is touched on a little later in this section.

To determine whether or not we can see a surface becomes a matter of deciding whether the normal vector associated with a surface has a *positive mathematical sign* or a *negative sign*. The mathematics of the method are fairly complex, but it is not out of place here to describe the method used to determine the mathematical sign of the normal vector.

Firstly you must know how a vector is evaluated from the data given in the computer program. Now, since you always view the objects in this chapter from the Z-direction, we are only concerned with the X- and Y-values of the vector. Consider for the moment the vector in Fig. 7.13*a* which starts at the point X1,Y1 and ends at X2,Y2. The X-component of the vector is given by

$$\text{X-component} = \text{final X component} - \text{initial X component}$$
$$= X2 - X1$$

and its Y-component is

$$\text{Y-component} = \text{final Y component} - \text{initial Y component}$$
$$= Y2 - Y1$$

Fig. 7.13 *a*) Determining the length of a vector. *b*) Front face vectors. *c*) Rear face vectors

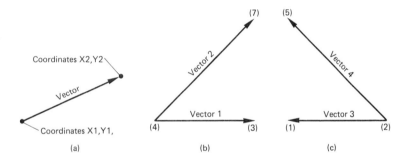

Now, consider the cube in Fig. 7.11*a*; the corners on the front face are (4), (3), (7) and (8). To determine the value of the vector which is normal to a point on the surface, i.e. the vector in the Z-direction (which may be either towards you or away from you), we need information about *any two vectors* on the surface. We will use corners (4), (3) and (7) as shown in Fig. 7.13*b*. The X- and Y- components of these corners are as follows (see also program *P7.1A* to *P7.1F*):

For corner (4)   X = −0.5, Y = −0.5
For corner (3)   X = 0.5, Y = −0.5
For corner (7)   X = 0.5, Y = 0.5

The X component of vector 1 is

X of corner (3) − X of corner (4) = 0.5 − (−0.5) = 1

The Y component of vector 1 is

Y of corner (3) − Y of corner (4) = −0.5 − (−0.5) = 0

Similarly, you can show that

X component of vector 2 = 1

and

Y component of vector 2 = 1

Also, it can be shown using vector algebra that the component of the vector in the Z-direction, i.e. the normal vector to the X-Y surface is given by

(X component of vector 1 ∗ Y component of vector 2)
    − (X component of vector 2 ∗ Y component of vector 1)

This is known as the **vector cross-product** of vectors 1 and 2. The numerical value of this cross-product for the front face is

$$(1 * 1) \times (1 * 0) = +1$$

The rule for this cross-product is that

If it has a positive sign, then you can see the surface. If it has a negative sign, you cannot see the surface.

Since the cross-product for the front face is positive, you can see the surface and the computer is allowed to draw it on the screen.

Let us now investigate the cross-product for the rear face of the cube (see Fig. 7.14). This surface has corners (2), (1), (5) and (6); however from your vantage point which faces the front face, the vectors on the rear face point in the opposite direction to those on the front face (see also Fig. 7.12). We will use corners (2), (1) and (5) as shown in Fig. 7.13c. The corresponding X and Y coordinates for these corners are

For corner (2)   X = 0.5, Y = −0.5
For corner (1)   X = −0.5, Y = −0.5
For corner (5)   X = −0.5, Y = 0.5

Fig. 7.14 The faces of the cube in program P7.4 and the directions of the vectors along the edges of the faces (using right-handed coordinates)

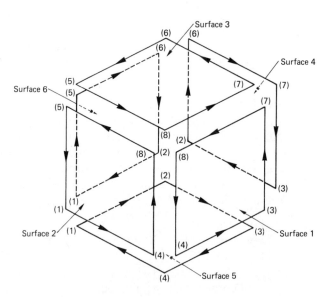

Using the method described above to calculate the X- and Y-components of vectors 3 and 4 (Fig. 7.13c), we get

X component of vector 3 = −0.5 − 0.5 = −1
Y component of vector 3 = −0.5 − (−0.5) = 0
X component of vector 4 = −0.5 − 0.5 = −1
X component of vector 4 = 0.5 − (−0.5) = 1

and the component of the vector in the Z-direction, i.e. the vector cross-product of vectors 3 and 4 is

(X component of vector 3 $*$ Y component of vector 4)
  $-$ (X component of vector 4 $*$ Y component of vector 3)
$= [(-1) * 1] - [(-1) * 0] = -1 + 0 = -1$

Since the cross-product for the rear surface has a negative sign, you cannot see the surface containing corners (2), (1), (5) and (6), and the computer must be prevented from displaying it on the monitor.

The above calculations ignore the effects of perspective, and are simplified compared with the numerical values used by the computer (which does, of course, account for perspective). However, the calculations above illustrate the principles involved.

Program *P7.4* (*listing 7.12*) lists the modifications needed to program *P7.1F* in order to eliminate hidden surfaces on a 'convex' shape. The coordinates of the cube are not listed in *P7.4* since they are the same as those used in program *P7.1F*. However, the data relating to the number of lines and the corners to be joined in *P7.1F* is replaced in *P7.4* by information referring to the surfaces on the shape (this form of data is necessary in order that the computer can calculate the vector sizes and cross-products). Line 140 in the program gives two items of data which are respectively the number of surfaces (6) and the number of corners per surface (4).

You should note that, in any programs you may develop using this programming technique,

each surface must have at least three corners, and the first three corners in any surface must not lie in a straight line.

The reason for this is that these conditions must be satisfied before the computer can calculate the normal vector for each surface.

Having read the number of corners and their coordinates, PROC_surfaces reads the values described above as total_surfaces (6) and corners_per_surface (4), and used them to DIMension an array called normal_z in line 690 and an array called surface in line 700. The former is used to store the value of the vector cross-products for each of the six surfaces of the cube; the latter stores the corner numbers taken in an anticlockwise direction associated with each surface (this needs to be done because we are using the right-handed coordinate system).

Figure 7.14 shows an exploded view of the cube, in which the faces and corners are numbered. Lines 160 and 170 of the program contain the data relating to the corners contained in each surface. For example, the corners associated with surface 1 are listed as (4), (3), (7) and (8); in fact, you can use *any corner* as the starting point, but you *must follow* the correct direction for the vectors, i.e. you could use the sequence (7), (8), (4), (3) or the sequence (3), (7), (8), (4).

A useful point to note is that the vector direction associated with, say, the top edge of surface 1 (which is from right to left in Fig. 7.14) is reversed in the adjacent surface (surface 3, in which the direction is from left to right); this applies to every vector along every edge of every face.

The REPEAT-UNTIL loop in lines 480–530 in the original listing now

Listing 7.12

```
  10  REM****PROGRAM "P7.4"****
  20  REM****SOLID 3-D DRAWING WITH HIDDEN FACES OMITTED****

 130  REM NUMBER OF SURFACES AND CORNERS PER SURFACE
 140  DATA 6,4
 150  REM CORNERS ON EACH SURFACE (ANTICLOCKWISE)
 160  DATA 4,3,7,8,  1,4,8,5,  6,5,8,7
 170  DATA 3,2,6,7,  3,4,1,2,  5,6,2,1
 180 :

 460  PROC_surfaces

 500  PROC_hidden_surfaces
 510  PROC_visible_surfaces

 660  DEF PROC_surfaces
 670  REM READ SURFACE CORNER NUMBERS (ANICLOCKWISE)
 680  READ total_surfaces,corners_per_surface
 690  DIM normal_z(total_surfaces)
 700  DIM surface(total_surfaces,corners_per_surface)
 710  FOR surface_number=1 TO total_surfaces
 720    FOR corner_number=1 TO corners_per_surface
 730      READ surface(surface_number,corner_number)
 740      NEXT corner_number
 750    NEXT surface_number
 760  ENDPROC
 770 :
 780  DEF PROC_draw3
 790  REM DRAW VISIBLE SURFACES
 800  switch=0:REM switch PREVENTS INFINITE LOOP
 810  FOR corner=1 TO corners_per_surface
 820    IF switch=1 ENDPROC
 830    MOVE scale*XS(surface(surface_number,corner)),scale*YS(surface(sur
face_number,corner))
 840    IF corner=corners_per_surface THEN corner=0:switch=1
 850    DRAW scale*XS(surface(surface_number,corner+1)),scale*YS(surface(s
urface_number,corner+1))
 860    NEXT corner
 870  ENDPROC
 880 :

1680  DEF PROC_hidden_surfaces
1690  REM CALCULATE NORMAL-Z VECTOR FOR EACH SURFACE
1700  FOR surface_number=1 TO total_surfaces
1710    corner1=surface(surface_number,1):corner2=surface(surface_number,2
):corner3=surface(surface_number,3)
1720    X1=XS(corner1):X2=XS(corner2):X3=XS(corner3)
1730    Y1=YS(corner1):Y2=YS(corner2):Y3=YS(corner3)
```

```
1740     X21=X2-X1:X31=X3-X1:Y21=Y2-Y1:Y31=Y3-Y1
1750     normal_z(surface_number)=X21*Y31-X31*Y21
1760    NEXT surface_number
1770  ENDPROC
1780  :
1790  DEF PROC_visible_surfaces
1800  REM CHECK FOR VISIBLE SURFACES
1810  CLG
1820  PRINT TAB(0,0);"VISIBLE SURFACES"
1830  FOR surface_number=1 TO total_surfaces
1840    IF normal_z(surface_number)>0 THEN PROC_draw3:PRINT;surface_number
1850     NEXT surface_number
1860  ENDPROC
1870  :
```

Fig. 7.15 The monitor
display of a 3-D cube with
hidden surfaces removed

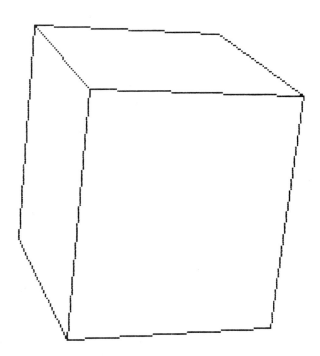

contains lines 500 and 510 in *P7.4* (see *listing 7.12*), which call on
PROC_hidden_surfaces and PROC_visible_surfaces to determine whether
you can see a particular surface. The function of PROC_hidden_surfaces
is, for the position in which you wish to view the cube, to calculate the
normal vector for each surface. PROC_visible_surfaces (uses the sign of
the normal vector to decide whether the surface can be seen. If the surface

can be seen, PROC_draw3 not only draws the surface but also prints the number of the surface on the screen. PROC_draw3 has a parameter called "switch" in it; this is simply a value which is set to 1 whenever the fourth corner in the surface is reached. When this occurs, the next line drawn by the computer connects the fourth corner in the surface to the first corner, completing the surface.

Fig. 7.15 shows a typical display provided by program *P7.4*. You will find that the extra demand placed on the computer by the calculations performed by this program imposes a time penalty, resulting in a reduction of speed when compared with program *P7.1F*.

7.16   Solid Three-dimensional Drawing with a Figure Embossed on one Face

Program *P7.4* can be modified to allow you to "emboss" a shape on one face (or all faces for that matter!). The technique adopted is a simple extension of the original process.

The embossed shape is defined as a "surface", and it must conform to the definition of a surface adopted by the remainder of the program; that is, it must have four corners and the first three must not be in a straight line. The shape to be embossed is, in this case, a triangle. But wait a moment, you say, a triangle only has three corners; quite true, but if you define the "fourth" corner of the surface (the triangle) to be at the same position as the third corner, then you satisfy the definition of a surface within program *P7.4*.

The modifications to program *P7.4* which allow you to emboss a triangle on one face are listed in *P7.4B* (*listing 7.13*). You will see that line 80 specifies that there are 12 corners (8 in the cube and 4 in the triangle), and line 115 contains the coordinates of the triangle (notice that the third and fourth corners are identical!) — see Fig. 7.16*a*. Line 140 specifies that there are 7 surfaces, surface 7 being the triangle which is embossed on

Listing 7.13

```
10  REM****PROGRAM "P7.4B"****
20  REM****SOLID 3-D DRAWING WITH CHARACTER ON ONE FACE****

70  REM NUMBER OF CORNERS
80  DATA 12
90  REM COORDINATES OF CORNERS
100 DATA -0.5,-0.5,-0.5,  0.5,-0.5,-0.5,  0.5,-0.5,0.5,  -0.5,-0.5,0.5
110 DATA -0.5,0.5,-0.5,  0.5,0.5,-0.5,  0.5,0.5,0.5,  -0.5,0.5,0.5
115 DATA -0.3,-0.3,0.5,  0.3,-0.3,0.5,  0,0.3,0.5,  0,0.3,0.5
120 :
130 REM NUMBER OF SURFACES AND CORNERS PER SURFACE
140 DATA 7,4
150 REM CORNERS ON EACH SURFACE (ANTICLOCKWISE)
160 DATA 4,3,7,8,  1,4,8,5,  6,5,8,7
170 DATA 3,2,6,7,  3,4,1,2,  5,6,2,1
180 DATA 9,10,11,12
190 :
```

Fig. 7.16 *a*) Defining a
triangle to be embossed on
one face of a 3-D cube. *b*)
One display on the monitor

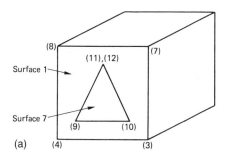

(a)

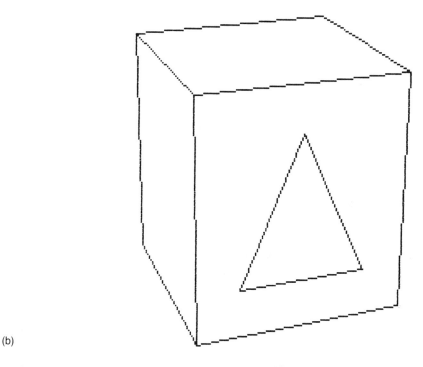

(b)

surface 1 of the cube. That is, surface 1 and surface 7 are simultaneously
either visible or invisible. The final modification in line 180 lists the "four"
corners of the embossed triangle in an anticlockwise direction. Figure
7.16*b* shows one form of display on the monitor.

7.17 Hidden Lines

So far you have looked at the removal of hidden surfaces from an object.
However, the real world is rather more complex, as depicted in the
diagram in Fig. 7.17.

Whilst you can write a program which will remove the hidden surfaces
from house A, the front of house B is only partly visible to the human eye.

Fig. 7.17 Hidden lines on a
diagram

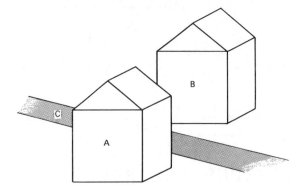

Fig. 7.18 *a*) One-point, *b*)
two-point, *c*) three-point
perspective projection

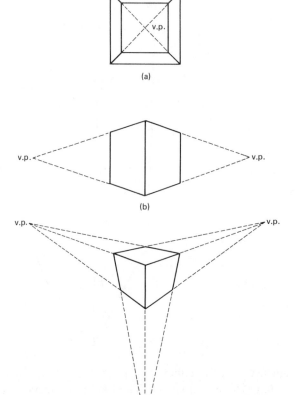

Similarly, road C becomes invisible when it passes behind house A.
Program *P7.4* cannot deal with this form of diagram.

A simple solution to this problem is to draw house B in colour, followed
by road C, followed by house A. Each colour covers up anything behind it
and makes it vanish. Hoever, this treatment has its limitations and does not

truly eliminate hidden lines for all viewing angles. Strictly speaking, the computer needs a **depth-of-view algorithm** to test whether it can see any or all of house B and road C. The treatment of this problem is beyond the scope of this book, but it is an interesting exercise you may like to pursue.

7.18 Other Forms of Projection

Architectural and engineering draughtsmen use several forms of projection to illustrate diagrams. You have already met **orthographic projection** (see program *P7.1A*) in which you view a complete face of the object; perspective is not involved in this method of projection.

The majority of this chapter has been concerned with **perspective projection** in which the edges of the object appear to have one, two or three vanishing points, each marked as v.p. in diagrams (a), (b) and (c), respectively, of Fig. 7.18.

Yet another form of projection is **isometric projection** (see Fig. 7.19) in which the axes are inclined to each other at an angle of 120°, with two of the axes being at 30° to the horizontal. This type of projection does not involve perspective, and *the length of each edge is shortened from its 3-D length by the same amount.* Two variants of this form of projection are **dimetric projection** and **axometric projection** or **trimetric projection** in which, respectively, two edges and three edges are shortened by differing amounts. In trimetric projection the axes are not equally inclined to the plane of projection.

Fig. 7.19 Isometric projection

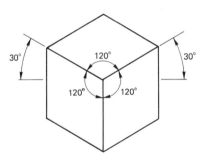

Fig. 7.20 Oblique projection

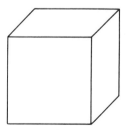

Yet another form of projection favoured by engineers is **oblique projection** (see Fig. 7.20). In this projection, the front elevation lies in the surface being viewed, other surfaces being at an angle to it. Once again, perspective is not involved.

You may like to take up the challenge of producing programs which enable you to display diagrams using these (and other) forms of projection.

A Computer-aided Drawing Package

8.1 Typical Functions Needed in a Computer-aided Drawing Package

The needs of a computer-aided drawing (CAD) program are many and varied. The following (and more) are contained in the program developed in this chapter.

1. Rubber band line drawing of lines, rectangles, polygons and circles.
2. Icon drawing.
3. Picking and dragging icons and other shapes.
4. Writing text at an angle on the screen.
5. Cross-hatching and filling shapes.
6. Drawing an arc.
7. Drawing and deleting a graticule.
8. Measuring the length and angle of a line.
9. Clearing the text window and/or the graphics window.
10. Providing a rubber which allows you to selectively rub out part of the graphics.
11. Drawing special features such as a dot, or a blob, or a dimensioning arrow (at any angle).
12. Saving the picture on the screen on either tape or disc.
13. Loading a picture which has been saved on tape or disc.

All the above features are obained using the **function keys** of the BBC micro; the method of programming these keys is described in section 8.4. In all, *over thirty user-defined keys are used, with provision for another ten* (memory space permitting).

The CAD program is quite lengthy and, whilst it is not possible to give a detailed description of each procedure, the general purpose of each one of them is outlined. It will prove an interesting and educational exercise for you to study and understand (and even improve!) the operation of each procedure.

8.2 Screen MODE Selection

A CAD program needs the best available line thickness, i.e. the smallest pixel size consistent with the amount of free memory to allow a long program to be stored. For the program in this chapter, MODE 4, which is a 2-colour mode, is the best. The default colour is white on a black background; you can alter this by changing some of the instructions in the executive program (or, at a later stage, you can modify the program to select your own foreground and background colours using a user-defined key).

8.3 The Executive Program

The executive of the CAD program (program *P8* see *listing 8.1*) is only ten lines long, the first four lines being generally similar to programs earlier in the book.

Line 50 allocates 31 bytes in the memory to the variable called "name". Its purpose is to allow you to give a name to the drawing you wish to save on tape or disc. You should note the difference between a DIM of this type which simply reserves a number of bytes in the memory of the computer, and DIMensioning an array in the BASIC language.

Listing 8.1

```
10  REM****PROGRAM "P8"****
20  REM****COMPUTER AIDED DRAWING PROGRAM****
30  *TV0,1
40  MODE 4
50  DIM name 30
60  PROC_initialize
70  ON ERROR PROC_error
80  PROC_keys
90  MODE 4:VDU 26:*FX4,0
100 END
110 :
120 DEF PROC_error
130 VDU4:CLS:REPORT:PRINT" AT LINE ";ERL
140 PRINT TAB(0,2)"Do you wish to continue (Y/N)"
150 REPEAT:ans$=GET$:UNTIL INSTR("YyNn",ans$)>0
160 IF ans$="Y" OR ans$="y" CLS:VDU5:ENDPROC
170 error=1:ENDPROC
180 :
190 DEF PROC_initialize
200 VDU23;8202;0;0;0;
210 *FX 4,2
220 *FX 225,130
230 *FX 226,146
240 *FX 227,162
250 *FX 228,178
260 x=445:y=421:line=0:circle=0:square=0:erase=0:n=0:poly=0:ruler=0:move
_poly=0:arc=0:icon=0:error=0
270 MOVE 0,0:DRAW 0,840:DRAW890,840:DRAW 890,0:DRAW 0,0
280 PROC_icon_frame
290 VDU 28,0,4,39,0
300 ENDPROC
310 :
320 DEF PROC_icon_frame
330 VDU 24,890;0;1240;844;
340 MOVE 890,840:DRAW 1240,840:DRAW 1240,0:DRAW 890,0:DRAW 890,840
350 FOR N=1 TO 3
360   MOVE 890,N*210:DRAW 1240,N*210
```

```
370    NEXT N
380    PRINT TAB(39,8);"1";TAB(39,15);"2";TAB(39,22);"3";TAB(39,28);"4";TAB
(0,0)
390    VDU 24,6;6;884;836;:ENDPROC
400    :
410    DEF PROC_keys
420    REPEAT
430      key=INKEY(0)
440      *FX 15,0
450      IF line=0 AND square=0 AND circle=0 AND poly=0 AND erase=0 AND rul
er=0 AND arc=0 xstart=x:ystart=y
460      test=key-129
470      ON test GOTO 600,610,620,630,640,650,660,670,680,690,430,1050,700,
710,720,730 ELSE 480
480      ON test-16 GOTO 740,750,760,770,780,790,800,810,820,830,430,1050,8
40,850,860,870 ELSE 490
490      ON test-32 GOTO 1080,880,890,900,910,920,930,940,950,960,430,1050,
970,980,990,1000 ELSE 500
500      ON test-48 GOTO 1050,1050,1050,1050,1050,1050,1050,1050,1050,1050,
430,1050,1010,1020,1030,1040 ELSE 510


510    IF line=1 PROC_line:PROC_cursor
520    IF square=1 PROC_rubber_square:PROC_cursor
530    IF erase=1 PROC_erase_on:PROC_cursor
540    IF circle=1 PROC_rubber_circle:PROC_cursor
550    IF poly=1 PROC_rubber_poly:PROC_cursor
560    IF ruler<>0 PROC_ruler:PROC_cursor
570    IF move_poly=1 PROC_move_poly1:PROC_cursor
580    IF icon<>0 PROC_rubber_icon:PROC_cursor
590    GOTO 1050
600    PROC_save:GOTO 1050
610    PROC_line:GOTO 1050
620    PROC_rubber_circle:GOTO 1050
630    PROC_rubber_poly:GOTO 1050
640    PROC_rubber_square:GOTO 1050
650    PROC_erase_on:GOTO 1050
660    PROC_text:GOTO 1050
670    m=1:PROC_hatch:GOTO 1050
680    PROC_start_arc:GOTO 1050
690    icon=NOT icon:PROC_icon:GOTO 1050
700    x=x-24:GOTO 1050
710    x=x+24:GOTO 1050
720    y=y-24:GOTO 1050
730    y=y+24:GOTO 1050
740    PROC_load:GOTO 1050
750    PROC_fix_line:GOTO 1050
760    PROC_fix_poly:GOTO 1050
770    PROC_move_poly1:GOTO 1050
```

```
 780  PROC_fix_square:GOTO 1050
 790  PROC_erase_off:GOTO 1050
 800  VDU4:CLS:VDU5:GOTO 1050
 810  m=2:PROC_hatch:GOTO 1050
 820  PROC_arc_rad:GOTO 1050
 830  PROC_centre:GOTO 1050
 840  x=x-4:GOTO 1050
 850  x=x+4:GOTO 1050
 860  y=y-4:GOTO 1050
 870  y=y+4:GOTO 1050
 880  PROC_off:GOTO 1050
 890  PROC_dot:GOTO 1050
 900  PROC_blob:GOTO 1050
 910  PROC_arrow:GOTO 1050
 920  CLG:GOTO 1050
 930  xstart=x:ystart=y:ruler=NOT ruler:PROC_ruler:GOTO 1050
 940  PROC_fill:GOTO 1050
 950  PROC_draw_arc:GOTO 1050
 960  PROC_grat:GOTO 1050
 970  step=-12:PROC_CL_R:GOTO 1050
 980  step=12:PROC_CL_R:GOTO 1050
 990  step=-12:PROC_CL_U:GOTO 1050
1000  step=12:PROC_CL_U:GOTO 1050
1010  step=-12:PROC_lin_R:GOTO 1050
1020  step=12:PROC_lin_R:GOTO 1050
1030  step=-12:PROC_lin_U:GOTO 1050
1040  step=12:PROC_lin_U:GOTO 1050
1050  PROC_cursor
1060  IF error=1 ENDPROC
1070  UNTIL 1=2
1080  ENDPROC
1090 :


1100  DEF PROC_delay
1110  FOR T= 1 TO 200:NEXT T
1120  ENDPROC
1130 :
1140  DEF PROC_cursor
1150  IF x<6 x=6
1160  IF x>884 x=884
1170  IF y<6 y=6
1180  IF y>836 y=836
1190  PROC_cross:PROC_cross:ENDPROC
1200 :
1210  DEF PROC_cross
1220 MOVE x,y+12:PLOT 6,x,y-12:MOVE x-12,y:PLOT 6,x+12,y:ENDPROC
1230 :
1240  DEF PROC_centre
```

```
1250  x=445:y=421:ENDPROC
1260 :
1270  DEF PROC_line
1280  IF line=0 xstart=x:ystart=y
1290  MOVE xstart,ystart:PLOT 6,x,y:PROC_delay:MOVE xstart,ystart:PLOT 6,x
,y:line=1
1300  IF arc=0 PROC_calc:VDU4:CLS:PRINT TAB(0,1)"Length=";len2;" Angle=";a
ng2;" degrees":VDU5
1310  ENDPROC
1320 :
1330  DEF PROC_fix_line
1340  PROC_off:MOVE xstart,ystart:DRAW x,y:ENDPROC
1350 :
1360  DEF PROC_off
1370  line=0:square=0:circle=0:poly=0:move_poly=0:icon=0:ENDPROC
1380 :
1390  DEF PROC_dot
1400  MOVE x,y:DRAW x,y:ENDPROC
1410 :
1420  DEF PROC_rubber_square
1430  IF square=0 xstart=x:ystart=y
1440  GCOL 4,1:PROC_square:PROC_delay:PROC_square:GCOL 0,1
1450  PROC_calc:VDU4:CLS:PRINT TAB(0,1)"Width=";X;" Height=";Y:VDU5:ENDPRO
C
1460 :
1470  DEF PROC_square
1480  MOVE xstart,ystart:DRAW x,ystart:DRAW x,y:DRAW xstart,y:DRAW xstart,
ystart:square=1:ENDPROC
1490 :
1500  DEF PROC_fix_square
1510  PROC_square:square=0:ENDPROC
1520  ENDPROC
1530 :
1540  DEF PROC_erase_on
1550  erase=1
1560  IF x<16 x=16
1570  IF x>872 x=872
1580  IF y<16 y=16
1590  IF y>824 y=824
1600  MOVE x-12,y-12:DRAW x-12,y+12:DRAW x+12,y+12:DRAW x+12,y-12:DRAW x-1
2,y-12
1610  VDU 24,x-12;y-12;x+12;y+12;
1620  VDU 16
1630  VDU 24,6;6;884;836;:ENDPROC
1640 :


1650  DEF PROC_erase_off
1660  erase=0:VDU 24,6;6;884;836;:ENDPROC
```

```
1670 :
1680  DEF PROC_rubber_circle
1690  IF poly=0 theta=2*PI/30:xcentre=x:ycentre=y:poly=1
1700  GCOL4,1:PROC_poly:PROC_delay:PROC_poly:GCOL0,1:ENDPROC
1710 :
1720  DEF PROC_poly
1730  X=x-xcentre:Y=y-ycentre:rad=SQR(X^2+Y^2)
1740  IF X=0 PROC_zero ELSE ang=ATN(Y/X)
1750  IF X<0 ang=ang+PI
1760  VDU4:CLS:PRINT TAB(0,2)"Angle = ";INT(DEG(ang)*100+.5)/100," Radius
= ";INT(rad*100+.5)/100:PRINT TAB(0,3)"Cursor x=";x,"Cursor y=";y:VDU5
1770  IF rad<10 ENDPROC
1780  MOVE x,y
1790  FOR alpha=ang TO (2*PI+ang+.05) STEP theta
1800    X=rad*COS(alpha):Y=rad*SIN(alpha)
1810    DRAW X+xcentre,Y+ycentre:NEXT alpha:ENDPROC
1820 :
1830  DEF PROC_fix_poly
1840  IF poly=1:poly=0:PROC_poly
1850  IF move_poly=1:move_poly=0:PROC_move_poly2
1860  ENDPROC
1870 :
1880  DEF PROC_rubber_poly
1890  IF poly=0 VDU4:CLS:INPUT TAB(0,1)"Number of sides? "sides:VDU5:theta
=2*PI/sides:xcentre=x:ycentre=y:poly=1
1900  GCOL 4,1:PROC_poly:PROC_delay:PROC_poly:GCOL 0,1:ENDPROC
1910 :
1920  DEF PROC_zero
1930  IF Y=0 ang=0
1940  IF Y>0 ang=PI/2
1950  IF Y<0 ang=3*PI/2
1960  ENDPROC
1970 :
1980  DEF PROC_move_poly1
1990  IF move_poly=0:poly=0:move_poly=1:x=xcentre:y=ycentre
2000  GCOL 4,1:PROC_move_poly2:PROC_delay:PROC_move_poly2:GCOL 0,1:ENDPROC
2010 :
2020  DEF PROC_move_poly2
2030  MOVE X+x,Y+y
2040  FOR alpha=ang TO (2*PI+ang+.05) STEP theta
2050    X=rad*COS(alpha):Y=rad*SIN(alpha)
2060    DRAW X+x,Y+y:NEXT alpha:ENDPROC
2070 :


2080  DEF PROC_ruler
2090  IF ruler=0 VDU4:PRINT TAB(0,0)"Ruler OFF":VDU5:ENDPROC
2100  PROC_calc:PROC_cursor
2110  VDU4:CLS:PRINT TAB(0,0)"Ruler ON ";TAB(0,1)"Cursor position: x=";x,"
y=";y
```

```
2120  PRINT TAB(0,2)"Length = ";INT(len*100+.5)/100:PRINT TAB(0,3)"Angle =
";INT(DEG(ang)*100+.5)/100;" degrees":VDU5
2130  ENDPROC
2140 :
2150  DEF PROC_fill
2160  xstart=x:ystart=y:fill=0
2170  IF POINT(x,y)=1 ENDPROC
2180  PROC_dot
2190  FOR N=1 TO 2
2200    IF N=1 n=4 ELSE n=-4
2210    REPEAT
2220      ypoint=POINT(x,y+n)
2230      IF ypoint<>0 THEN fill=1
2240      IF fill=0 y=y+n:MOVE x,y:PROC_dot
2250      UNTIL fill=1
2260    MOVE xstart,ystart:x=xstart:y=ystart:fill=0
2270    NEXT N
2280  x=x+4:y=ystart:xpoint=POINT(x,y)
2290  IF xpoint<>0 x=xstart:GOTO 2310
2300  GOTO 2160
2310  MOVE x,y:PROC_cursor:ENDPROC
2320 :
2330  DEF PROC_clear_icons
2340  VDU 24,890;0;1240;894;:CLG:PROC_icon_frame:CLS:MOVE 1100,0:DRAW 1100
,844:VDU 24,890;0;1240;894;:ENDPROC
2350 :
2360  DEF PROC_hatch
2370  xstart=x:ystart=y:hatch=0
2380  IF POINT(x,y)<>0 ENDPROC
2390  PROC_dot
2400  IF m=1 r=4:u=4
2410  IF m=2 r=-4:u=4
2420  FOR N=1 TO 2
2430    IF N=2 r=-r:u=-u
2440    REPEAT
2450      xpoint=POINT(x+r,y):ypoint=POINT(x,y+u):xypoint=POINT(x+r,y+u)
2460      IF (xpoint<>0 AND ypoint<>0) OR xypoint<>0 hatch=1
2470      IF hatch=0 x=x+r:y=y+u:MOVE x,y:PROC_dot
2480      UNTIL hatch=1
2490    x=xstart:y=ystart:hatch=0
2500    NEXT N
2510  x=xstart:y=ystart:move=0
2520  REPEAT
2530    move=move+1
2540    x=x+4:xpoint=POINT(x,y)
2550    IF xpoint<>0 x=xstart:y=ystart:move=6
2560    UNTIL move=6
2570  IF xpoint<>0 GOTO 2590
2580  GOTO 2370
```

```
2590   MOVE x,y:PROC_cursor:ENDPROC
2600 :



2610   DEF PROC_blob
2620   MOVE x-4,y+4:DRAW x+4,y+4:DRAW x+4,y-4:DRAW x-4,y-4:DRAW x-4,y+4:PRO
C_dot:ENDPROC
2630 :
2640   DEF PROC_arrow
2650   VDU4:CLS:PRINT TAB(0,1)"Angle in which the arrow points"
2660   INPUT TAB(0,3)"in degrees = "ang:CLS:VDU5:ang=ang+180
2670   x1=16*COS(RAD(ang+30)):y1=16*SIN(RAD(ang+30)):x2=16*COS(RAD(ang-30))
:y2=16*SIN(RAD(ang-30))
2680   MOVE x+x1,y+y1:MOVE x,y:PLOT 85,x+x2,y+y2:ENDPROC
2690 :
2700   DEF PROC_text
2710   PROC_cross
2720   VDU4:CLS:PRINT TAB(0,1)"Type in text string":INPUT TAB(0,2) str$
2730   IF LEN(str$)=1 CLS:VDU5:PROC_cross:MOVE x,y:PRINT str$:ENDPROC
2740   PRINT TAB(0,3)"Angle of text (in the range 90 to -90"
2750   INPUT TAB(0,4)"degrees) = "angt:sgn=SGN(angt):CLS:VDU5
2760   PROC_cross
2770   IF angt>90.01 OR angt<-90.01 ENDPROC
2780   IF angt=90 OR angt=-90 OR angt=270 PROC_string3:ENDPROC
2790   IF angt>45 AND angt<90 PROC_string2:ENDPROC
2800   IF angt<-45 AND angt>=-90 angt=angt+180:PROC_string2:ENDPROC
2810   IF angt<=45 OR angt<=-45 PROC_string1:ENDPROC
2820 :
2830   DEF PROC_string1
2840   FOR N=1 TO LEN(str$)
2850     MOVE x+32*(N-1),y+32*(N-1)*TAN(RAD(angt)):PRINT MID$(str$,N,1):NEX
T N
2860   ENDPROC
2870 :
2880   DEF PROC_string2
2890   FOR N=1 TO LEN(str$)
2900     MOVE x+sgn*32*(N-1)/TAN(RAD(angt)),y+sgn*32*(N-1):PRINT MID$(str$,
N,1):NEXT N:ENDPROC
2910 :
2920   DEF PROC_string3
2930   FOR N=1 TO LEN(str$)
2940     MOVE x,y-32*(N-1):PRINT MID$(str$,N,1):NEXT N:ENDPROC
2950 :
2960   DEF PROC_CL_R
2970   MOVE x,y:x=x+step:DRAW x,y:x=x+step:MOVE x,y
2980   FOR N=1 TO 6
2990     x=x+step:DRAW x,y
3000     NEXT N:x=x+step:ENDPROC
```

```
3010 :
3020  DEF PROC_CL_U
3030  MOVE x,y:y=y+step:DRAW x,y:y=y+step:MOVE x,y
3040  FOR N=1 TO 6
3050    y=y+step:DRAW x,y
3060    NEXT N:y=y+step:ENDPROC
3070 :
3080  DEF PROC_calc
3090  X=x-xstart:Y=y-ystart:len=SQR(X^2+Y^2)
3100  IF X=0 PROC_zero ELSE ang=ATN(Y/X)
3110  IF X<0 ang=ang+PI
3120  len2=INT(100*len+.5)/100:ang2=INT(DEG(100*ang))/100
3130  ENDPROC
3140 :
3150  DEF PROC_start_arc
3160  xstart=x:ystart=y:GCOL 4,1:PROC_dot:GCOL 0,1
3170  IF arc=1 arc=0:ENDPROC
3180  VDU4:CLS:PRINT TAB(0,0)"Arc centre: x=";x;" y=";y:VDU5:arc=1:ENDPROC
3190 :
3200  DEF PROC_arc_rad
3210  x1=x:y1=y:PROC_dot:PROC_calc:rad=len:line=1:PROC_line
3220  IF ang<0 ang=ang+2*PI
3230  ang1=ang:VDU4
3240  PRINT TAB(0,1)"Radius = ";INT(rad*100+.5)/100;"  Angle 1 = ";INT(DEG
(ang1*100))/100;" degrees":VDU5:ENDPROC
3250 :
3260  DEF PROC_draw_arc
3270  x2=x:y2=y:PROC_dot:PROC_calc
3280  IF ang<0 ang=ang+2*PI
3290  ang2=ang
3300  IF ang2=0 ang2=2*PI
3310  arc_ang=ang2-ang1
3320  VDU4:PRINT TAB(0,2)"Angle 2 =";INT(DEG(ang2*100))/100;" degrees";TAB
(0,3)"Arc angle = ";INT(DEG(arc_ang*100))/100;" degrees":VDU5
3330  IF arc_ang<0 arc_ang=2*PI-ang1+ang2
3340  VDU4:PRINT TAB(0,2)"Angle 2 =";INT(DEG(ang2*100))/100;" degrees";TAB
(0,3)"Arc angle = ";INT(DEG(arc_ang*100))/100;" degrees":VDU5
3350  arc_step=arc_ang/INT(.5+arc_ang*36/2*PI)
3360  MOVE x1,y1
3370  IF ang1>3*PI/2 AND ang2>3*PI/2 AND ang2<2*PI GOTO 3400
3380  IF ang1>3*PI/2 THEN ang1=-2*PI+ang1
3390  IF ang1<=3*PI/2 AND ang2>0 AND (ang2-ang1<0) PROC_last_quad:GOTO 344
0
3400  FOR alpha=ang1 TO ang2 STEP arc_step
3410    X=rad*COS(alpha):Y=rad*SIN(alpha)
3420    DRAW X+xstart,Y+ystart:NEXT alpha
3430  IF arc_ang=2*PI GOTO 3450
3440  x=x2:y=y2:GCOL 4,1:PROC_dot:GCOL 0,1
```

```
3450  x=xstart:y=ystart:PROC_start_arc:arc=0:line=0:ENDPROC
3460 :


3470  DEF PROC_last_quad
3480  FOR alpha=ang1 TO 2*PI+.05 STEP arc_step
3490    X=rad*COS(alpha):Y=rad*SIN(alpha)
3500    DRAW X+xstart,Y+ystart:NEXT alpha
3510  MOVE xstart+rad,ystart
3520  FOR alpha=0TO ang2 STEP arc_step
3530    X=rad*COS(alpha):Y=rad*SIN(alpha)
3540    DRAW X+xstart,Y+ystart:NEXT alpha
3550  ENDPROC
3560 :
3570  DEF PROC_icon
3580  IF icon=0 PROC_fix_icon:ENDPROC
3590  xstart=x:ystart=y:PROC_cross
3600  VDU4:CLS:PRINT TAB(0,1)"SELECT ICON GROUP";TAB(0,2)"House (1), Circu
its (2), Circuits (3)"
3610  INPUT TAB(0,4)"Your choice (1,2 or 3) = "select1:CLS:PROC_clear_icon
s:PROC_icons
3620  INPUT TAB(0,1)"Your selected icon (1,2,3 or 4) = "select2:CLS:VDU5
3630  VDU 24,6;6;884;836;;x=xstart:y=ystart:PROC_cross:ENDPROC
3640 :
3650  DEF PROC_icons
3660  IF select1=1 x=910:y=640:PROC_icon11:y=450:PROC_icon12:y=260:PROC_ic
on13:y=100:PROC_icon14
3670  IF select1=2 x=1000:y=735:PROC_icon21:x=1065:y=465:PROC_icon22:x=103
0:y=300:PROC_icon23:x=1065:y=70:PROC_icon24
3680  IF select1=3 x=1065:y=700:PROC_icon31:x=1020:y=525:PROC_icon32:x=106
5:y=330:PROC_icon33:x=1030:y=105:PROC_icon34
3690  ENDPROC
3700 :
3710  DEF PROC_icon11
3720  MOVE x,y:PLOT1,296,0:PLOT1,0,180:PLOT1,-296,0:PLOT1,0,-180:ENDPROC
3730 :
3740  DEF PROC_icon12
3750  MOVE x,y:PLOT1,296,0:PLOT1,-50,96:PLOT1,-200,0:PLOT1,-50,-96:PLOT0,1
38,100:PLOT1,0,46:PLOT1,21,0:PLOT1,0,-50:ENDPROC
3760 :
3770  DEF PROC_icon13
3780  MOVE x,y:PLOT1,36,0:PLOT1,0,76:PLOT1,-36,0:PLOT1,0,-76:ENDPROC
3790 :
3800  DEF PROC_icon14
3810  MOVE x,y:PLOT1,46,0:PLOT1,0,46:PLOT1,-46,0:PLOT1,0,-46:PLOT0,4,30:PL
OT1,42,0:PLOT0,-23,-30:PLOT1,0,38:PLOT1,0,8:ENDPROC
3820 :
3830  DEF PROC_icon21
3840  MOVE x,y:PLOT1,24,0:PLOT0,0,-12:PLOT1,0,24:PLOT1,72,0:PLOT1,0,-24:PL
OT1,-72,0:PLOT0,72,12:PLOT1,24,0:ENDPROC
```

```
3850 :
3860 DEF PROC_icon22
3870 MOVE x,y:PLOT1,0,24:PLOT0,-12,0:PLOT1,24,0:PLOT1,0,72:PLOT1,-24,0:PL
OT1,0,-72:PLOT0,12,72:PLOT1,0,24:ENDPROC
3880 :
3890 DEF PROC_icon23
3900 MOVE x,y:PLOT1,24,0:PLOT0,0,-12:PLOT1,0,24:PLOT0,16,0:PLOT1,0,-24:PL
OT0,0,12:PLOT1,24,0:ENDPROC
3910 :


3920 DEF PROC_icon24
3930 MOVE x,y:PLOT1,0,24:PLOT0,-12,0:PLOT1,24,0:PLOT0,0,16:PLOT1,-24,0:PL
OT0,12,0:PLOT1,0,24:ENDPROC
3940 :
3950 DEF PROC_icon31
3960 MOVE x,y:PLOT1,0,24:PLOT0,-8,0:PLOT1,16,0:PLOT0,0,4:PLOT1,-16,0:PLOT
0,-12,8:PLOT1,40,0:PLOT0,-20,0:PLOT1,0,24:ENDPROC
3970 :
3980 DEF PROC_icon32
3990 MOVE x,y:PLOT1,24,0:PLOT0,0,-48:PLOT1,0,96:PLOT1,72,-48:PLOT1,-72,-4
8:PLOT0,72,48:PLOT1,24,0:ENDPROC
4000 :
4010 DEF PROC_icon33
4020 MOVE x,y:PLOT1,0,-24:PLOT0,-20,0:PLOT1,40,0:PLOT0,-32,-8:PLOT1,24,0:
PLOT0,-16,-8:PLOT1,8,0:ENDPROC
4030 :
4040 DEF PROC_icon34
4050 MOVE x,y:PLOT1,24,0:PLOT0,0,-12:PLOT0,0,24:PLOT81,24,-12:PLOT0,4,-12
:PLOT1,0,24:PLOT0,0,-12:PLOT1,24,0:ENDPROC
4060 :
4070 DEF PROC_rubber_icon
4080 IF icon=0 ENDPROC
4090 GCOL4,1:PROC_icon_select:PROC_delay:PROC_icon_select:GCOL0,1:ENDPROC
4100 :
4110 DEF PROC_icon_select
4120 IF select1=1 AND select2=1 PROC_icon11
4130 IF select1=1 AND select2=2 PROC_icon12
4140 IF select1=1 AND select2=3 PROC_icon13
4150 IF select1=1 AND select2=4 PROC_icon14
4160 IF select1=2 AND select2=1 PROC_icon21
4170 IF select1=2 AND select2=2 PROC_icon22
4180 IF select1=2 AND select2=3 PROC_icon23
4190 IF select1=2 AND select2=4 PROC_icon24
4200 IF select1=3 AND select2=1 PROC_icon31
4210 IF select1=3 AND select2=2 PROC_icon32
4220 IF select1=3 AND select2=3 PROC_icon33
4230 IF select1=3 AND select2=4 PROC_icon34
4240 ENDPROC
```

```
4250 :
4260 DEF PROC_fix_icon
4270 PROC_icon_select:ENDPROC
4280 :
4290 DEF PROC_grat
4300 xstart=x:ystart=y:GCOL 4,1:y=106:MOVE 6,y
4310 FOR N=1 TO 8
4320   DRAW 884,y:y=y+100:MOVE 6,y:NEXT N
4330 x=106:MOVE x,6
4340 FOR N=1 TO 8
4350   DRAW x,836:x=x+100:MOVE x,6:NEXT N
4360 GCOL 0,1:x=xstart:y=ystart:ENDPROC
4370 :


4380 DEF PROC_load
4390 VDU4:CLS:PRINT TAB(0,2)"Name of file to be loaded (use no"
4400 INPUT"more than 7 characters) ="$name
4410 $name="LOAD "+$name+" 5800"
4420 X%=name:Y%=X%DIV256:CALL &FFF7
4430 CLS:VDU5:ENDPROC
4440 :
4450 DEF PROC_save
4460 VDU4:CLS:PRINT TAB(0,1)"Name of file to be saved (use no more"
4470 INPUT"than 7 characters) = "$name:CLS
4480 $name="SAVE "+$name+" 5800,7FFF"
4490 X%=name:Y%=X% DIV256:CALL &FFF7
4500 VDU5:ENDPROC
4510 :
4520 DEF PROC_lin_R
4530 MOVE x,y:x=x+step:DRAW x,y:x=x+step:ENDPROC
4540 :
4550 DEF PROC_lin_U
4560 MOVE x,y:y=y+step:DRAW x,y:y=y+step:ENDPROC
4570 :
```

Line 60 calls on PROC_initialize, which performs several functions, including the following: enabling the function keys and cursor keys to produce ASCII codes, establishing the values of variables and flags in the program, drawing a frame around the graphics area, drawing frames or cells in which a selection of icons can be drawn, and, finally, establishing a text window.

Line 70 of the executive program introduces a method of dealing with errors in the program which, hitherto, has not been used. When an error occurs while you are running the program (as, for example, when you input data which produces a "division by zero" error), the type of error is printed in the text window, and you are given the option either of continuing with the program or of quitting the program [you are asked to give a simple Y (Yes) or N (No) answer].

At line 80 you enter the main program proper at PROC_keys (see lines 410–1080 inclusive). This procedure contains an endless REPEAT-UNTIL loop which is terminated by the impossible condition UNTIL 1 = 2. To escape from the program you have one of three options:

1 Press ⟨CTRL−f0⟩.
2 Answer N or n when an error occurs.
3 Press the BREAK key (to restore the program you should type NEW followed by RUN).

On quitting the program using either method 1 or 2 above, line 90 restores the computer to its normal operating condition.

8.4   Use of the Red Function Keys

Practical computer-aided drawing software makes extensive use of programmable function keys to produce special effects. The BBC micro has a nubmer of *FX commands which allow you to program the red function keys and the cursor control keys to generate special ASCII codes (the normal ASCII codes have a value of 128 or less).

When the computer identifies that one of the special codes has been produced by the keyboard, it transfers program control to a procedure which produces the special effect you require. For example, one of the keys is associated with drawing a circle; when that key is pressed, it generates an ASCII code which is greater than 128. The computer recognizes this code and automatically transfers control to the circle-drawing procedure. Program lines 210–250 inclusive set up the function keys to produce the ASCII codes as follows.

*FX 225 sets the base number for the function ⟨FN⟩ keys.
*FX 226 sets the base number for ⟨SHIFT-FN⟩ keys.
*FX 227 sets the base number for ⟨CTRL-FN⟩ keys.
*FX 228 sets the base number for ⟨SHIFT-CTRL-FN⟩ keys.

These put over 40 user-defined keys at your command!

Line 220 sets the base number for the function keys alone to 130, so that when key f0 is pressed it returns the value 130 to the computer; f1 returns 131, f2 returns 132, etc. Sixteen keys are affected by this instruction and include the ten function keys, the break key, the copy key, and the four cursor control keys.

Each of the above keys can also be programmed to generate another ASCII code when used in association with the SHIFT key, or the CTRL key, or with both the SHIFT and CTRL keys simultaneously.

For example, line 230 sets the ⟨SHIFT-FN⟩ key combination base number to 146 (this is selected because it is the value 130 + 16). When the SHIFT key is held down and f0 is pressed (described as ⟨SHIFT-f0⟩), the ASCII value 146 is returned to the computer; ⟨SHIFT-f1⟩ returns 147, etc.

Lines 240 and 250 set the base numbers for the user-defined keys to 162 (= 146 + 16) and 178 (= 162 + 16), respectively, so that when ⟨CTRL−f0⟩ is pressed the value 162 is returned, and when ⟨SHIFT-CTRL−f0⟩ is pressed 178 is returned.

In this way, each of the user-defined keys (and the cursor control keys)

Fig. 8.1 A reduced-size prompt card for the CAD program

	f0	f1	f2	f3	f4	f5	f6	f7	f8	f9	CURSOR KEYS
CTRL SHIFT & fn key											Dotted line
CTRL & fn key	Quit program	Rubber band OFF	Dot	Blob	Arrow	Clear graphics	Toggle ruler	Fill shape	Draw arc	Toggle graticule	Centre line
SHIFT & fn key	Load screen	Fix line	Fix polygon and circle	Move polygon and circle	Fix rectangle	Eraser OFF	Clear text window	Cross hatch (-45 deg)	Set arc radius	Centre cursor	Pixel step
fn key only	Save screen	Rubber band line	Rubber band circle	Rubber band polygon	Rubber band rectangle	Eraser ON	Text	Cross hatch (45 deg)	Centre arc	Select/fix ion	Normal step

Fig. 8.2 Screen display of
the CAD program

```
Ruler OFF
Cursor position: x=692          y=788
Length = 519.2
Angle = 33.69 degrees
```

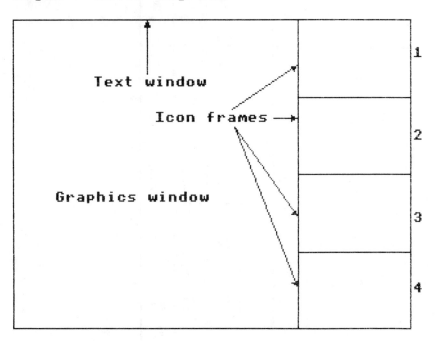

can be used to perform several different functions.

Line 430 of PROC_keys reads the value returned by the key which is pressed, and lines 460–500 inclusive decide which procedure is requested by the key. You will note that each of the ⟨SHIFT-CTRL-FN⟩ keys simply transfers control to PROC_cursor, causing the flashing cursor to be drawn on the screen. This provides you with ten keys which you can use to develop your own procedures at a later date. For example, you can use one of them to dump the diagram on the screen either to a printer or a drafting table; you could use another to, say, draw ellipses, etc.

There now follows a brief description of the procedures in the program. Since many procedures are nested, the chapter is written in an order which enables you to build up an understanding of the program.

A key prompt card is shown in Fig. 8.1, which lists the functions performed by the red function keys (you should refer to section 8.5 for the function of the cursor control keys).

8.5 The Cursor Control Keys

When you run the program, you will see the graphics window together with the four icon frames (see Fig. 8.2); at this time you will see the flashing cursor at the centre of the graphics area. The blank area above the graphics window is the text window (this is shown in Fig. 8.2 with some text in it).

At this time, the four cursor control keys enable you to move the cursor around the screen in steps equal to the cursor width, but you are prevented from moving the cursor outside the limits of the graphics window.

When you hold the SHIFT key down and press one of the cursor control keys, the cursor moves by only one pixel. This enables you to select any pixel position on the screen as a starting or finishing point for a line or a shape.

You can use each of the cursor control keys to draw a chain-dotted line for centre-line purposes simply by holding the CTRL key down and pressing one of the cursor control keys. Also, you can draw a broken (dotted or dashed) line by holding both the SHIFT and CTRL keys down and pressing one of the cursor control keys. Examples of these lines and other features are shown in Fig. 8.3.

Fig. 8.3 Examples of some of the features available using the CAD program

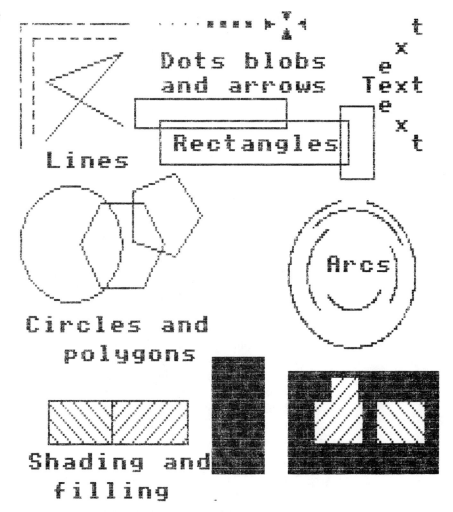

Summary of cursor control key functions

Cursor control keys alone — cursor movement in six pixel steps.
⟨SHIFT-cursor control⟩ — cursor movement in one pixel steps.
⟨CTRL-cursor control⟩ — draws chain-dotted line.
⟨SHIFT-CTRL-cursor control⟩ — draws a dotted line.

8.6   Centring the Cursor

Should you need to return the cursor to the centre of the screen, simply press ⟨**SHIFT-f9**⟩.

8.7   Rubber-band Drawing

Rubber-band drawing is the name given to the technique which allows you to draw either a line or a shape as though it were being done with a rubber band, allowing you to stretch its size to suit your requirements.

There are six rubber-band routines in program *P8* [although method (f) below is, strictly speaking, not a rubber-band drawing method]:

(a)   draw a line
(b)   draw a circle
(c)   draw a regular (equal-sided) polygon
(d)   move a polygon or a circle which is being rubber-banded around the screen
(e)   draw a rectangle
(f)   move icons around the screen.

Two flowcharts illustrating the basis of the rubber-band technique are shown in Fig. 8.4. Diagram 8.4*a* is a simplified flowchart for PROC_keys, showing how a branch to a rubber-banding procedure is brought about by presing one of the following keys:

f1 – rubber-band draw a line
f2 – rubber-band draw a circle
f3 – rubber-band draw a regular polygon
f4 – rubber-band draw a rectangle
f9 – rubber-band move an icon (marked as select/fix icon in Fig. 8.1)

Key f9 differs from the others in that it operates as a toggle which, when pressed once, turns the rubber-band process ON and, when pressed a second time turns it OFF.

When one of the above keys is pressed, say ⟨f3⟩, control is transferred to the appropriate rubber-banding procedure (PROC_rubber_poly in the case of ⟨f3⟩). The first instruction in the procedure tests the condition of a variable to see if its value is zero (see also Fig. 8.4*b*); in the case of PROC_rubber_poly this is the variable "poly", which was initially set to zero in line 260. If the variable has the value zero, the computer asks for data as follows:

Key	*Question*
f3	The number of sides of the polygon
f9	Select one of a group of icons, after which you are asked to select an icon from the group.

At the same time, the value of the variable is set to 1, i.e. poly = 1 (see line 1890); this action prevents the question associated with that procedure being asked again whilst you are using it.

The next step in the procedure is to draw the shape or line specified by the key (the polygon in this case). This is drawn (see line 1900) in inverse

Fig. 8.4 Simplified
flowchart for the rubber-
banding process

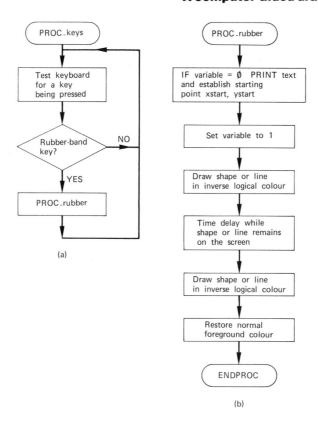

(a)

(b)

colour by PROC_poly, so that the polygon is drawn in white except where
one line crosses another line, when the crossing point is in black. The
computer then executes a delay routine to allow you to see the shape or
line, after which the polygon is drawn once more in inverse colour so that it
vanishes from view; at the same time it restores any black holes produced
by the first line in the original diagram. In this way, a flashing black and
white image is drawn on the screen. Before returning to the main program,
the normal foreground colours are restored (see line 1900).

When a return is made to the main program, the value of the procedure
variable remains at logic 1, and its value is tested in lines 510 to 580
inclusive during each pass of PROC_keys. Each time that the value of the
variable is found to be 1, program control is transferred to the associated
rubber-banding procedure once more. In this way, the shape or the line
drawn by the rubber-band procedure is made to follow the cursor
movement. Features to note for the procedure are as follows.

Line ⟨f1⟩   The length of the line in graphics units (you increase the length
by moving the cursor) and its angle in degrees are printed out, and are
updated as you move the cursor.
Circle ⟨f2⟩   Whilst the circle is being rubber-banded (you increase the
diameter by moving the cursor) and whilst it is small, it looks like a series
of random dots; do not worry about this, it will be O.K. when you fix it
(see later). The radius of the circle is displayed on the screen together with

the angle of the line between the centre of the circle and the starting point of the circle. The current values of the X- and Y-position of the cursor are also displayed.

The circle is perhaps the slowest of the graphics routines in this program (you may like to adapt the faster circle drawing routine outlined in the final chapter of the book), and is drawn in the form of a regular polygon having 30 sides.

You should draw a circle using key ⟨f2⟩, either if you are not sure what diameter you need or where you want to position the circle on the screen. However, if you know exactly where the centre of the circle needs to be on the screen and what its diameter is, it is quicker to use the arc procedure described in section 8.18.

Polygon ⟨f3⟩ The procedure controlling the drawing of polygons is also used to draw the circle, and the same data is displayed on the screen. The angle information on the screen refers to the angle between the centre and the line drawn to the starting corner; the radius is the distance between the centre of the polygon and the cursor position. You can use the cursor control keys to rotate the polygon about its centre. The method of fixing the polygon is described later.

An interesting feature of the polygon procedure is that you can draw a line on the screen by specifying that the polygon has two sides. The polygon procedure then draws a line of equal length about its centre; this is useful if you want to draw a long line by setting the cursor at the centre of the line, the complete line being drawn by moving the cursor to one end of the line.

You can also produce a dot by specifying that the polygon has one side (a polygon having "zero" sides causes an error message to be printed).

Moving a polygon or circle ⟨SHIFT–f3⟩ Once you have drawn a circle or polygon using the rubber-band method, *but have not yet fixed it* on the screen, you can move it or "drag" it to any point you like by pressing ⟨SHIFT–f3⟩ (the flashing cursor is now positioned at the centre of the polygon) following which you press the appropriate cursor control keys. This process is technically known as **picking and dragging**.

Rectangle ⟨f4⟩ After you have pressed this key, you use the cursor control keys to alter the width and height (both dimensions being printed in the text area) of the rectangle which is rubber-banded on the screen. This feature is useful, for example, for drawing a box around text for titling a drawing.

8.8 Deleting a Rubber-band Drawing

If you have entered a rubber-band drawing process (line, circle, polygon, rectangle or icon) and wish to delete the shape or line *whilst you are still rubber-banding it,* you can do so by pressing ⟨**CTRL–f1**⟩. This has the effect of setting to zero the variable in the rubber-banding process, which prevents an automatic return to the rubber-banding procedure.

8.9 Fixing a Rubber-band Shape or Line on the Screen

When you are rubber-banding a shape and it has the correct size or position, you can fix it on the screen by the following operations:

⟨SHIFT–f1⟩ – fix a line
⟨SHIFT–f2⟩ – fix a circle or a polygon
⟨SHIFT–f4⟩ – fix a rectangle
⟨f9⟩ – fix the icon which is being dragged around the screen (remember: this key is a toggle).

8.10 Centring the Cursor

Should you need to return the cursor to the centre of the screen, simply press ⟨**SHIFT–f9**⟩. This has the effect of restoring the default X- and Y-position of the cursor.

8.11 The Ruler

If, during the process of drawing a diagram, you need either to determine the position of a point on the diagram in graphics units, or to measure the length of a line, or to determine the angle of inclination of a line, the ruler enables you to do it.

Simply move the cursor to the first point on the line or diagram and press ⟨**CTRL–f6**⟩, and the current position of the cursor is reported on the screen, the length and angle of the line are also reported but, at this stage, they are both zero. As you move the cursor around the screen, the length and angle of the measured line are calculated to two decimal places and displayed on the screen.

The ruler is yet another toggle; that is, pressing ⟨CTRL–f6⟩ once turns the ruler ON, and pressing it a second time turns it OFF (leaving the measurements displayed).

8.12 Clearing the Text Window

For display purposes, you may wish to clear any text from the text window (as, for example, when you have toggled the ruler OFF). You can do this by pressing ⟨**SHIFT–f6**⟩.

8.13 Picking and Dragging Icons

When you first press key ⟨**f9**⟩, the cursor freezes on the screen and you are given a choice of any one of the three sets of icons (you can amend both the choice and type of icon by modifying the appropriate procedures in the program). The icons which are available from within the program are shown in Fig. 8.5.

You type in your selection of icon group, followed by ⟨RETURN⟩, and the icon group is displayed in the frames on the right-hand side of the screen. You now have to choose an icon from the group. When you type in the icon number, followed by ⟨RETURN⟩, the selected icon is rubber-banded at the cursor position.

You can now drag the icon to any position on the screen under the control of the cursor keys. When the icon is in position, you fix it on the screen by pressing key ⟨f9⟩ once more, that is ⟨f9⟩ is a toggle.

8.14 Deleting the Complete Diagram

If you need to delete the complete drawing on the screen, simply press

Fig. 8.5 Illustrating the icons which are available in the CAD program (you can design your own and include them in the program)

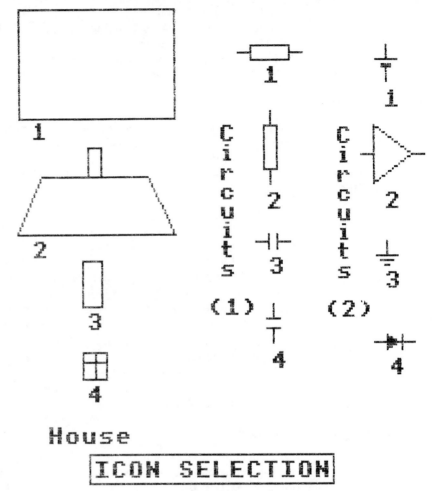

House

ICON SELECTION

⟨**CTRL–f5**⟩. This has the effect of clearing the graphics area of the screen, which also includes any text in that area.

8.15 The Eraser

When you press key ⟨**f5**⟩, you will momentarily see the cursor surrounded by a frame, which is immediately rubbed out; this process is repeated continuously. The frame outlines the size of the rubber, and anything within the eraser is rubbed out (including the frame itself). Using the eraser, you can rub anything out within the graphics area of the screen; using the cursor control keys in conjunction with the ⟨SHIFT⟩ key enables you to move the rubber one pixel at a time. The program prevents the rubber from moving outside the graphics area.

The eraser can be turned OFF at any time by pressing ⟨**SHIFT–f5**⟩.

8.16 Adding Text to the Diagram

You can add text to your diagram at any angle in the range $+90°$ to $-90°$ by pressing key ⟨**f6**⟩. First, you must move the cursor the position where you want the text to be printed, and then press ⟨f6⟩.

You are then prompted to type in the text string (typing errors can be removed at this stage using the ⟨DELETE⟩ key), after which you press ⟨RETURN⟩. If you have typed in only one character, it is printed on the screen *in the fourth quadrant of the cursor cross.*

If you have typed in more than one character, you are asked for the angle in degrees (which can be determined using the ruler ⟨CTRL–f6⟩) at which the text is to be printed. The default angle is zero degrees, and if you simply press the ⟨RETURN⟩ key, the string is printed horizontally. Once again, the first character is printed in the fourth quadrant of the cursor cross.

An interesting feature about this procedure is that, if you specify an angle of +90°, the text is printed at an angle of −90°, i.e. downwards, so that the first character is at the top of the string. The reason is simply to give a better presentation of data on the drawing. Examples of printing are illustrated in Fig. 8.3.

To increase the speed at which text is presented compared with the programs earlier in the book, an upright presentation of text has been adopted. However, should you wish to print text at an angle, you can incorporate some of the procedures outlined in Chapter 4; this, of course, imposes a time penalty on the printing process.

8.17 Dots, Blobs and Arrows

It is often useful to be able to fill a small gap in a drawing by adding a dot on the screen. If you press ⟨CTRL–f2⟩, a **dot** is drawn at the current cursor position.

A **blob** is often useful to point out an item on the diagram; ⟨CTRL–f3⟩ does this for you.

An **arrow** is needed either when you need to dimension a diagram or where you want to point out a feature on the diagram. You select the arrow mode as follows. Firstly, you *position the cursor where the tip of the arrow is to appear on the diagram,* and then press ⟨CTRL–f4⟩. Next, you are prompted to type in the angle in degrees in which the arrow points (the default direction is zero degrees, that is, towards the right-hand side of the screen). When you have typed the value of the angle, you press the ⟨RETURN⟩ key and the arrow is printed at the point specified.

8.18 Drawing an Arc

To draw an **arc**, the function key **f8** is used in association with the SHIFT and CTRL keys. The steps are as follows:

1 Move the cursor to the centre of curvature of the arc and press key ⟨f8⟩. This prints a dot on the screen, and causes the X- and Y-coordinates of the centre to be printed in the text area of the screen.
2 Using the cursor control keys, move the cursor to the point where you wish the arc to begin, and press ⟨SHIFT–f8⟩. This causes the computer to calculate the radius of the arc, and to draw a flashing line from the centre of the arc to the current position of the cursor. The computer also prints the value of angle1 – see Fig. 8.6.
3 Move the cursor to *any point on the finishing angle of the arc;* you will

Fig. 8.6 Drawing an arc

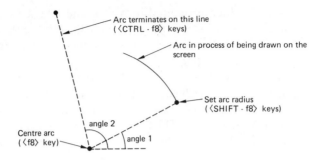

notice at this time that the screen has a second dot on it which corresponds to the starting point of the arc. You now press ⟨CTRL–f8⟩; three events now occur. Firstly, the computer begins to draw the arc, secondly a dot is printed on the line of the angle at which the arc is to terminate, and, thirdly, the computer prints the values of angle2 and the angle of the arc. When the computer has drawn the arc, it rubs out the two remaining dots on the screen, leaving only the arc.

You can also use the arc procedure to draw a circle as follows:
1 Fix the centre of the circle using key ⟨f8⟩.
2 Move the cursor *horizontally* to a point on the radius of the circle and press ⟨SHIFT–f8⟩.
3 *Without moving the cursor,* press ⟨CTRL–f8⟩.

8.19 Filling a Shape and Shading

In order to reduce the memory requirement of the program, a relatively simple filling and cross-hatching or shading procedure is used here.

To **fill a shape**, move the cursor to a point *one pixel inside* the left-hand edge of the shape to be filled and press ⟨**CTRL–f7**⟩. The inside of the shape is then filled vertically (up and down) from left to right; you should choose a starting point which gives the longest left-to-right run possible in the shape. If some areas are left unfilled (as they will be in an irregular shape), simply move the cursor to a point which is one pixel inside the unfilled area and press ⟨CTRL–f7⟩ once more.

To **cross-hatch** or **shade** a shape, position the cursor as described above and press ⟨**f7**⟩ for shading at an angle of 45°, or ⟨**SHIFT–f7**⟩ for shading at an angle of −45°. The shading lines are one normal cursor step apart. Should the shading procedure miss any areas out due to an obstruction in the diagram, simply position the cursor one normal cursor step inside the unshaded area, and press the appropriate key or key combination again.

8.20 Drawing a Graticule

If you need to draw a graticule on the screen, simply press ⟨**CTRL–f9**⟩. The graticule spacing in both the X- and Y-direction is 100 graphics units; it is drawn in inverse logical colour, and does not affect your drawing when it is turned OFF by pressing ⟨CTRL–f9⟩ once more, i.e. the graticule key is a toggle.

8.21   Saving and Loading the Diagram on Tape or Disc

To **save a diagram** on the screen on tape or disc, simply press ⟨**f0**⟩. This causes the computer to ask for the name under which the diagram is to be saved (the restriction of not more than 7 characters is intended for disc users). You type in the filename and press ⟨RETURN⟩.

The recording system then records the file under the nominated filename. If you are using a tape system, you must obey the screen prompts (remember, you are saving every pixel on the screen and, with a tape system, this may take a little time).

You can **load a diagram** onto the screen by pressing ⟨**SHIFT–f0**⟩. You are prompted to enter the filename, after which you press the ⟨RETURN⟩ key. The recording system then returns the diagram to the screen.

When using a tape system, obey the prompts on the screen. Tape is, of course, slower than disc and you will see the recorded diagram gradually grow from the top of the graphics area.

Computer Graphics Mathematics

9.1 Degrees and Radians

Angular rotation can be expressed either in **degrees** or in **radians** (rad); one complete revolution is represented by 360° or 2π (6.283...) radians. The angle A in Fig. 9.1 can be expressed either in degrees or radians, and the relationship between them is

$$\frac{A \text{ in degrees}}{360} = \frac{A \text{ in radians}}{2\pi}$$

hence

$$A° = A \ (rad) * 360/(2*\pi) = 57.2958 * A \ (rad)$$

That is   one radian = 57.2958 degrees.
and

$$A \ (rad) = A° * 2\pi/360 = 0.01745 * A°$$

Fig. 9.1 Angles in degrees and radians

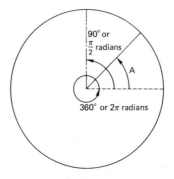

The BBC micro has the value PI = 3.14159265 stored in ROM, and the instruction DEG enables you to convert an angle expressed in radians into degrees. Thus, the instruction PRINT DEG(PI/2) prints 90 (degrees). The instruction RAD allows you to convert an angle in degrees into radians; the instruction PRINT RAD(360) prints the radian equivalent of 360°.

Whilst most of us think of angular displacements in degrees, most scientific and engineering calculations are performed in radians. Unless told otherwise, all computers assume that angles are in radians.

9.2 Trigonometric Ratios

When rotating an object on the monitor screen, the computer needs to know how the horizontal component (X) and the vertical component (Y) of the object vary with the angle of rotation A (see Fig. 9.2*a*), and its length H. The relationship between the elements of the triangle is given by the trigonometric ratios of the triangle.

Fig. 9.2 *a*) Trigonometric ratios of angle A. *b*) Calculation of the tangent of *a*) 90°, *b*) 270° (or −90°)

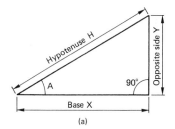

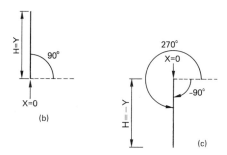

The ratio Y/X is known as the **tangent** (tan) of the angle; the ratio X/H is known as the **cosine** (cos) of the angle, and the ratio Y/H is the **sine** (sin) of the angle. That is

$$\tan A = Y/X \quad \text{or} \quad Y = X * \tan A$$
$$\cos A = X/H \quad \text{or} \quad X = H * \cos A$$
$$\sin A = Y/H \quad \text{or} \quad Y = H * \sin A$$

It is interesting to note that whilst mathematics books use the lower-case names tan, cos and sin to represent the trigonometric ratios, you **must use** the upper-case names TAN, COS and SIN when using the ratios in a BASIC program.

You should also note that difficulties sometimes arise in computer programs when the tangents of 90° and 270° have to be calculated (see Fig. 9.2*b* and *c*). In this case, the length of the base of the triangle is zero, resulting in the computer giving a "divide by zero" error message when it attempts to calculate the tangent (Y/X) of these angles. One method of overcoming this is illustrated in the computer-aided drawing program *P8*; in this program the problem is handled by the procedure PROC_zero.

The length of the hypotenuse (H) is calculated either from one of the above formulae, or from Pythagoras rule as follows:

$$H = \sqrt{(X^2 + Y^2)}$$

Hence, a knowledge of any two of the factors X, Y, H and A enables the remaining two to be calculated.

9.3 Cartesian and Polar Representation of a Line or Vector

The length and angular position of a line (see Fig. 9.3) can be represented in either of two ways, namely by its cartesian coordinates or by its polar coordinates.

In the **cartesian form**, it is represented by the X- and Y-values of the line relative to its starting point. In the case of the line in Fig. 9.3, we merely say that the end of the line, Q, is +X1 to the right of the origin, O, and +Y1 above it.

Fig. 9.3 Representation of a vector

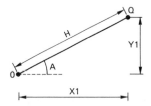

The line or *vector* H in Fig. 9.3 would be represented in what is known as **complex number** form as

$$H = X1 + i\,Y1 \quad \text{or} \quad H = X1 + j\,Y1$$

where both i and j in these equations can be thought of as meaning "in an upward direction". That is, H has a horizontal component of X1 and an upward component of Y1.

The line or vector H can be represented in its **polar form** in terms of its length H and angle A from the horizontal as

$$H\underline{/A}$$

where $\underline{/A}$ means "at angle A". The relationship between the two forms of representation is

$$H = \sqrt{[(X1)^2 + (Y1)^2]}$$

and

$$\tan A = Y1/X1$$

Also

$$X1 = H \cos A \quad \text{and} \quad Y1 = H \sin A$$

These relationships are very useful when dealing with the manipulation of shapes in both two and three dimensions.

9.4 Similar Triangles

Triangles are said to be **similar to one another** when they have the same included angles. For example, the two triangles in Fig. 9.4 are similar to one another because they have included angles of 30°, 60° and 90°. For this reason, the ratios of similar sides of the triangles have the same ratio. That is

$$\frac{L1}{L4} = \frac{L2}{L5} = \frac{L3}{L6}$$

We shall refer to this relationship in section 9.5.

Fig. 9.4 Similar triangles

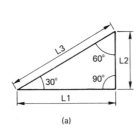

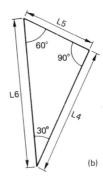

(a)

(b)

9.5 Rotating a Line — Compound Angle Formulae

When a line is to be rotated about a point on the monitor screen, the computer must use the initial coordinates of the line in order to calculate the final coordinates of the line.

In this section we will develop the basis on which suitable formulae can be produced. Suppose that line OQ in Fig. 9.5, which is at angle A to the horizontal, is to be rotated through angle B (remember: the positive direction of angular movement is anticlockwise).

The coordinates of point Q relative to point O are X1 and Y1. When the line is rotated through angle B, it takes up positon OZ (see Fig. 9.5a). If a line is projected from Z to OQ which is at right-angles to OQ, it cuts OQ at R (see diagram b). Furthermore, the line projected from R to the base of the triangle OPQ cuts it as S. Now, since triangles OPQ and OSR contain the same angles, they are similar to one another so that

$$\frac{X12}{X1} = \frac{Y12}{Y1} = \frac{H12}{H}$$

or

$$X12 = \frac{H12}{H} * X1 = \frac{H}{H} * \frac{H12}{H} * X1 = H * \frac{H12}{H} * \frac{X1}{H}$$

$$= H*cosB*cosA \tag{9.1}$$

and

$$Y12 = \frac{H12}{H} * Y1 = \frac{H}{H} * \frac{H12}{H} * Y1 = H * \frac{H12}{H} * \frac{Y1}{H}$$

$$= H*cosB*sinA \tag{9.2}$$

If the line RS is projected upwards to T, triangles OPQ and RTZ are seen to be similar so that

$$\frac{X13}{Y1} = \frac{Y13}{X1} = \frac{H13}{H} \qquad \text{(see Fig. 9.5}c\text{)}$$

Fig. 9.5 Rotating a line form
OQ to OZ

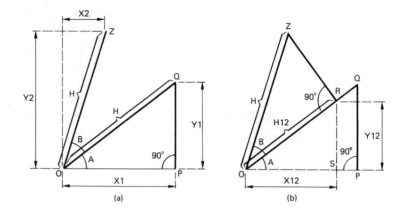

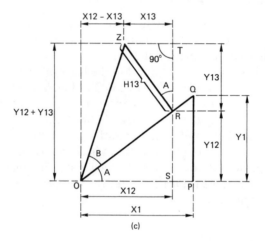

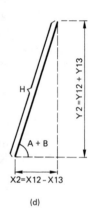

or

$$X13 = \frac{H13}{H} * Y1 = \frac{H}{H} * \frac{H13}{H} * Y1 = H * \frac{H13}{H} * \frac{Y1}{H}$$

$$= H*sinB*sinA \tag{9.3}$$

and

$$Y13 = \frac{H13}{H} * X1 = \frac{H}{H} * \frac{H13}{H} * X1 = H * \frac{H13}{H} * \frac{X1}{H}$$

$$= H*sinB*cosA \tag{9.4}$$

Referring now to the total angular movement $(A + B)$ in Fig. 9.5d, the sine of the compound angle is

$$sin\ (A+B) = \frac{Y12 + Y13}{H} = \frac{H}{H} * (cosB*sinA + sinB*cosA)$$

$$= cosB*sinA + sinB*cosA \tag{9.5}$$

and the cosine of the compound angle is

$$\cos\,(A+B)\;=\;\frac{X12\,-\,X13}{H}\;=\;\frac{H}{H}\;*\;(\cos B * \cos A\;-\;\sin B * \sin A)$$

$$=\cos B * \cos A\,-\,\sin B * \sin A \qquad\qquad (9.6)$$

It can also be shown that

$$\sin\,(A-B) = \sin A * \cos B\,-\,\cos A * \sin B \qquad\qquad (9.7)$$

and

$$\cos\,(A-B) = \cos A * \cos B\,+\,\sin A * \sin B \qquad\qquad (9.8)$$

Equations (9.5) to (9.8), inclusive, are vital not only to an understanding of the mathematics of rotating two- and three-dimensional shapes, but to methods of drawing shapes. An example of this is given in section 9.6, in which some of the equations are used to draw a circle on the screen faster than has been drawn hitherto.

9.6   A Faster Circle Drawing Program

Circle-drawing programs used earlier in the book have involved the proces of calculating the sine and cosine of every angle of the coordinates of many points on a circle (typicaly 30 or more angles). Trigonometrical calcula-tioins are notoriously slow to perform, and therefore slow down the drawing process. Program *P9.1* (*listing 9.1*) illustrates the use of eqns. (9.5) and (9.6) to reduce the time taken to draw a circle.

Listing 9.1

```
 10  REM****PROGRAM "P9.1"****
 20  *TV0,1
 30  MODE 4
 40  x0=500:y0=500:r=500:x1=r:y1=0
 50  ang=2*PI/60:cos=COS(ang):sin=SIN(ang)
 60  MOVE x0+x1,y0+y1
 70  FOR N=1 TO 60
 80    X=x1*cos-y1*sin:Y=x1*sin+y1*cos
 90    DRAW x0+X,y0+Y:x1=X:y1=Y
100    NEXT N
110  END
```

The program draws a circle of radius 500 graphics units centred at x0 = 500, y0 = 500 graphics units (see line 40 of the program) in steps of 2*PI/60 radians (6 degrees) – given as the variable "ang" in line 50. Line 50 is the one and only point in the program where the computer is used to determine the value of a trigonometrical ratio. Line 80 calculates the new value of the X-coordinate and Y-coordinate of the point to which the arc of the circle is to be drawn.

The circle is drawn by the FOR-NEXT loop in lines 70–100 inclusive, and since trigonometical calculations are not performed in this loop, the circle is drawn very quickly.

Program *P9.1* can be modified to draw a circle drawn in dots at 6° intervals by adding the following lines.

```
62   FOR M = 1 TO 2
64   IF M = 1 GCOL 0,1 ELSE GCOL 4,1
102 NEXT M
```

9.7   The "Best" Straight Line to Fit a Set of Results

When you plot a set of results for an experiment, say for the change in length of a metal bar with variation in temperature, the results may not lie in a straight line. However, it may be possible to draw a straight line through the points giving the "best" estimate of how the length varies with temperature. If several groups of people perform the same experiment, it is likely that there will be variations between their results, each group producing its own version of the "best" line to fit the results. One way of overcoming the widest interpretation of the results is to carry out a statistical study of the results.

As has been shown earlier in the book, if you have a set of results which relate two variables X and Y, there are two possible straight-line equations which relate them:

$$Y = mX + c \tag{9.9}$$

and

$$X = MY + C \tag{9.10}$$

where m and M are the slopes of the respective graphs, and c and C are the intercepts on the Y- and X-axis, respectively. Which equation you choose depends on which you decide is the independent variable. Moreover,

Fig. 9.6 *a*) Best fit to the slope of a graph, but a bad fit to the intercept on the Y-axis. *b*) Best fit to the Y-axis intercept, but a bad fit to the slope of the graph

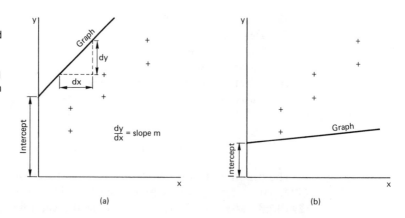

depending on the data, you can draw a graph which gives either the best fit to the slope of the graph (see Fig. 9.6*a*) or the best fit to the intercept (see Fig. 9.6*b*). Statistics take a lot of the guesswork out of the process of drawing the graph, and the **correlation coefficient** gives an indication of the relationship between the two straight lines satisfied by eqns. (9.9) and (9.10) both for the best slope and intercept.

9.8   Fitting a Straight Line to a Set of Results — the Least Squares Method

Let us assume for the moment that Y is the dependent variable, and that any errors in the result are likely to be in the measured value of Y rather that in X.

Figure 9.7 illustrates how differences or errors can occur. At a particular value x_1 of the variable X, the measured value of the dependent variable Y is y_1. However, when all the results have been obtained and the graph plotted, the value of Y corresponding to x_1 predicted from the best straight line graph is y_2. The difference between the two is $(y_2 - y_1)$.

Fig. 9.7 Error in measured values

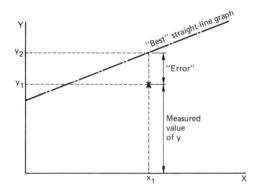

Depending on the value of y_1, the difference could have either a positive mathematical sign or a negative sign. For this reason, mathematicians have devised a **method of least squares**, in which the least possible square value of the error, i.e. $(error)^2$, is calculated. This ensures that, whatever the mathematical sign of the error, its squared value is always positive.

The best straight line is one giving a net error or zero, that is the **average value** of the error of all pairs of X- and Y-values on the graph is zero. The resulting line is known as the **line of regression of X on Y** or the **line of prediction for Y**.

To illustrate how this is done, consider a graph having the values in Table 9.1. The method of least squares shows that the slope m of the line of prediction for Y is given by the expression

$$m = \frac{(N * \Sigma XY) - \Sigma X \ \Sigma Y}{[N*\Sigma(X^2)] - (\Sigma X)^2} \qquad (9.11)$$

and the intercept c of the line on the y-axis is

$$c = [\Sigma Y - (m*\Sigma X)]/N \qquad (9.12)$$

where

N = the number of points on the graph (4 in the case of table 9.1)
ΣX = sum of all the X-values
ΣY = sum of all the Y-values
ΣXY = sum of all the products of X and Y
$\Sigma(X^2)$ = sum of all the square values of X

Table 9.1

X	0	1	2	3
Y	2	4	4	6

Table 9.2

					Sum
X	0	1	2	3	$\Sigma X = 6$
Y	2	4	4	6	$\Sigma Y = 16$
XY	0	4	8	18	$\Sigma XY = 30$
X^2	0	1	4	9	$\Sigma(X^2) = 14$
Y^2	4	16	16	36	$\Sigma(Y^2) = 72$

Table 9.2 shows how these values are computed. Substituting the appropriate values into eqns. (9.11) and (9.12) gives

$$m = \frac{(4 * 30) - (6 * 16)}{(4 * 14) - 6^2} = \frac{24}{20} = 1.2$$

and

$$c = [16 - (1.2 * 6)]/4 = 8.8/4 = 2.2$$

This gives the law for the graph as

$$Y = 1.2X + 2.2 \tag{9.13}$$

The law of least squares also allows you to determine the best line which assumes that Y is the independent variable, the law of the line being

$$X = MY + C$$

The values are calculated as follows:

$$M = \frac{(n * \Sigma XY) - \Sigma X \, \Sigma Y}{(N * \Sigma(Y^2)) - (\Sigma Y)^2} \tag{9.14}$$

and

$$C = (\Sigma X - (M \, \Sigma Y))/N \tag{9.15}$$

The equation above is known as the **line of regression of X on Y** or the **line of prediction for X**. In the case of the example in Table 9.1 (see also Table 9.2), the predicted values of M and C are

$$M = \frac{(4 * 30) - (6 * 16)}{(4 * 72) - 16^2} = 0.75$$

and

$$C = [6 - (0.75 * 16)]/4 = 1.5$$

so that the line of prediction for X is

$$X = 0.75Y - 1.5 \tag{9.16}$$

You therefore have two straight-line laws for the results in Table 9.1. Which of these is the best law is a matter for debate, and you must choose between them.

The above equations are used in program *P5.1* to determine the laws of regression of the line, the equations being printed on the screen and the two straight lines are plotted.

9.9   The Correlation Coefficient

It was explained in Chapter 5 that the correlation between the two lines of regression for a set of results was indicated by the **correlation coefficient** r. The value of this coefficient is calculated in line 1530 of program *P5.1* from the equation

$$r = \frac{\Sigma XY - (\Sigma X \Sigma Y / N)}{\sqrt{[(\Sigma(X^2) - (\Sigma X)^2 / N * (\Sigma(Y^2) - (\Sigma Y)^2 / N)]}}$$

In the case of the results in Table 9.2, the correlation coefficient is

$$r = \frac{30 - (6 * 16/4)}{\sqrt{[(14 - 6^2/4) * (72 - 16^2/4)]}} = 0.9487$$

9.10   Matrices (Arrays)

If you have a set of algebraic equations of the form

$$3x + 2y + 4z = 5$$
$$2x + y + 5z = 7$$
$$4x + 3y + 2z = 3$$

they can be represented in the following **matrix** form:

$$\begin{bmatrix} 3 & 2 & 4 \\ 2 & 1 & 5 \\ 4 & 3 & 2 \end{bmatrix} \bullet \begin{bmatrix} x \\ y \\ z \end{bmatrix} = \begin{bmatrix} 5 \\ 7 \\ 3 \end{bmatrix}$$

The left-hand matrix contains the coefficients of the variables x, y and z; this form of matrix is known as a **3×3 square matrix** having three rows and three columns. The variables x, y and z are stored in the **column matrix** to the left of the equals sign; that is, the variables are presented in the form of a column. The values on the right-hand side of the equals sign are also stored in another column matrix. In the BBC micro, a matrix is called an **array**.

Other forms of matrices include **row matrices**, for example

$$[2 \quad 4 \quad 6] \quad \text{and} \quad [a \quad b \quad c]$$

A **rectangular matrix** may take the form

$$\begin{bmatrix} 6 & 1 & 4 \\ 5 & 0 & 3 \end{bmatrix} \quad \text{or} \quad \begin{bmatrix} a_1 & b_1 & c_1 \\ a_2 & b_2 & c_2 \end{bmatrix}$$

An element in a matrix is positioned according to which row and column it is in. In mathematical terms, an element in an array "a" is given the value a_{ij}, where

$$i = \text{row number} \quad \text{and} \quad j = \text{column number}$$

In the BBC micro, the 1st row is **row zero** ($\emptyset$), and the 1st column is **column zero** ($\emptyset$). Thus if a 2×2 square array is represented in the form

$$\begin{bmatrix} 2 & 6 \\ 4 & -3 \end{bmatrix}$$

you could write it down in the form

$$\begin{bmatrix} a_{\emptyset\emptyset} & a_{\emptyset 1} \\ a_{1\emptyset} & a_{11} \end{bmatrix}$$

where $a_{\emptyset\emptyset}$ = the element in row zero, column zero = 2
$a_{\emptyset 1}$ = the element in row zero, column one = 6
$a_{1\emptyset}$ = the element in row one, column zero = 4
a_{11} = the element in row one, column one = -3.

9.11 Addition and Subtraction of Matrices

Matrices of the same order can be added together or subtracted from one another. That is, you can add a 3×2 matrix to another 3×2 matrix, but you cannot add it to a 2×3 matrix, or to a 2×2 matrix, or a 3×3 matrix, etc.

To form the new matrix, you simply add the corresponding elements together as follows:

$$\begin{bmatrix} 1 & 2 & 3 \\ 4 & -5 & 6 \end{bmatrix} + \begin{bmatrix} 11 & 22 & 33 \\ 44 & 55 & 66 \end{bmatrix} = \begin{bmatrix} 1+11 & 2+22 & 3+33 \\ 4+44 & -5+55 & 6+66 \end{bmatrix}$$

$$= \begin{bmatrix} 12 & 24 & 36 \\ 48 & 5\emptyset & 72 \end{bmatrix}$$

When subtracting one matrix from another, you simply subtract the corresponding elements from one another.

9.12 Multiplying Matrices

A matrix can be multiplied by a scalar (a number or a scaling factor) simply by multiplying each element in the marix by the scalar as follows:

$$3 \times \begin{bmatrix} 1 & 2 \\ 3 & 4 \end{bmatrix} = \begin{bmatrix} 3\times1 & 3\times2 \\ 3\times3 & 3\times4 \end{bmatrix} = \begin{bmatrix} 3 & 6 \\ 9 & 12 \end{bmatrix}$$

A rectangular matrix can be multiplied by a column matrix as follows:

$$\begin{bmatrix} a_{\emptyset\emptyset} & a_{\emptyset 1} \\ a_{1\emptyset} & a_{11} \end{bmatrix} \bullet \begin{bmatrix} x \\ y \end{bmatrix} = \begin{bmatrix} a_{\emptyset\emptyset}x & a_{\emptyset 1}y \\ a_{1\emptyset}x & a_{11}y \end{bmatrix}$$

$$\begin{bmatrix} 2 & 1 \\ 4 & 3 \end{bmatrix} \bullet \begin{bmatrix} 5 \\ 6 \end{bmatrix} = \begin{bmatrix} 2\times5 & 1\times6 \\ 4\times5 & 3\times6 \end{bmatrix} = \begin{bmatrix} 1\emptyset & 6 \\ 2\emptyset & 18 \end{bmatrix}$$

The element in row r and column c of the rectangular matrix is multiplied by the element in the column r of the column matrix.

The two matrices can only be multiplied if the rectangular matrix has as many columns as the column matrix has rows in it.

A row matrix can be multiplied by a rectangular matrix as follows:

$$[x \quad y] \bullet \begin{bmatrix} a_{00} & a_{01} \\ a_{10} & a_{11} \end{bmatrix} = [a_{00}x + a_{10}y \quad a_{01}x + a_{11}y]$$

$$[5 \quad 6] \bullet \begin{bmatrix} 2 & 1 \\ 4 & 3 \end{bmatrix} = [5 \times 2 + 6 \times 4 \quad 5 \times 1 + 6 \times 3] = [34 \quad 23]$$

More complex matrices can be multiplied together, and you should refer to specialized books on mathematics for further details.

9.13 Transformations

The position and size of an object on the screen of your monitor can be changed using the procedures outlined in Chapter 7, but more universal methods involve the use of matrices, the mathematical operations involved being called **transformations**.

A transformation involves transposing a point which has coordinates x,y to a new set of coordinates xt,yt. This is written down mathematically in the form

$$[xt \quad yt] = [x \quad y] \times \text{transformation matrix}$$

The nature of the **transformation matrix** depends on the purpose of the transformation. That is, it may be for scaling (enlarging or reducing), or for moving the object on the screen (translation), or for rotation, etc.

A number of transformations which are important in computer-aided drawing are described in the following sections.

9.14 The Identity Transformation

This transformation is one which produces an identical diagram to the one you have already drawn, that is there is no change in the diagram. At this point you will ask the question: "what is the point of this transformation?". Quite simply, the answer is that it provides an understanding of the transformation technique.

The identity transformation for a point in plane is

$$\begin{bmatrix} 1 & 0 \\ 0 & 1 \end{bmatrix}$$

Suppose that you specify a point having the coordinates x,y. The transformed values xt and yt of x and y are obtained using the identity matrix as follows:

$$[xt \quad yt] = [x \quad y] \bullet \begin{bmatrix} 1 & 0 \\ 0 & 1 \end{bmatrix} = [x.1 + y.0 \quad x.0 + y.1]$$

$$= [x \quad y]$$

That is to say, the transformed values, xt and yt, are the same as the original values.

9.15   The Scaling Transformation

This transformation allows you to alter the scale of an object on the screen; it enables you to modify the scale independently in both the X- and Y-direction. The transformation therefore allows you to map between the original point [x y] and a transformed point [xt yt]. The scaling transformation for a two-dimentional object is

$$\begin{bmatrix} sx & 0 \\ 0 & sy \end{bmatrix}$$

where sx is the scaling factor you wish to use in the X-direction, and sy is the scaling factor in the Y-direction. The transformed values of x and y are

$$[xt \quad yt] = [x \quad y] \bullet \begin{bmatrix} sx & 0 \\ 0 & sy \end{bmatrix} = [x.sx + y.0 \quad x.0 + y.sy]$$

$$= [x.sx \quad y.sy]$$

If, for example, you wish to double the scaling factor in the X-direction, and increase it to 1.1 in the Y-direction, then sx = 2 and sy = 1.1. The scales values of x and y after the scaling transformation has been applied are

$$[xt \quad yt] = [x \quad y] \bullet \begin{bmatrix} 2 & 0 \\ 0 & 1.1 \end{bmatrix} = [2x \quad 1.1y]$$

That is, the value of the new (transformed) X-coordinate of the point is twice the value of the old coordinate, and the new Y-coordinate is 1.1 times the old coordinate.

If you compare the scaling transformation with the identity transformation, you will find the latter is simply a scaling transformation with a scaling factor of 1.0 in both the X- and Y-direction!

Program *P9.2* (*listing 9.2*) incorporates the scaling transformation using sx = 2 and sy = 1.1. Line 50 of the program establishes the graphics origin at the centre of the screen, and line 60 calls for PROC_axes which draws graphic axes (in red) on the screen through the graphics origin.

Lines 70–100 inclusive of the program draw the original square shape (in white) which is to be scaled; the number of corners is given in line 170 and the coordinates of the corners of are specified in the DATA statement in line 180.

The FOR-NEXT loop in lines 140 and 150 applies the scaling transformation [see PROC_scale(x,y)] to each corner in turn, and also draws the scaled shape (in yellow). The resulting diagram is shown in Fig. 9.8*a*; in this case, both shapes have the same origin, namely the graphics origin, and part of the scaled rectangle lies on top of the original square.

However, this scaling technique has a disadvantage, as can be seen if you move the original shape from the graphics origin. You can check this by altering line 180 to

180DATA 100,150, 300,150, 300,350, 100,350, 100,150

When you run the program, the original square is drawn in white at the correct position on the screen, but the scaled rectangle (in yellow) is moved

Listing 9.2

```
10   REM ****PROGRAM "P9.2"****
20   REM THE SCALING TRANSFORMATION
30   *TV0,1
40   MODE 1
50   VDU 29,640;512;
60   PROC_axes
70   READ no_of_corners
80   READ x,y:MOVE x,y
90   FOR N=2 TO no_of_corners
100    READ x,y:DRAW x,y:NEXT N
110  GCOL 0,2:RESTORE
120  READ no_of_corners
130  READ x,y:PROC_scale(x,y):MOVE xt,yt
140  FOR N=2 TO no_of_corners
150    READ x,y:PROC_scale(x,y):DRAW xt,yt:NEXT N
160  GCOL 0,3:VDU 29,0;0;
170  DATA 5
180  DATA 0,0,  200,0,  200,200,  0,200,  0,0
190  END
200  :
210  DEF PROC_axes
220  GCOL 0,1
230  MOVE -640,0:DRAW 640,0:MOVE 0,-512:DRAW 0,512
240  GCOL 0,3
250  ENDPROC
260  :
270  DEF PROC_scale(x,y)
280  xt=2*x+0*y:yt=0*x+1.1*y
290  ENDPROC
```

upwards and to the right relative to the original shape (see Fig. 9.8*b*). The reason for this is that each point (including the origin) is scaled relative to the original point. For example, the starting point of the diagram (whose coordinates are x = 100, y = 150) is moved to xt = $100 \times 2 = 200$, yt = $1.1 \times 150 = 165$ graphics units. A method of overcoming the change in the origin when scaling is applied is discussed in sections 9.16 onwards.

9.16   The Translation Transformation — Homogeneous Coordinates

If the starting point of the shape to be scaled is at the graphics origin, then program *P9.2* allows you to scale it without shifting the starting point of the shape on the screen. However, if the starting point is not at the origin, then scaling shifts the starting point on the screen.

Hence, it is generally the case that you need to move or to **translate** the starting point of the object to the graphics origin before you scale it. Having scaled it, you then need to translate the scaled shape back to its correct position on the screen. We must therefore study the mechanics of translation at this time.

Fig. 9.8 *a*) Scaling with the
starting point at the
graphics origin. *b*) Scaling
with the starting point not at
the graphics origin

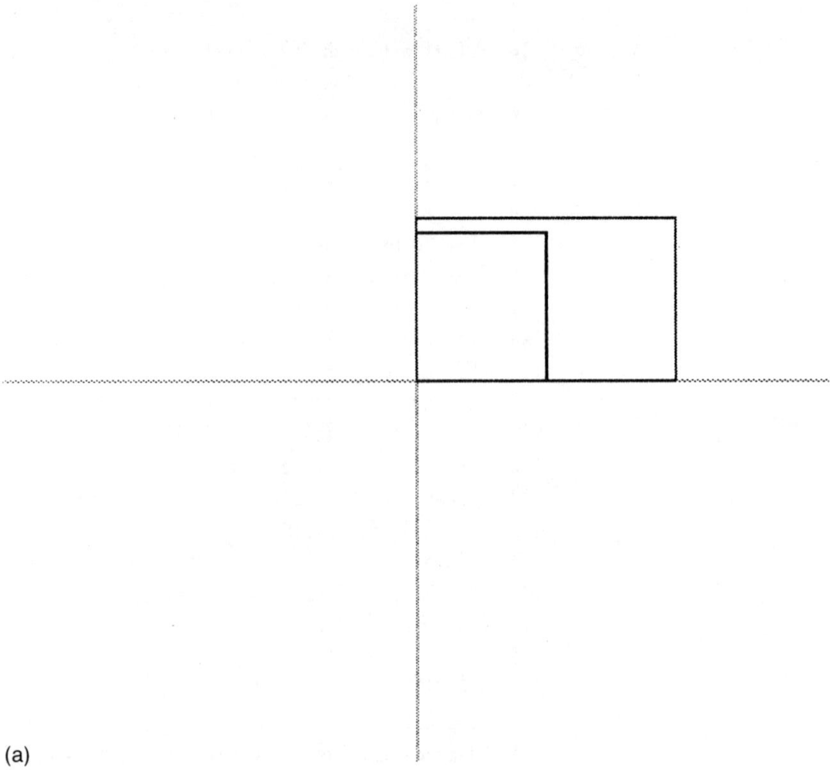

(a)

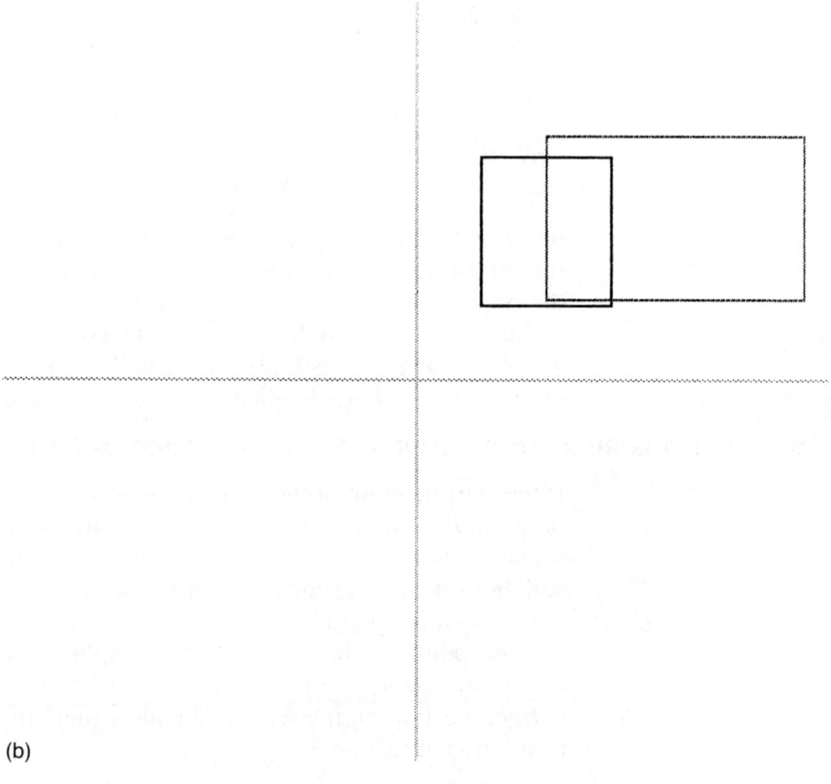

(b)

If you need to move or to translate object A in Fig. 9.9 to a new position B, you must add an amount Tx in the X-direction to every point, and an amount Ty in the Y-direction. That is, if point L has the coordinates x_1,y_1, then point M in the translated shape has the coordinates

$$x_2 = x_1 + Tx \qquad y_2 = y_1 + Ty$$

Unfortunately, this relationship is not presented in matrix form, so that it cannot be combined with other transformations. However, there is a way around the problem using what are known as **homogeneous coordinates**.

Using these, a point in a two-dimensional space, i.e. on a surface, is specified by three numbers instead of the usual two, i.e. X and Y. When dealing with translation in three dimensions, each point in a 3-dimensional space is represented by four numbers instead of the usual three, i.e. X, Y and Z. We will limit ourselves here to studying 2-D diagrams.

Fig. 9.9 The translation transformation

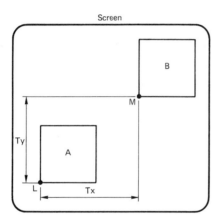

A point whose coordinates are x,y in a 2-dimensional space is represented by the three homogeneous coordinates (xh,yh,h), where h is a "dummy" coordinate. If you make h = 1, the homogeneous coordinates of the point (x,y) are (x,y,1). Using these coordinates, the **translation matrix** is

$$\begin{bmatrix} 1 & \emptyset & \emptyset \\ \emptyset & 1 & \emptyset \\ Tx & Ty & 1 \end{bmatrix}$$

where Tx is the translation (movement in graphics units) of each point in the X-direction, and Ty is the translation of each point in the Y-direction. Multiplying the homogeneous coordinate of one point by the translation matrix gives

$$[x \quad y \quad 1] \bullet \begin{bmatrix} 1 & \emptyset & \emptyset \\ \emptyset & 1 & \emptyset \\ Tx & Ty & 1 \end{bmatrix} = [x + Tx \quad y + Ty \quad 1]$$

That is, each point (x,y) is translated on the screen to the point (x+Tx,y+Ty). The calculation is simplified if you omit the right-hand column of the translation matrix; when you do this, the above calculation becomes

$$[x \quad y \quad 1] \bullet \begin{bmatrix} 1 & \emptyset \\ \emptyset & 1 \\ Tx & Ty \end{bmatrix} = [x+Tx \quad y+Ty]$$

In the remainder of this chapter we will look at other important transformation matrices, and it will be seen that they all reduce to the form

$$\begin{bmatrix} A & B \\ C & D \\ E & F \end{bmatrix}$$

where A, B, C, D, E and F are parameters or variables in the transformation. The effect of multiplying the homogeneous coordinates of a point by the above matrix is

$$[x \quad y \quad 1] \bullet \begin{bmatrix} A & B \\ C & D \\ E & F \end{bmatrix} = [A*x + C*y + E \quad B*x + D*y + F]$$

hence the transformed value xt and yt are given by

$$xt = A*x + C*y + E \qquad (9.17)$$
$$yt = B*x + D*y + F \qquad (9.18)$$

Equations (9.17) and (9.18) form the basis on which many 2-dimensional graphics manipulations are performed. It only remains to pass the values of the parameters to a matrix multiplication procedure to obtain a special effect on the screen.

9.17 Other Forms of Transformation

Any 2-dimensional transformation can be represented by a 2*2 matrix of the form

$$\begin{bmatrix} A & B \\ C & D \end{bmatrix}$$

where A, B, C and D are paremeters used to transform an original set of coordinates (x,y) to a transformed set (xt,yt) – see section 9.13 for an example of this. The naure of A, B, C and D depends on the required transformation.

The most commonly used transformations are translation and scaling. However, other important transformations include reflection, rotation and shear.

The 2*2 matrix described above can be converted into a 3*3 homogeneous coordinate matrix of the form

$$\begin{bmatrix} A & B & \emptyset \\ C & D & \emptyset \\ E & F & 1 \end{bmatrix}$$

which, for 2-D diagrams, can be reduced to

$$\begin{bmatrix} A & B \\ C & D \\ E & F \end{bmatrix}$$

In the remained of this section we will develop a number of 2∗2 matrices which refer to specific transformations, and the results are summarized in Table 9.3 (see page 211).

The reflection transformation

A 2-D shape which is drawn on the screen in position (i) in Fig. 9.10, can be

(*a*) relected in the Y-axis to give image (ii)
(*b*) relected in the X-axis to give image (iii)
(*c*) relected in the origin to give image (iv)

The corresponding 2∗2 matrices are

Reflection in the Y-axis $\quad \begin{bmatrix} -1 & \emptyset \\ \emptyset & 1 \end{bmatrix}$

Reflection in the X-axis $\quad \begin{bmatrix} 1 & \emptyset \\ \emptyset & -1 \end{bmatrix}$

Reflection in the origin $\quad \begin{bmatrix} -1 & \emptyset \\ \emptyset & -1 \end{bmatrix}$

You will find it an interesting exercise to mathematically verify these transformations.

Fig. 9.10 Reflection in (ii) the Y-axis, (iii) the X-axis, (iv) the origin

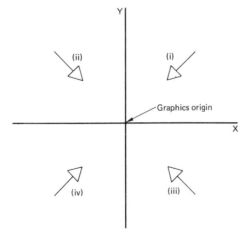

In order to combine transformations, the 2∗2 matrix form must be converted to a 3∗2 homogeneous coordinate matrix, which is achieved by adding (for 2-dimensional shapes) the parameters $E = \emptyset$ and $F = \emptyset$. The value of the parameters for the homogeneous coordinate reflection transformations are given in Table 9.3.

You can also reflect an object about any line of your own choosing. For example, the 2∗2 matrix for reflection in the line $Y = X$ (see Fig. 9.11*a*) is

Reflection in $Y = X \quad \begin{bmatrix} \emptyset & 1 \\ 1 & \emptyset \end{bmatrix}$

Fig. 9.11 Reflection in the
line *a*) y = x, *b*) y = −x

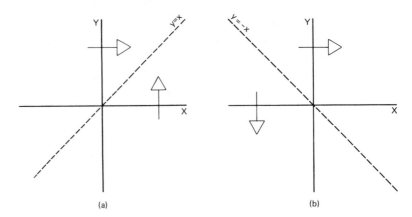

(a)   (b)

and for reflection in the line $Y = -X$ (see Fig. 9.11*b*) is

Reflection in $Y = X$ $\begin{bmatrix} 0 & -1 \\ -1 & 0 \end{bmatrix}$

These transformations can be combined with yet other transformations to produce many intersting graphics effects (see section 9.18).

The rotation transformation

The following 2∗2 linear transformation, based on eqns (9.5) to (9.8), can be used to rotate an object through angle θ:

Clockwise rotation $\begin{bmatrix} \cos\theta & -\sin\theta \\ \sin\theta & \cos\theta \end{bmatrix}$

Counter-clockwise
rotation $\begin{bmatrix} \cos\theta & \sin\theta \\ -\sin\theta & \cos\theta \end{bmatrix}$

The shear transformation

A 2-dimensional object can be sheared or twisted in both the X- and the Y-direction, as shown in Fig. 9.12. The shear transformation is very useful when illustrating the physical effect of a force on, say, a mechanical object. The corresponding 2∗2 transformation matrices are

Shear in the Y-direction $\begin{bmatrix} 1 & Sy \\ 0 & 1 \end{bmatrix}$

Shear in the X-direction $\begin{bmatrix} 1 & 0 \\ Sx & 1 \end{bmatrix}$

Where Sy and Sx are **shear scaling factors**. If the shape of the object is unchanged by the force applied to it, then the value of the scaling factor is zero (the shear transformation then becomes an identity transformation – see section 9.14). Depending on the direction of the shear, the scaling factor may have either a positive sign or a negative sign.

Summary

Table 9.3 summarizes the values of the parameters A, B, C, D, E and F developed for the transformations in this chapter.

Fig. 9.12 Shear in a) the
Y-direction, b) the X-
direction

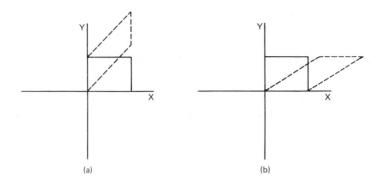

(a)   (b)

Table 9.3   Homogeneous coordinate matrix parameters

Transformation	Parameter					
	A	B	C	D	E	F
Scaling	sx	∅	∅	sy	∅	∅
Translation	1	∅	∅	1	Tx	Ty
Reflection in the Y-axis	−1	∅	∅	1	∅	∅
Reflection in the X-axis	1	∅	∅	−1	∅	∅
Reflection in the origin	−1	∅	∅	−1	∅	∅
Reflection in Y = X	∅	1	1	∅	∅	∅
Reflection in Y = −X	∅	−1	−1	∅	∅	∅
Clockwise rotation	$\cos\theta$	$-\sin\theta$	$\sin\theta$	$\cos\theta$	∅	∅
Counter-clockwise rotation	$\cos\theta$	$\sin\theta$	$-\sin\theta$	$\cos\theta$	∅	∅
Shear in the Y-direction	1	Sy	∅	1	∅	∅
Shear in the X-direction	1	∅	Sx	1	∅	∅

9.18   Combining Transformations

Each transformation described above transforms the X- and Y-value for
each point in a 2-dimensional diagram into its transformed values xt and yt.
If you need to perform several manipulations on a shape, such as rotating
and scaling it, it is simply a matter of performing a sequence of transformations on each point on the diagram.

To do this, the coordinates of the original diagram need to be stored in a
data matrix or array and, each time that a transformation is to be
performed on the coordinates, they are taken out of the matrix and the
transformed value is determined using eqns. (9.17) and (9.18). The
transformed values are then returned to the data matrix. The parameters

listed in Table 9.3 are, of course, those used in eqns. (9.17) and (9.18). Program *P9.3*, which is described in section 9.19, illustrates this process.

9.19 An Application of Homogeneous Coordinates to Graphics

Program *P9.3* applies the principle outlined above to produce a number of effects on the screen. It takes a rectangle, whose coordinates are listed in line 260, and manipulates it in various ways. Methods of altering the methods of manipulation are discussed later.

Line 50 of the program sets the graphics origin to the centre of the screen, and line 70 draws (in red) a set of axes through this origin. Lines 80 to 110 inclusive draw the original shape specified in line 260 [you can alter the shape by altering the data in lines 250 (the number of corners in the shape) and 260 (the X- and Y-coordinates of the corners)].

Lines 130 to 170 inclusive read the X- and Y-data relating to each corner of the object and store them in a data matrix called "save". [If you want to draw a diagram having a different number of corners than a square has (remember: the starting point needs to be specified twice!), you will need to redefine the DIMensions of "save" in line 60.]

The important part of the program is situated in lines 180 to 200 inclusive. These lines call on PROC_read_matrix, and pass the parameters A, B, C, D, E and F [see also Table 9.3 and eqns. (9.17) and (9.18)] to the procedure. This procedure extracts the current X- and Y-values from the data array, and calls on PROC_mult_matrix to transform the coordinates of each corner from (x,y) to (xt,yt). Line 370 of PROC_read_matrix returns the transformed values to the data array.

Program *P9.3* calls on PROC_read_matrix three times for the following reason. Line 180 takes the original shape (see Fig. 9.13*a*) and translates it to the origin (Fig. 9.13*b*); you should note that Tx = −100 graphics units and Ty = −150 graphics units. Line 190 scales the shape — see Fig. 9.13*c* — with sx = 2 and sy = 1.1, and line 200 translates the scaled shape back to its original starting point using Tx = 100 and Ty = 150 — see Fig. 9.13*d*. You will, of course, see only the original shape, which is quickly replaced by the final shape.

Should you wish to scale or enlarge the shape about its origin, it merely becomes a matter of translating the 'centre' of the original shape to the graphics origin. To do this, alter lines 180 and 200 as follows:

    180 PROC_read_matrix(1,0,0,1,−200,−250)
    200 PROC_read_matrix(1,0,0,1,200,250)

You will find that the enlarged object does not appear to be quite symmetrical about the centre in the Y-direction, and this is due to the width of the lines in MODE 1.

Using other sets of A, B, C, D, E and F parameters you can perform many sequences on the object. For example, the following sequence translates, scales, rotates clockwise (30°) and retranslates the shape:

    180 PROC_read_matrix(1,0,0,1,−100,−150)
    190 PROC_read_matrix(2,0,0,1.1,0,0)
    195 PROC_read_matrix(0.866,−0.5,0.5,0.866,0,0)
    200 PROC_read_matrix(1,0,0,1,100,150)

Listing 9.3

```
 10  REM ****PROGRAM "P9.3"****
 20  REM TRANSPOSE AND SCALE SHAPE****
 30  *TV0,1
 40  MODE 1
 50  VDU 29,640;512;
 60  DIM save(3,1)
 70  PROC_axes
 80  READ no_of_corners
 90  READ x,y:MOVE x,y:GCOL 0,2
100  FOR N=2 TO no_of_corners
110    READ x,y:DRAW x,y:NEXT N
120  RESTORE
130  READ no_of_corners:row=0
140  FOR corner=2 TO no_of_corners
150    READ x:save(row,0)=x:READ y:save(row,1)=y
160    row=row+1
170    NEXT corner
180  PROC_read_matrix(1,0,0,1,-100,-150):REM TRANSLATE TO ORIGIN
190  PROC_read_matrix(2,0,0,1.1,0,0):REM SCALE
200  PROC_read_matrix(1,0,0,1,100,150):REM TRANSLATE TO ORIGINAL POSITION
210  xt=save(3,0):yt=save(3,1):MOVE xt,yt:GCOL 0,3
220  FOR N=0 TO (no_of_corners-2)
230    xt=save(N,0):yt=save(N,1):DRAW xt,yt:NEXT N
240  GCOL 0,3:VDU 29,0;0;
250  DATA 5
260  DATA 100,150,   300,150,   300,350,   100,350,   100,150
270  END
280 :
290  DEF PROC_axes
300  GCOL 0,1
310  MOVE -640,0:DRAW 640,0:MOVE 0,-512:DRAW 0,512
320  ENDPROC
330 :
340  DEF PROC_read_matrix(A,B,C,D,E,F)
350  FOR row=0 TO (no_of_corners-2)
360    x=save(row,0):y=save(row,1):PROC_mult_matrix
370    save(row,0)=xt:save(row,1)=yt
380    NEXT row
390  ENDPROC
400 :
410  DEF PROC_mult_matrix
420  xt=A*x+C*y+E:yt=B*x+D*y+F
430  ENDPROC
```

Fig. 9.13 Combining transformations: *a*) the original shape, *b*) translation to the origin, *c*) scaling at the origin, *d*) translation to the starting position

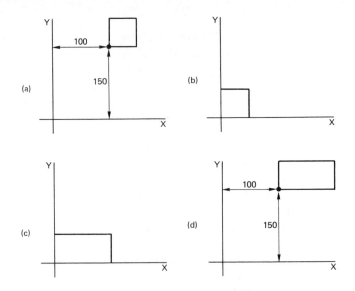

Altering lines 18Ø and 2ØØ in the above four lines to the following, causes the shape to be scaled and rotated about is centre:

18Ø PROC_read_matrix(1,Ø,Ø,1,−2ØØ,−25Ø)
2ØØ PROC_read_matrix(1,Ø,Ø,1,2ØØ,25Ø)

In general, you should note that when you use reflection transformations, they are used on their own without the translation transformations (which are in lines 18Ø and 2ØØ of *P9.3*), but some interesting effects are obtained when they are used with the translation transformations!

Appendix 1 ASCII code as applied to the BBC micro keyboard characters

Hex Code	Decimal Code	Normal Name	Hex Code	Decimal Code	Normal Name	Hex Code	Decimal Code	Normal Name
20	32	SPACE	40	64	@	60	96	£
21	33	!	41	65	A	61	97	a
22	34	"	42	66	B	62	98	b
23	35	#	43	67	C	63	99	c
24	36	$	44	68	D	64	100	d
25	37	%	45	69	E	65	101	e
26	38	&	46	70	F	66	102	f
27	39	'	47	71	G	67	103	g
28	40	(	48	72	H	68	104	h
29	41	)	49	73	I	69	105	i
2A	42	*	4A	74	J	6A	106	j
2B	43	+	4B	75	K	6B	107	k
2C	44	,	4C	76	L	6C	108	l
2D	45	−	4D	77	M	6D	109	m
2E	46	.	4E	78	N	6E	110	n
2F	47	/	4F	79	O	6F	111	o
30	48	0	50	80	P	70	112	p
31	49	1	51	81	Q	71	113	q
32	50	2	52	82	R	72	114	r
33	51	3	53	83	S	73	115	s
34	52	4	54	84	T	74	116	t
35	53	5	55	85	U	75	117	u
36	54	6	56	86	V	76	118	v
37	55	7	57	87	W	77	119	w
38	56	8	58	88	X	78	120	x
39	57	9	59	89	Y	79	121	y
3A	58	:	5A	90	Z	7A	122	z
3B	59	;	5B	91	[	7B	123	{
3C	60	<	5C	92	\	7C	124	¦
3D	61	=	5D	93	]	7D	125	}
3E	62	>	5E	94	^	7E	126	~
3F	63	?	5F	95	_	7F	127	DEL

Note: DEL means DELete

Appendix 2 VDU codes

Decimal	Hex	CTRL	ASCII abbrev.	Bytes extra	Meaning
0	0	@	NUL	0	does nothing
1	1	A	SOH	1	send next character to printer only
2	2	B	STX	0	enable printer
3	3	C	ETX	0	disable printer
4	4	D	EOT	0	write text at text cursor
5	5	E	ENQ	0	write text at graphics cursor
6	6	F	ACK	0	enable VDU drivers
7	7	G	BEL	0	make a short beep
8	8	H	BS	0	backspace cursor one character
9	9	I	HT	0	forwardspace cursor one character
10	A	J	LF	0	move cursor down one line
11	B	K	VT	0	move cursor up one line
12	C	L	FF	0	clear text area
13	D	M	CR	0	move cursor to start of current line
14	E	N	SO	0	page mode on
15	F	O	SI	0	page mode off
16	10	P	DLE	0	clear graphics area
17	11	Q	DC1	1	define text colour
18	12	R	DC2	2	define graphics colour
19	13	S	DC3	5	define logical colour
20	14	T	DC4	0	restore default logical colours
21	15	U	NAK	0	disable VDU drivers or delete current line
22	16	V	SYN	1	select screen mode
23	17	W	ETB	9	re-program display character
24	18	X	CAN	8	define graphics window
25	19	Y	EM	5	PLOT K,x,y
26	1A	Z	SUB	0	restore default windows
27	1B	[	ESC	0	does nothing
28	1C	\	FS	4	define text window
29	1D	]	GS	4	define graphics origin
30	1E	^	RS	0	home text cursor to top left
31	1F	_	US	2	move text cursor to x,y
127	7F		DEL	0	backspace and delete

Appendix 3 INKEY numbers

Key	Number	Key	Number
f0	−33	1	−49
f1	−114	2	−50
f2	−115	3	−18
f3	−116	4	−19
f4	−21	5	−20
f5	−117	6	−53
f6	−118	7	−37
f7	−23	8	−22
f8	−119	9	−39
f9	−120	0	−40
A	−66	−	−24
B	−101	^	−25
C	−83	\	−121
D	−51	@	−72
E	−35	[	−57
F	−68	_	−41
G	−84	;	−88
H	−85	:	−73
I	−38	]	−89
J	−70	'	−103
K	−71	.	−104
L	−87	/	−105
M	−102	ESCAPE	−113
N	−86	TAB	−97
O	−55	CAPS LOCK	−65
P	−56	CTRL	−2
Q	−17	SHIFT LOCK	−81
R	−52	SHIFT	−1
S	−82	SPACE BAR	−99
T	−36	DELETE	−90
U	−54	COPY	−106
V	−100	RETURN	−74
W	−34	↑	−58
X	−67	↓	−42
Y	−69	←	−26
Z	−98	→	−122

Index of Listings

*Complete program contained on a disc available from Pitman Publishing. For example, program P5.1 contains listings 5.1 to 5.10, inclusive.

Index